WITHDRAWN

ULTIMATE
CAPTAIN AMERICA

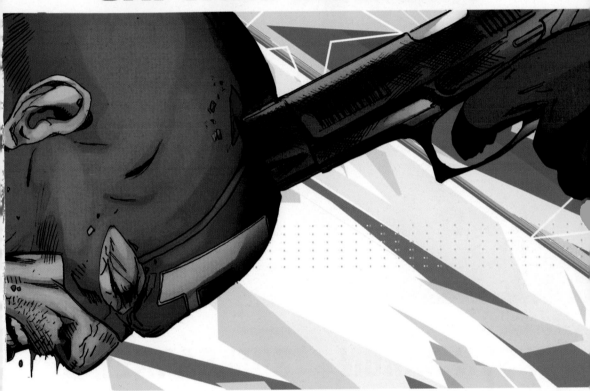

ULTIMATE CAPTAIN AMERICA

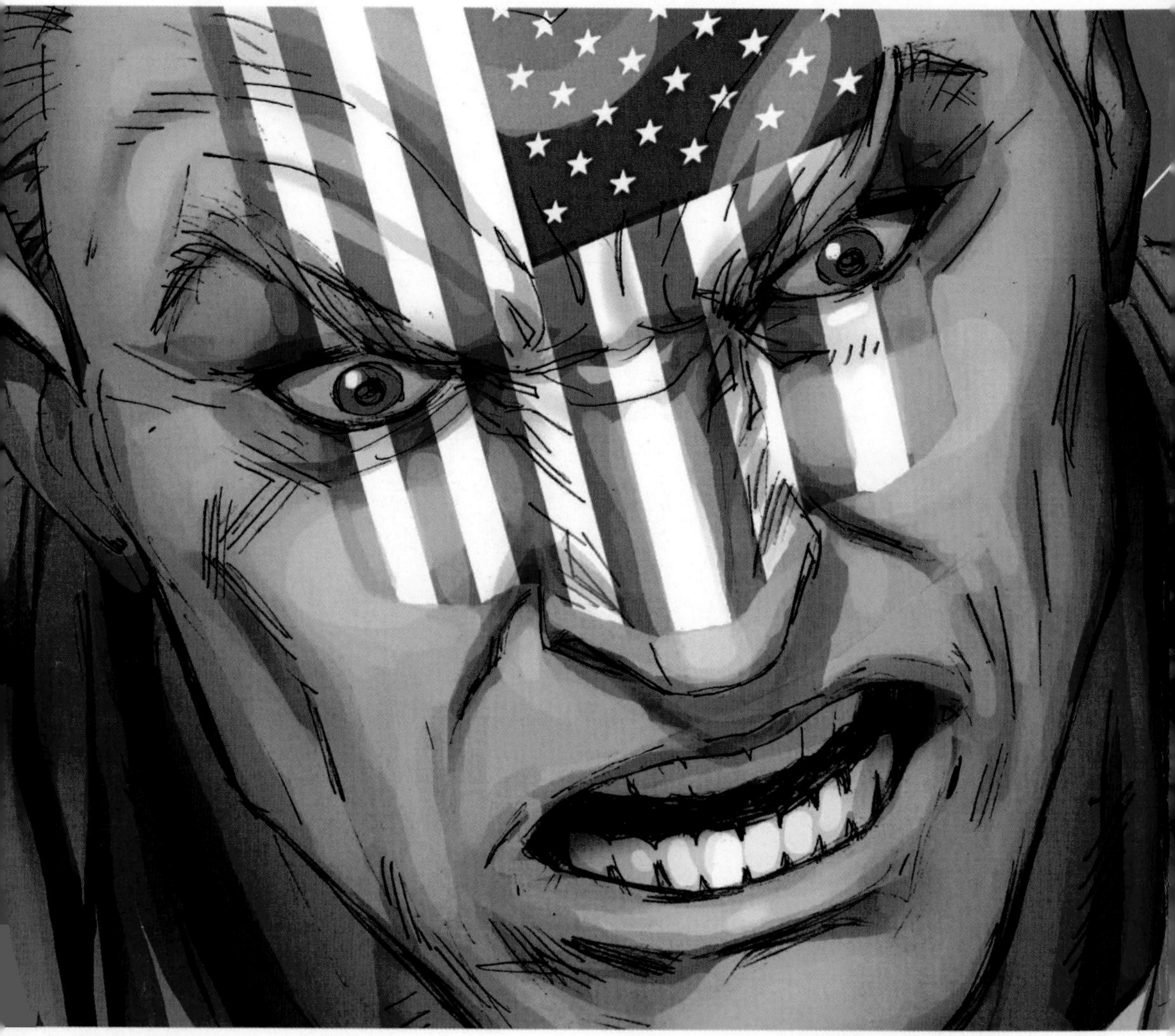

WRITER:
JASON AARON

ARTIST:
RON GARNEY

COLORIST: **JASON KEITH**
WITH **JIM CHARALAMPIDIS** & **MATT MILLA**
LETTERER: **VC'S CLAYTON COWLES**
COVER ART: **RON GARNEY** & **JASON KEITH**
ASSISTANT EDITOR: **SANA AMANAT**
EDITOR: **MARK PANICCIA**

CAPTAIN AMERICA CREATED BY **JOE SIMON** & **JACK KIRBY**

3 1526 04018217 9

COLLECTION EDITOR: **JENNIFER GRÜNWALD**

EDITORIAL ASSISTANTS: **JAMES EMMETT** & **JOE HOCHSTEIN**

ASSISTANT EDITORS: **ALEX STARBUCK** & **NELSON RIBEIRO**

EDITOR, SPECIAL PROJECTS: **MARK D. BEAZLEY**

SENIOR EDITOR, SPECIAL PROJECTS: **JEFF YOUNGQUIST**

SENIOR VICE PRESIDENT OF SALES: **DAVID GABRIEL**

SVP OF BRAND PLANNING & COMMUNICATIONS: **MICHAEL PASCIULLO**

EDITOR IN CHIEF: **AXEL ALONSO**   CHIEF CREATIVE OFFICER: **JOE QUESADA**

PUBLISHER: **DAN BUCKLEY**   EXECUTIVE PRODUCER: **ALAN FINE**

ULTIMATE COMICS CAPTAIN AMERICA. Contains material originally published in magazine form as ULTIMATE COMICS CAPTAIN AMERICA #1-4 and CAPTAIN AMERICA SPOTLIGHT. First printing 2011. ISBN# 978-0-7851-5194-4. Published by MARVEL WORLDWIDE, INC., a subsidiary of MARVEL ENTERTAINMENT, LLC. OFFICE OF PUBLICATION: 135 West 50th Street, New York, NY 10020. Copyright © 2009 and 2011 Marvel Characters, Inc. All rights reserved. $19.99 per copy in the U.S. and $21.99 in Canada (GST #R127032852); Canadian Agreement #40668537. All characters featured in this issue and the distinctive names and likenesses thereof, and all related indicia are trademarks of Marvel Characters, Inc. No similarity between any of the names, characters, persons, and/or institutions in this magazine with those of any living or dead person or institution is intended, and any such similarity which may exist is purely coincidental. **Printed in the U.S.A.** ALAN FINE, EVP - Office of the President, Marvel Worldwide, Inc. and EVP & CMO Marvel Characters B.V.; DAN BUCKLEY, Publisher & President - Print, Animation & Digital Divisions; JOE QUESADA, Chief Creative Officer; JIM SOKOLOWSKI, Chief Operating Officer; DAVID BOGART, SVP of Business Affairs & Talent Management; TOM BREVOORT, SVP of Publishing; C.B. CEBULSKI, SVP of Creator & Content Development; DAVID GABRIEL, SVP of Publishing Sales & Circulation; MICHAEL PASCIULLO, SVP of Brand Planning & Communications; JIM O'KEEFE, VP of Operations & Logistics; DAN CARR, Executive Director of Publishing Technology; JUSTIN F. GABRIE, Director of Publishing & Editorial Operations; SUSAN CRESPI, Editorial Operations Manager; ALEX MORALES, Publishing Operations Manager; STAN LEE, Chairman Emeritus. For information regarding advertising in Marvel Comics or on Marvel.com, please contact John Dokes, SVP Integrated Sales and Marketing, at jdokes@marvel.com. For Marvel subscription inquiries, please call 800-217-9158. **Manufactured between 4/11/2011 and 5/9/2011 by R.R. DONNELLEY, INC., SALEM, VA, USA.**

10 9 8 7 6 5 4 3 2 1

PREVIOUSLY

America's first Super-Soldier, Steve Rogers,
became a living legend in the trenches of
World War II before being frozen for more
than fifty years beneath the Atlantic Ocean.

Now, after being found by Tony Stark, Steve
Rogers continues his fight to defend his country
along with the New Ultimates. In this, or any
other time, Steve Rogers is Captain America.

1

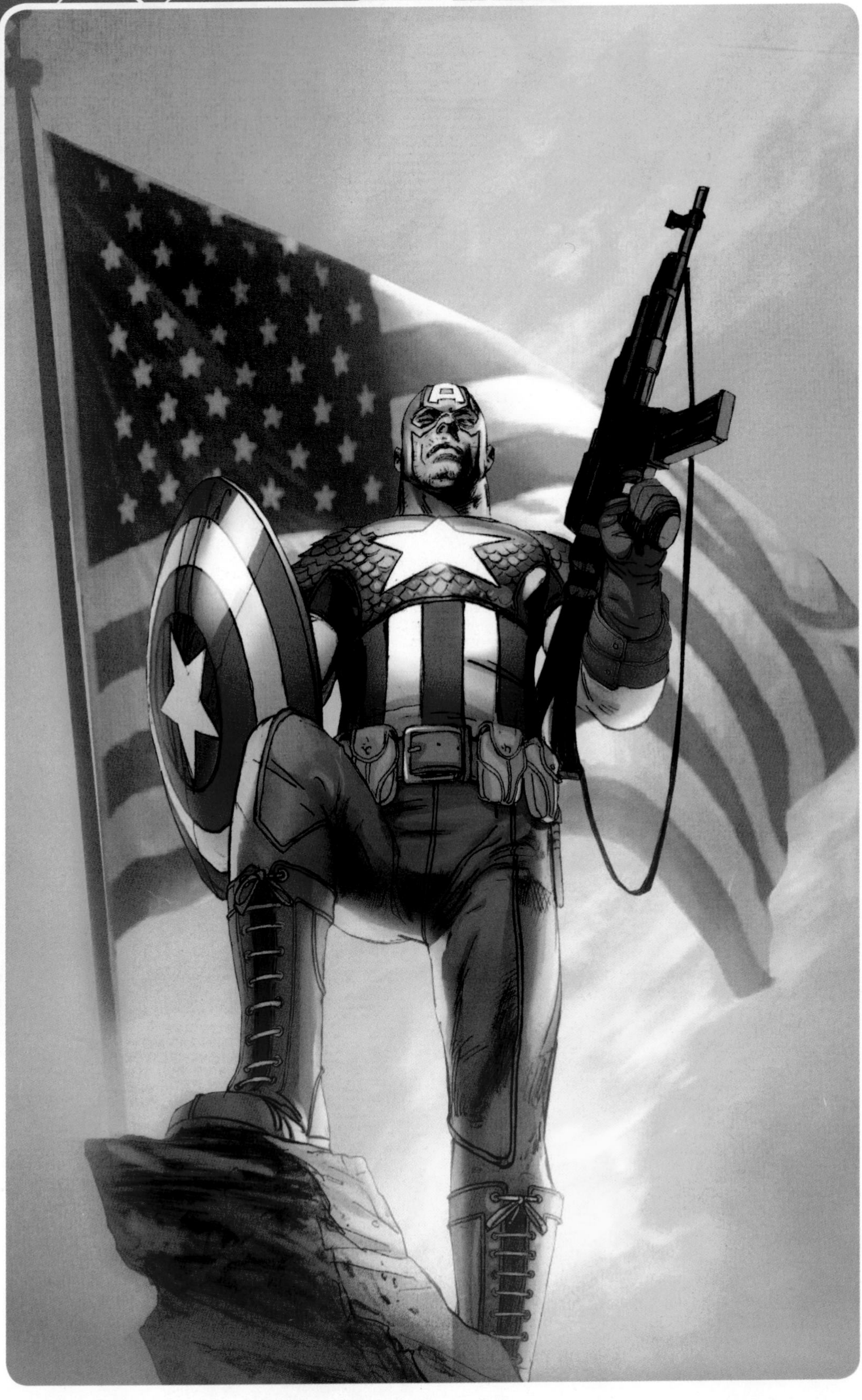

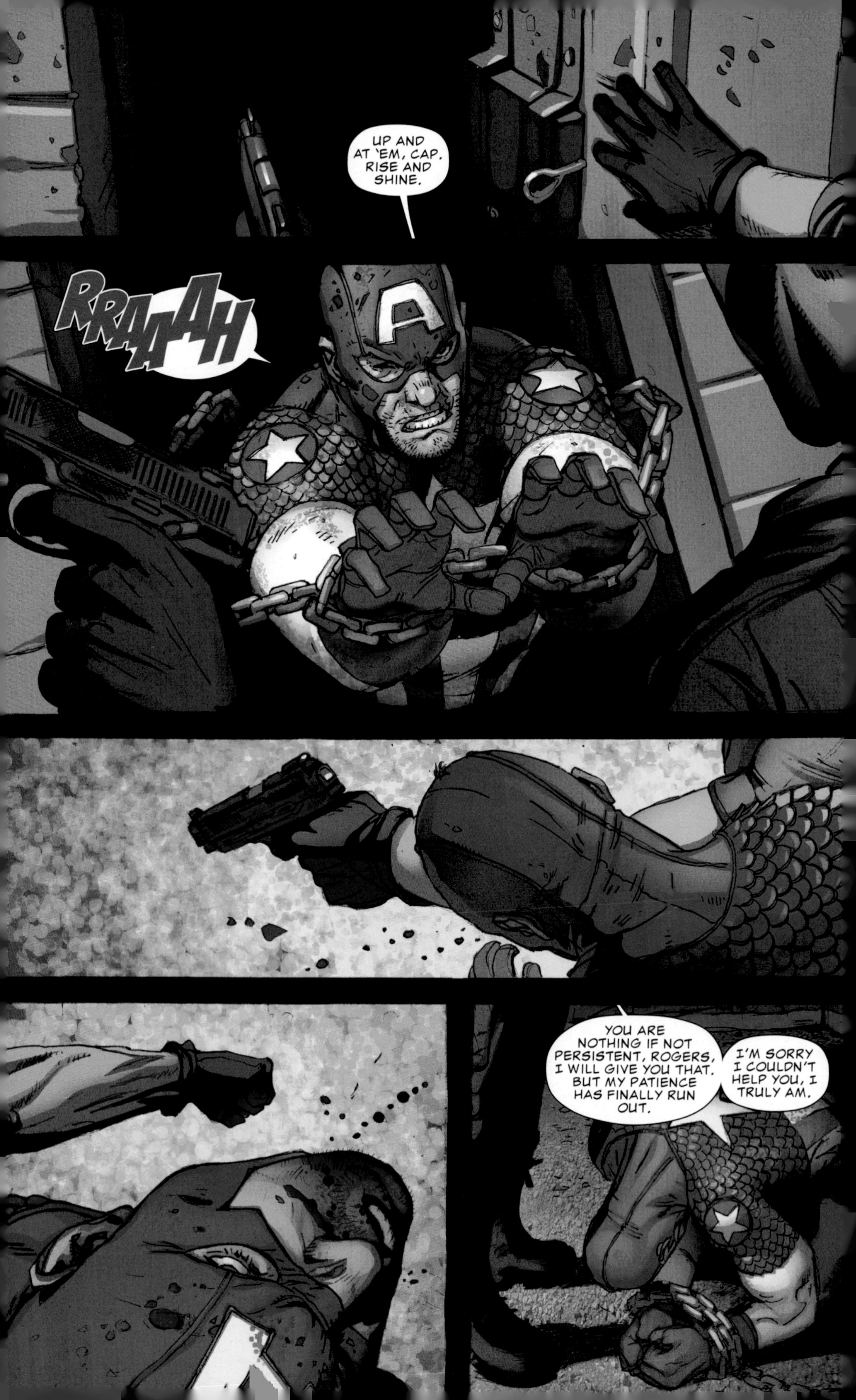
UP AND AT 'EM, CAP. RISE AND SHINE.
RRAAAAH
YOU ARE NOTHING IF NOT PERSISTENT, ROGERS, I WILL GIVE YOU THAT. BUT MY PATIENCE HAS FINALLY RUN OUT.
I'M SORRY I COULDN'T HELP YOU, I TRULY AM.

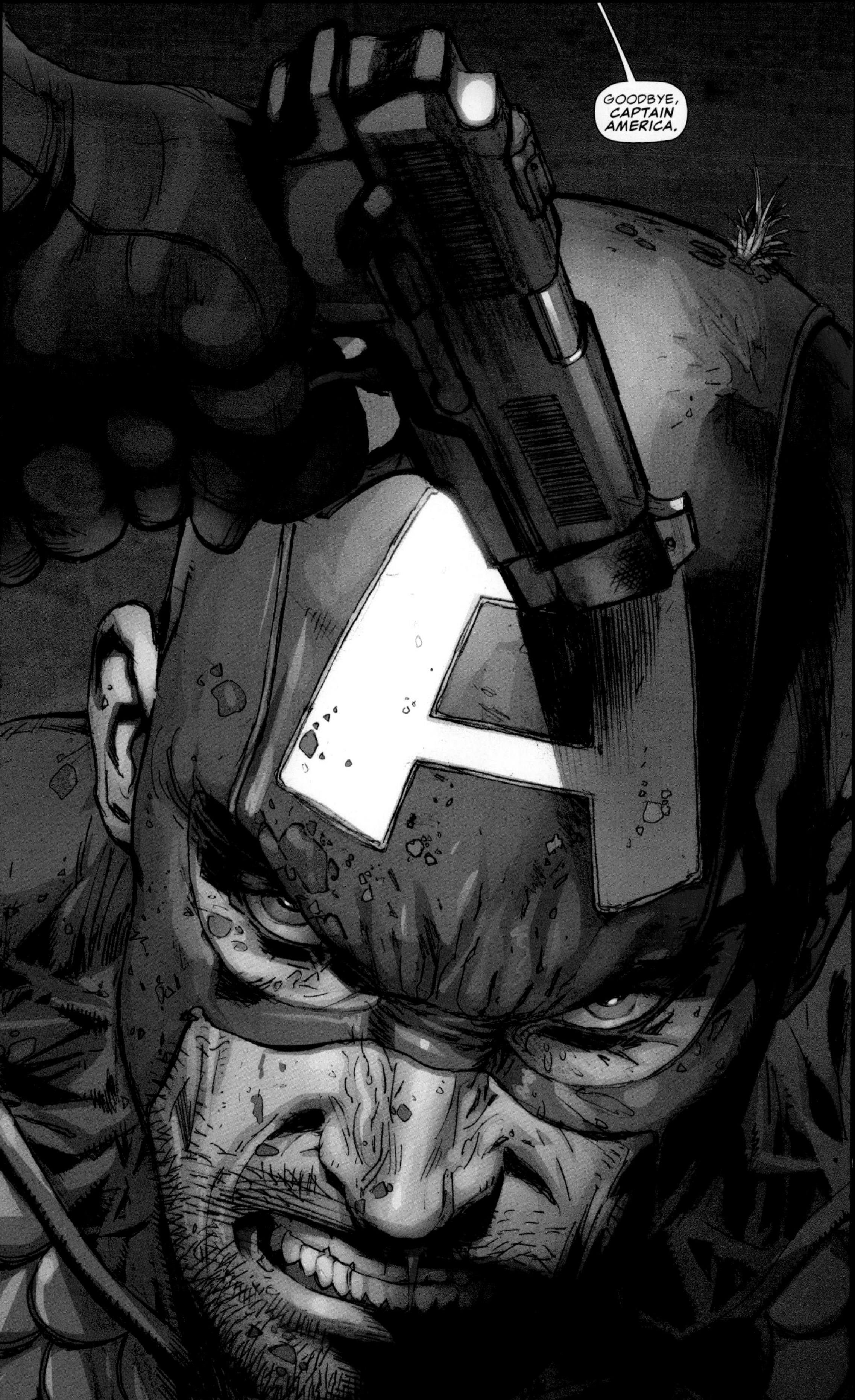
GOODBYE, CAPTAIN AMERICA.

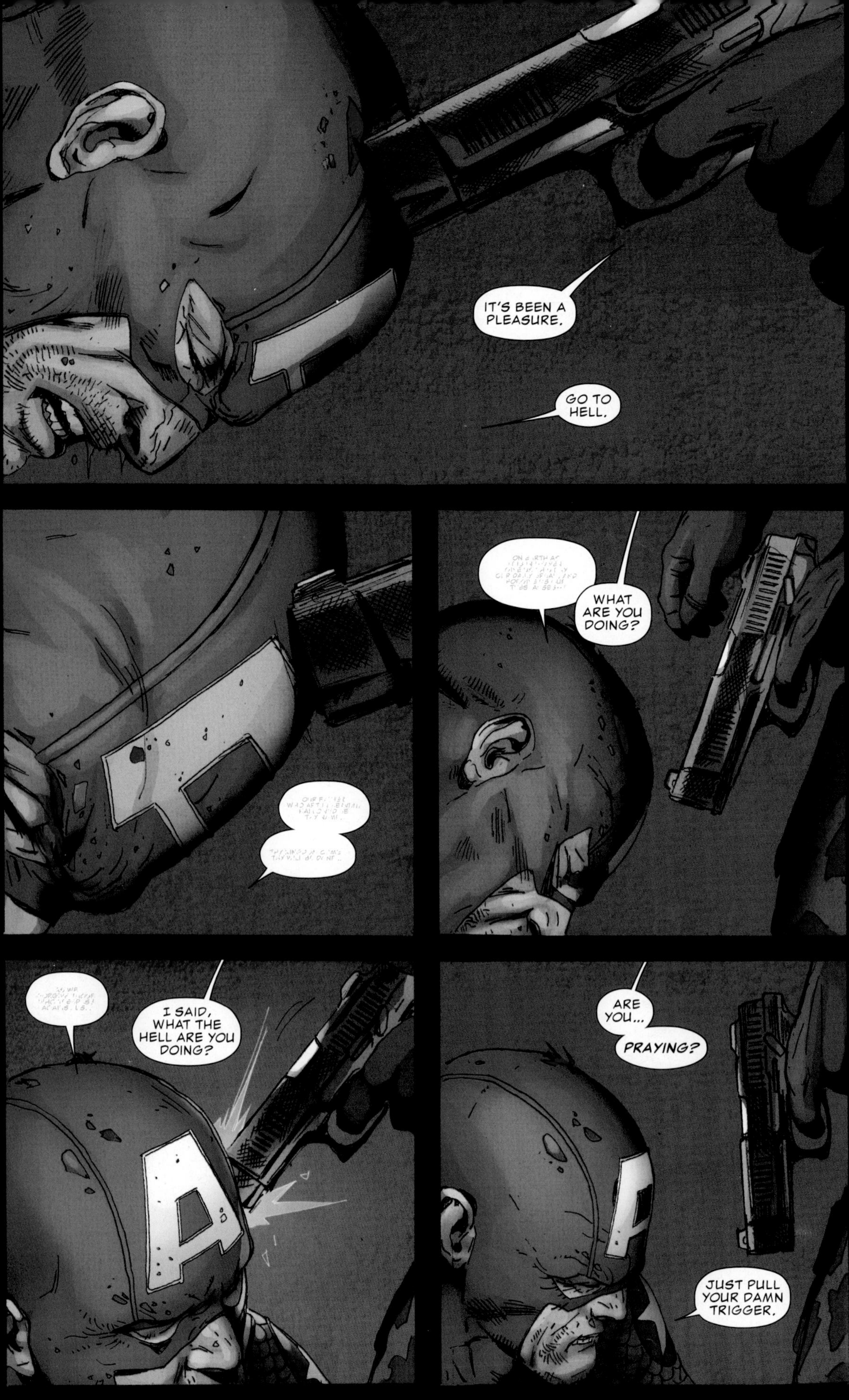
IT'S BEEN A PLEASURE.
GO TO HELL.
WHAT ARE YOU DOING?
I SAID, WHAT THE HELL ARE YOU DOING?
ARE YOU...
PRAYING?
JUST PULL YOUR DAMN TRIGGER.

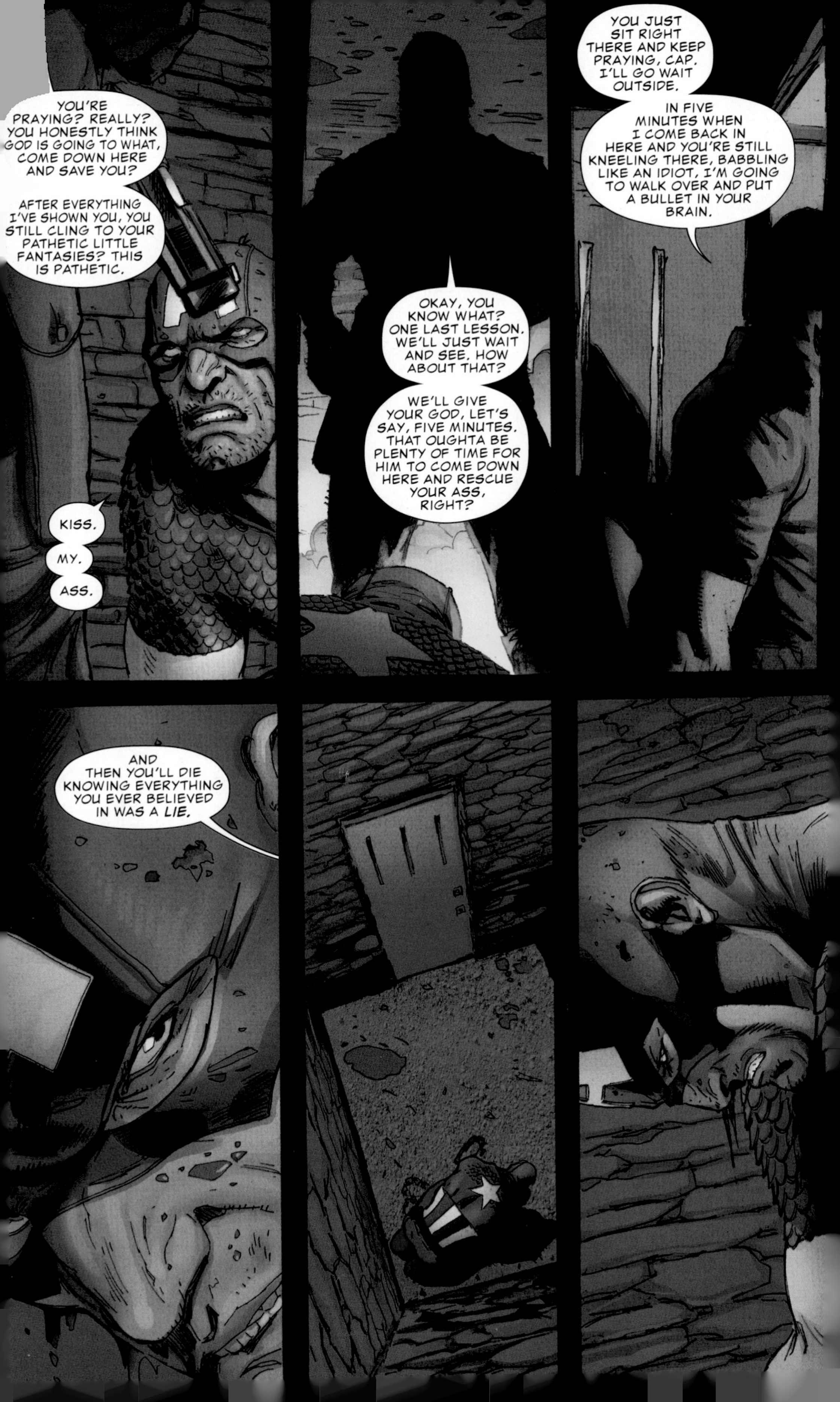

YOU'RE PRAYING? REALLY? YOU HONESTLY THINK GOD IS GOING TO WHAT, COME DOWN HERE AND SAVE YOU?
AFTER EVERYTHING I'VE SHOWN YOU, YOU STILL CLING TO YOUR PATHETIC LITTLE FANTASIES? THIS IS PATHETIC.
KISS.
MY.
ASS.
OKAY, YOU KNOW WHAT? ONE LAST LESSON. WE'LL JUST WAIT AND SEE. HOW ABOUT THAT?
WE'LL GIVE YOUR GOD, LET'S SAY, FIVE MINUTES. THAT OUGHTA BE PLENTY OF TIME FOR HIM TO COME DOWN HERE AND RESCUE YOUR ASS, RIGHT?
YOU JUST SIT RIGHT THERE AND KEEP PRAYING, CAP. I'LL GO WAIT OUTSIDE.
IN FIVE MINUTES WHEN I COME BACK IN HERE AND YOU'RE STILL KNEELING THERE, BABBLING LIKE AN IDIOT, I'M GOING TO WALK OVER AND PUT A BULLET IN YOUR BRAIN.
AND THEN YOU'LL DIE KNOWING EVERYTHING YOU EVER BELIEVED IN WAS A *LIE.*

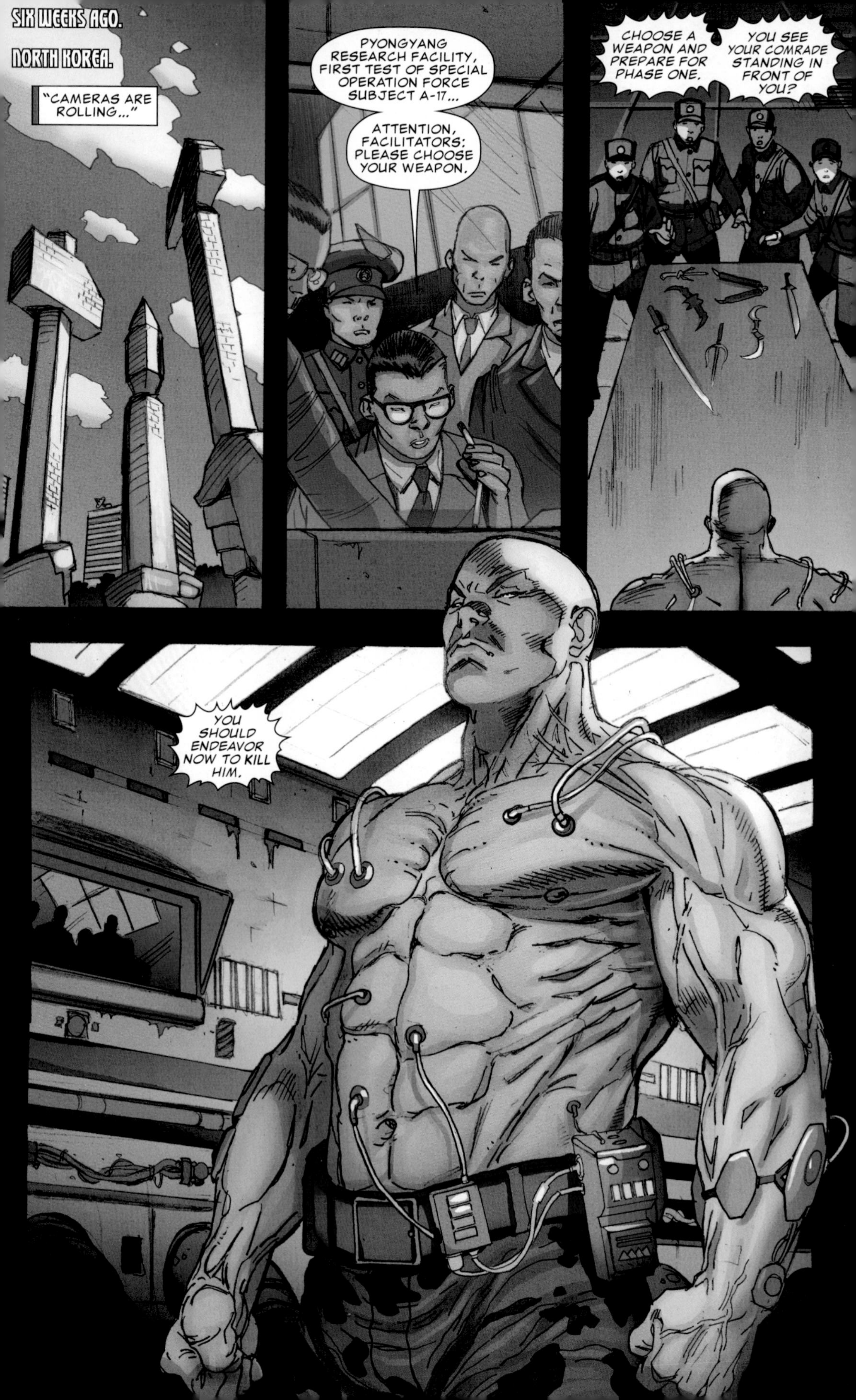
SIX WEEKS AGO.
NORTH KOREA.
"CAMERAS ARE ROLLING..."
PYONGYANG RESEARCH FACILITY, FIRST TEST OF SPECIAL OPERATION FORCE SUBJECT A-17...
ATTENTION, FACILITATORS: PLEASE CHOOSE YOUR WEAPON.
CHOOSE A WEAPON AND PREPARE FOR PHASE ONE.
YOU SEE YOUR COMRADE STANDING IN FRONT OF YOU?
YOU SHOULD ENDEAVOR NOW TO KILL HIM.

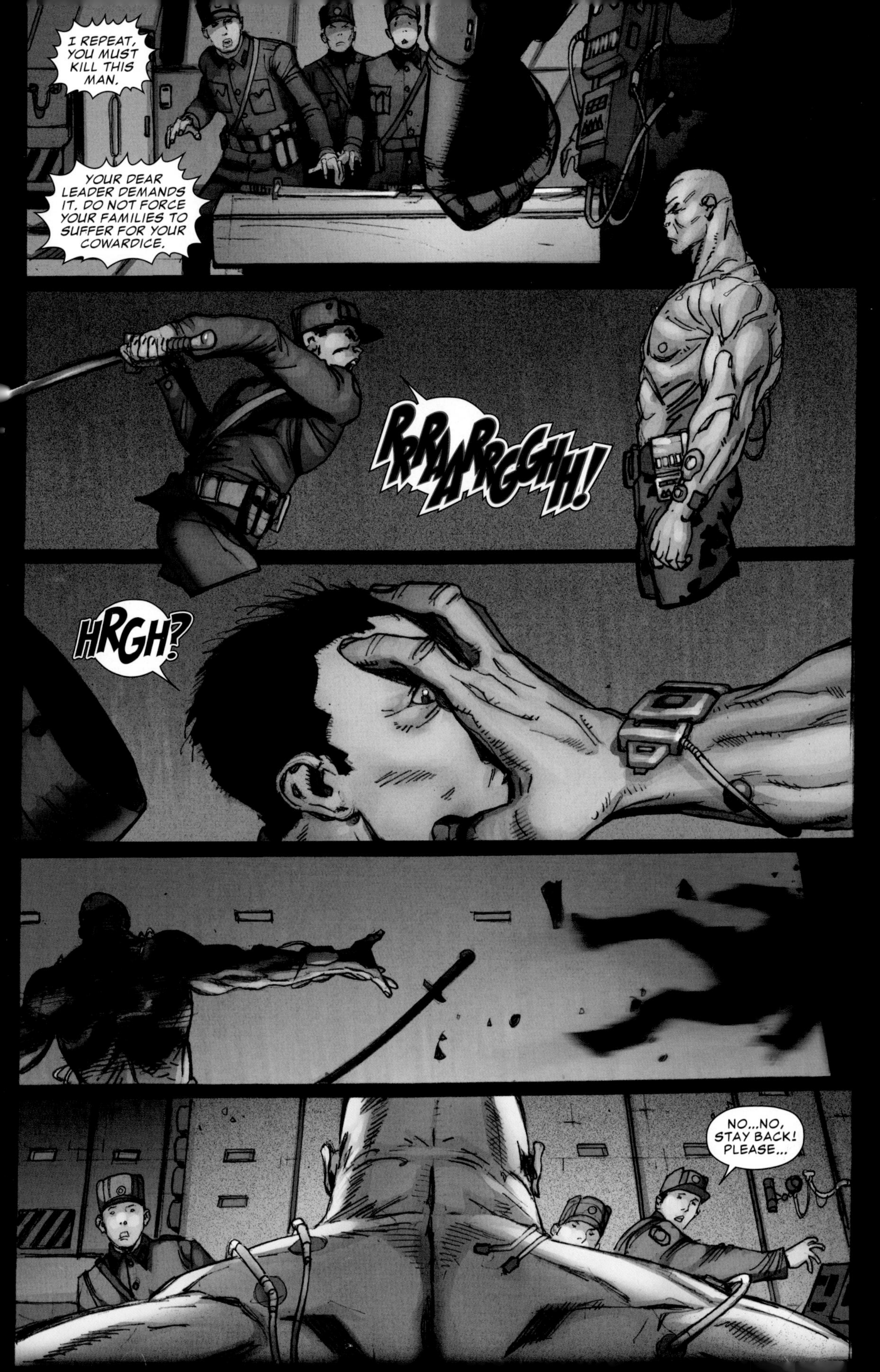
I REPEAT, YOU MUST KILL THIS MAN.
YOUR DEAR LEADER DEMANDS IT. DO NOT FORCE YOUR FAMILIES TO SUFFER FOR YOUR COWARDICE.
RRRAARRGGHH!
HRGH?
NO...NO, STAY BACK! PLEASE...

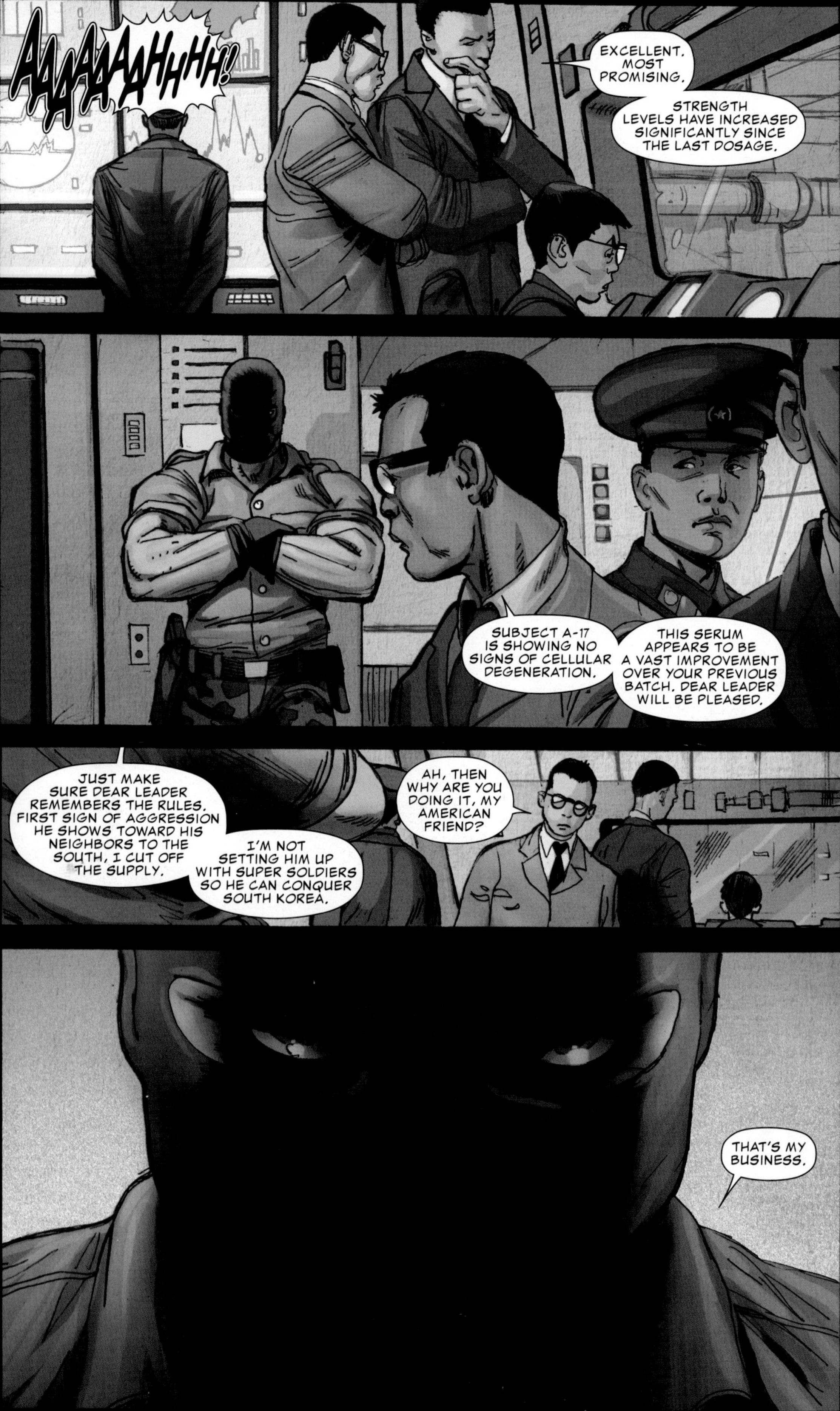
AAAAAAAHHHHH!
EXCELLENT. MOST PROMISING.
STRENGTH LEVELS HAVE INCREASED SIGNIFICANTLY SINCE THE LAST DOSAGE.
SUBJECT A-17 IS SHOWING NO SIGNS OF CELLULAR DEGENERATION.
THIS SERUM APPEARS TO BE A VAST IMPROVEMENT OVER YOUR PREVIOUS BATCH. DEAR LEADER WILL BE PLEASED.
JUST MAKE SURE DEAR LEADER REMEMBERS THE RULES. FIRST SIGN OF AGGRESSION HE SHOWS TOWARD HIS NEIGHBORS TO THE SOUTH, I CUT OFF THE SUPPLY.
I'M NOT SETTING HIM UP WITH SUPER SOLDIERS SO HE CAN CONQUER SOUTH KOREA.
AH, THEN WHY ARE YOU DOING IT, MY AMERICAN FRIEND?
THAT'S MY BUSINESS.

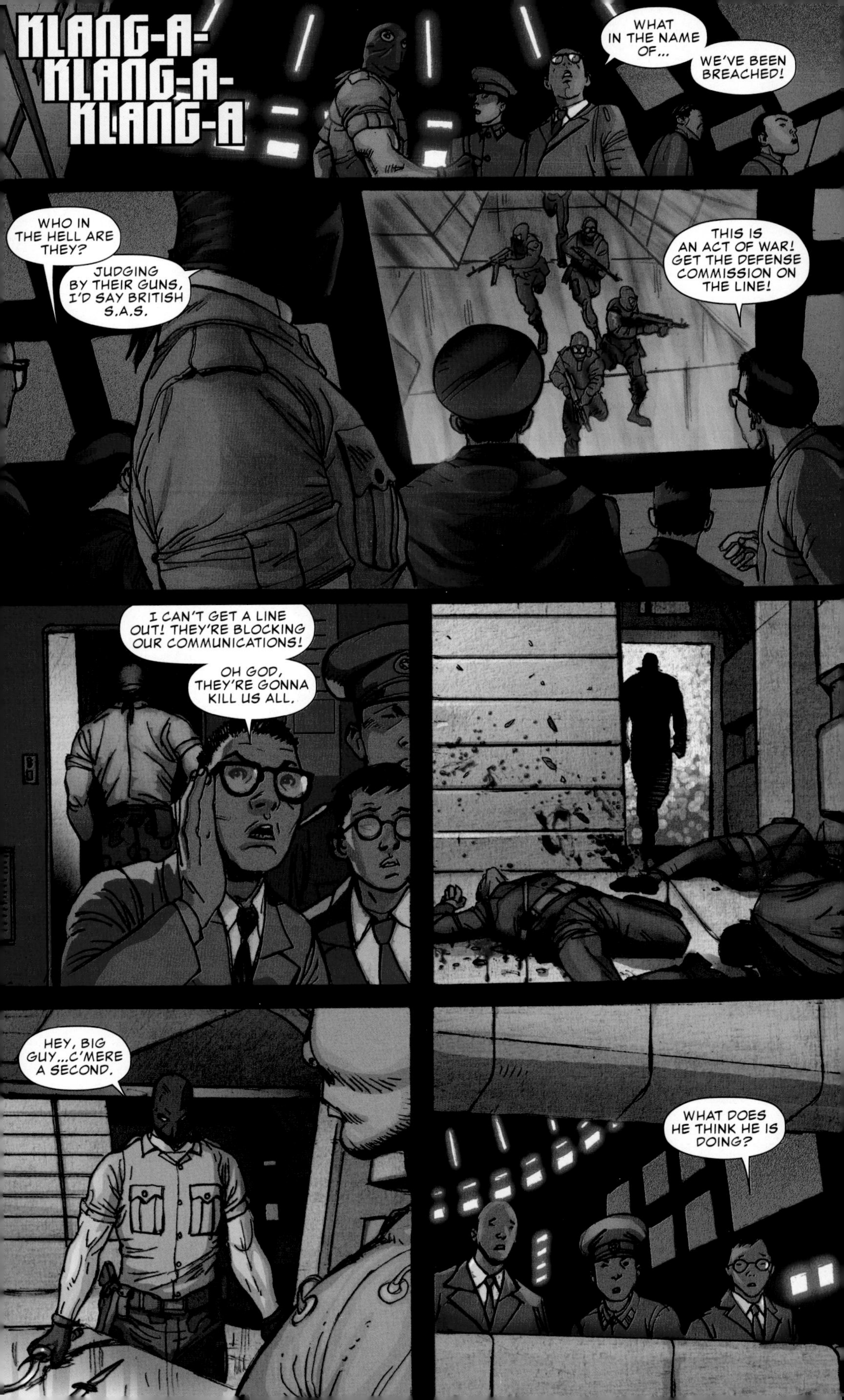
KLANG-A-KLANG-A-KLANG-A
WHAT IN THE NAME OF...
WE'VE BEEN BREACHED!
WHO IN THE HELL ARE THEY?
JUDGING BY THEIR GUNS, I'D SAY BRITISH S.A.S.
THIS IS AN ACT OF WAR! GET THE DEFENSE COMMISSION ON THE LINE!
I CAN'T GET A LINE OUT! THEY'RE BLOCKING OUR COMMUNICATIONS!
OH GOD, THEY'RE GONNA KILL US ALL.
HEY, BIG GUY...C'MERE A SECOND.
WHAT DOES HE THINK HE IS DOING?

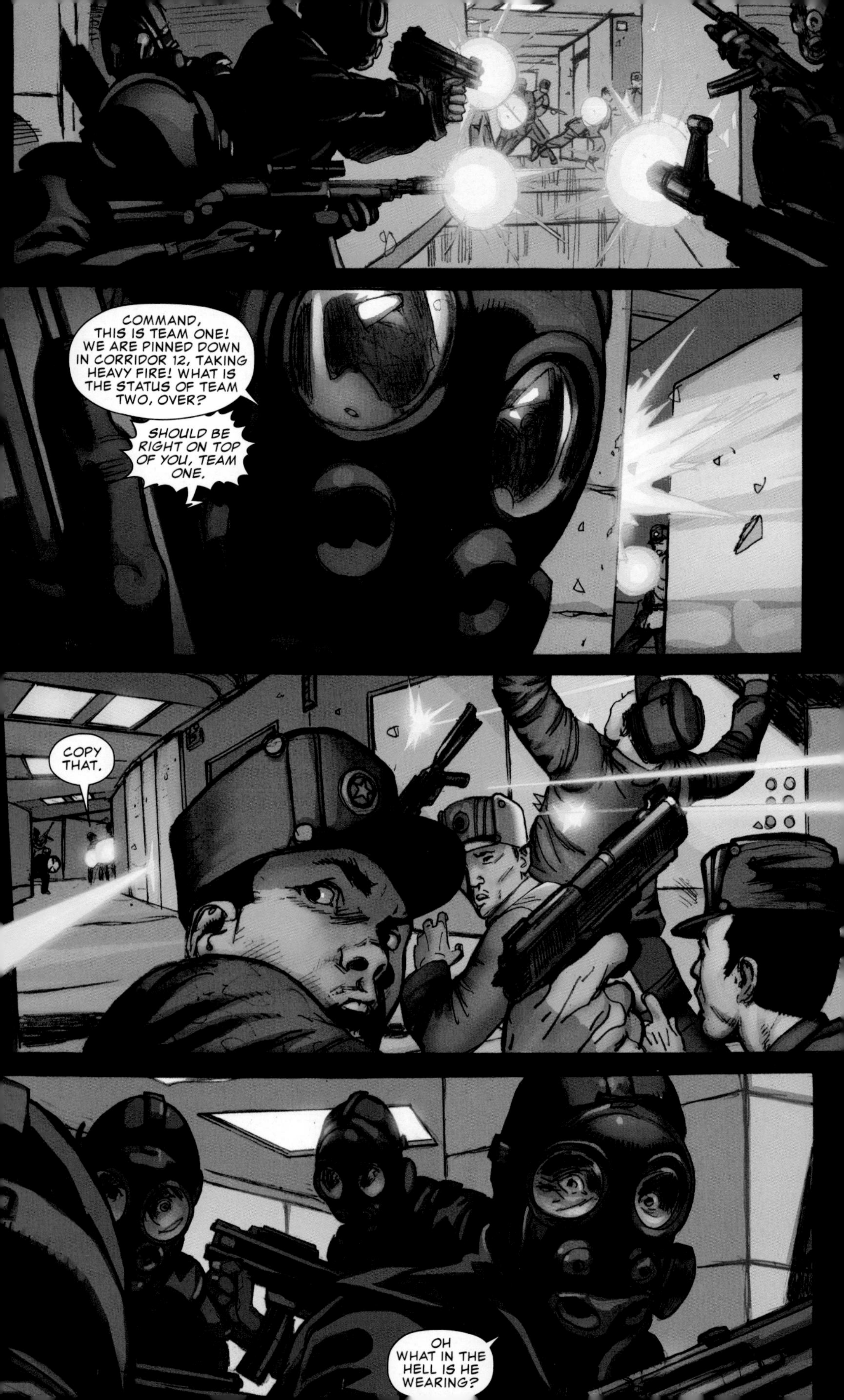
COMMAND, THIS IS TEAM ONE! WE ARE PINNED DOWN IN CORRIDOR 12, TAKING HEAVY FIRE! WHAT IS THE STATUS OF TEAM TWO, OVER?
SHOULD BE RIGHT ON TOP OF YOU, TEAM ONE.
COPY THAT.
OH WHAT IN THE HELL IS HE WEARING?

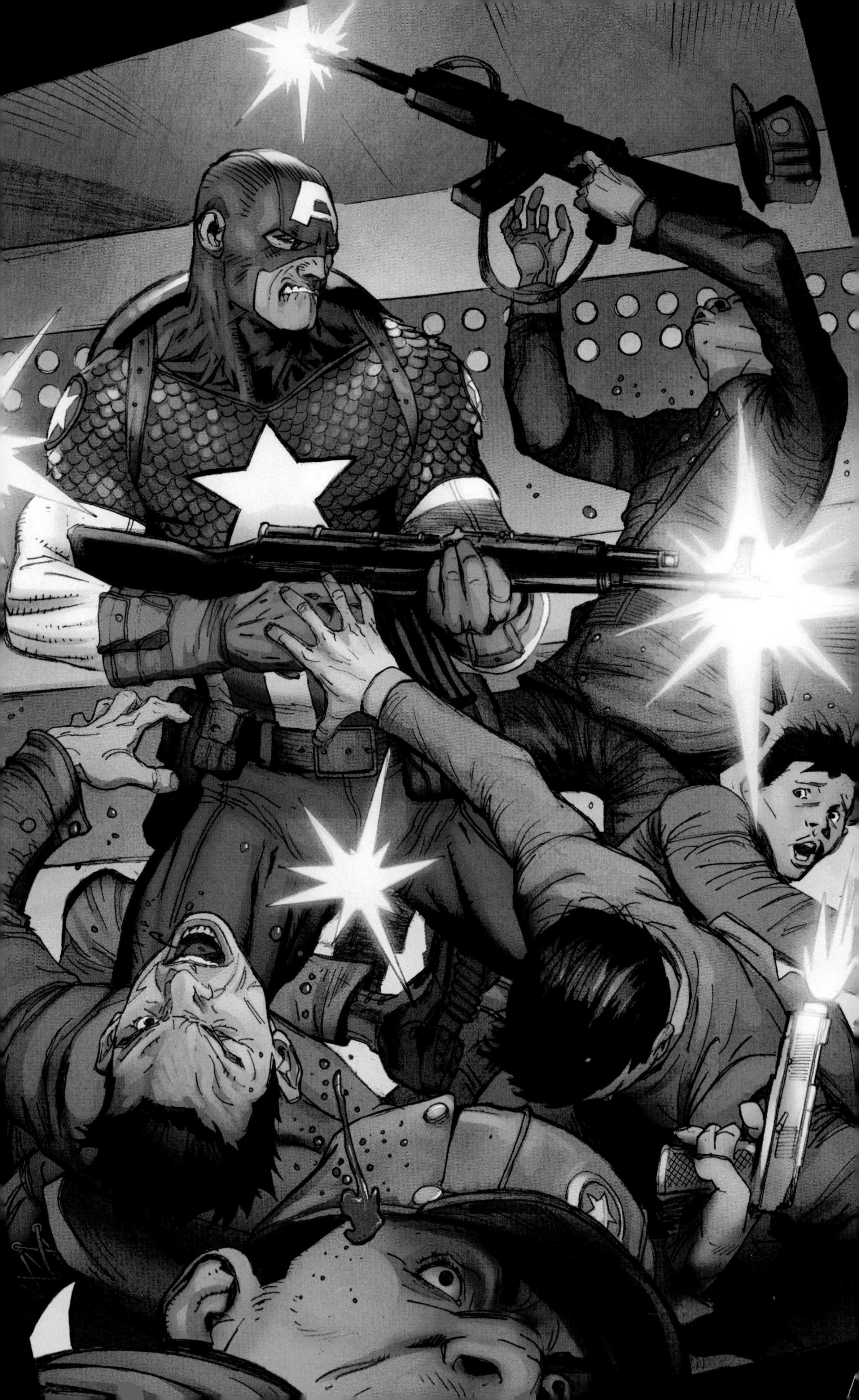

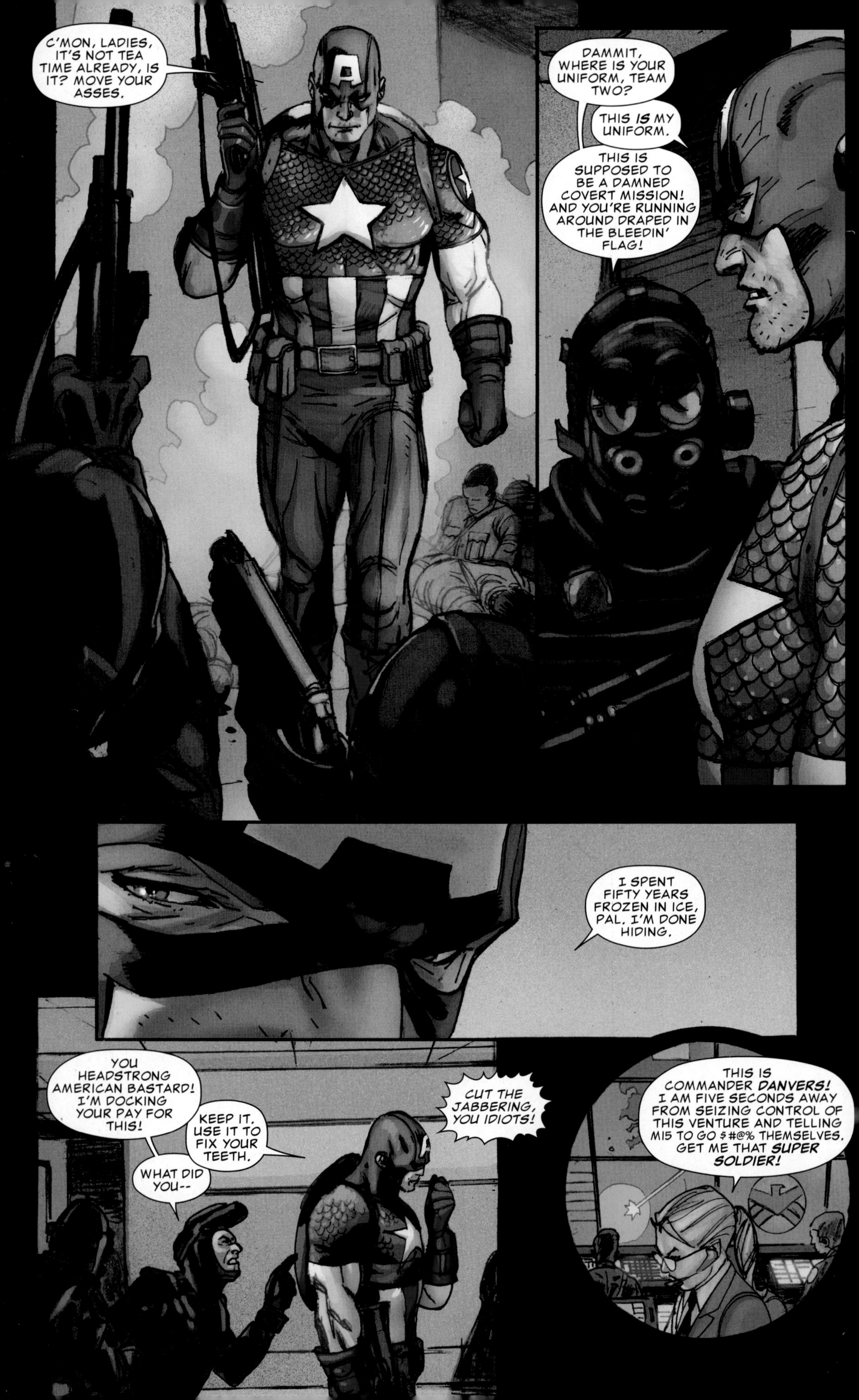
C'MON, LADIES, IT'S NOT TEA TIME ALREADY, IS IT? MOVE YOUR ASSES.
DAMMIT, WHERE IS YOUR UNIFORM, TEAM TWO?
THIS IS MY UNIFORM.
THIS IS SUPPOSED TO BE A DAMNED COVERT MISSION! AND YOU'RE RUNNING AROUND DRAPED IN THE BLEEDIN' FLAG!
I SPENT FIFTY YEARS FROZEN IN ICE, PAL. I'M DONE HIDING.
YOU HEADSTRONG AMERICAN BASTARD! I'M DOCKING YOUR PAY FOR THIS!
KEEP IT. USE IT TO FIX YOUR TEETH.
WHAT DID YOU--
CUT THE JABBERING, YOU IDIOTS!
THIS IS COMMANDER DANVERS! I AM FIVE SECONDS AWAY FROM SEIZING CONTROL OF THIS VENTURE AND TELLING MI5 TO GO $#@% THEMSELVES. GET ME THAT SUPER SOLDIER!

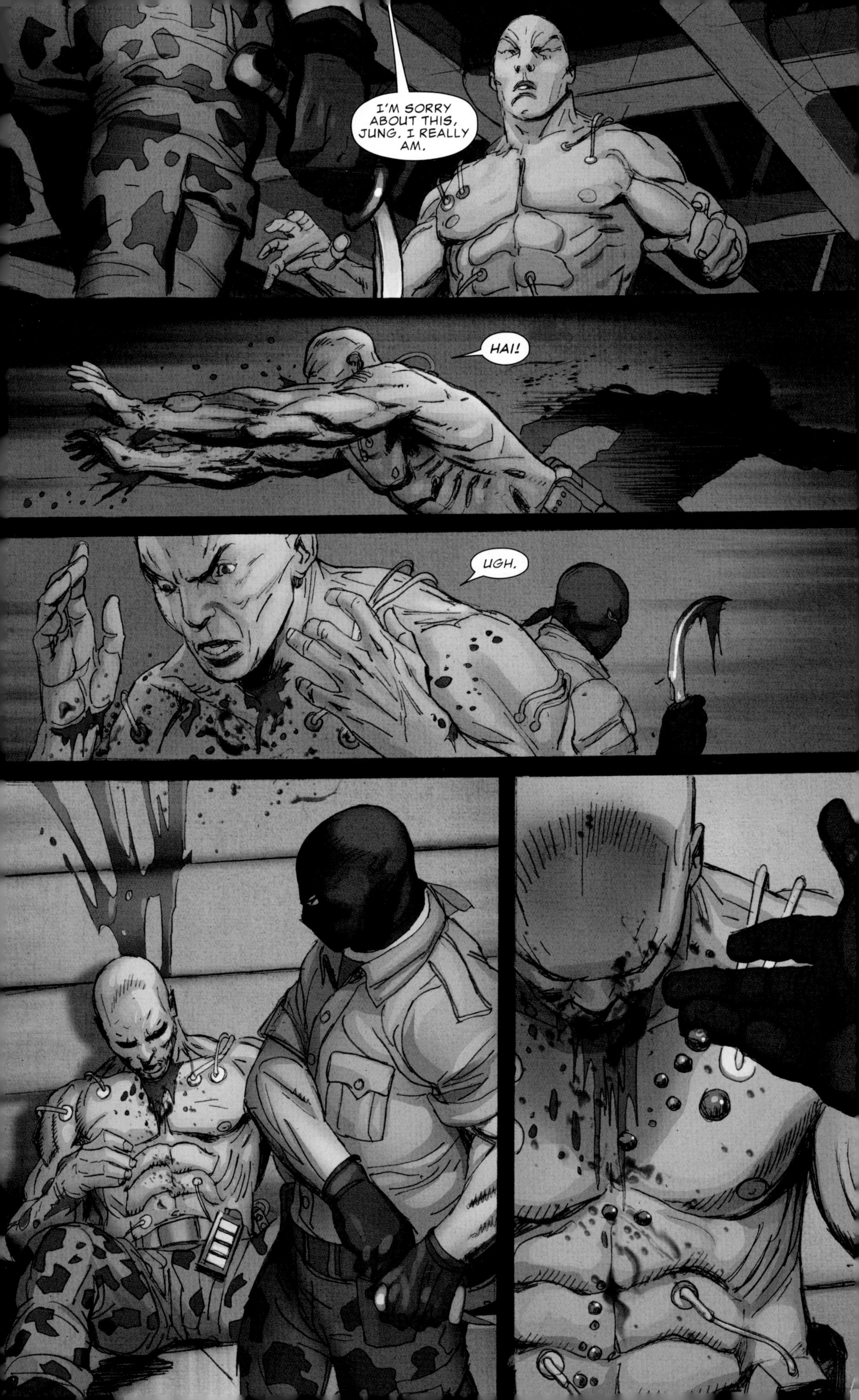
I'M SORRY ABOUT THIS, JUNG. I REALLY AM.
HAI!
UGH.

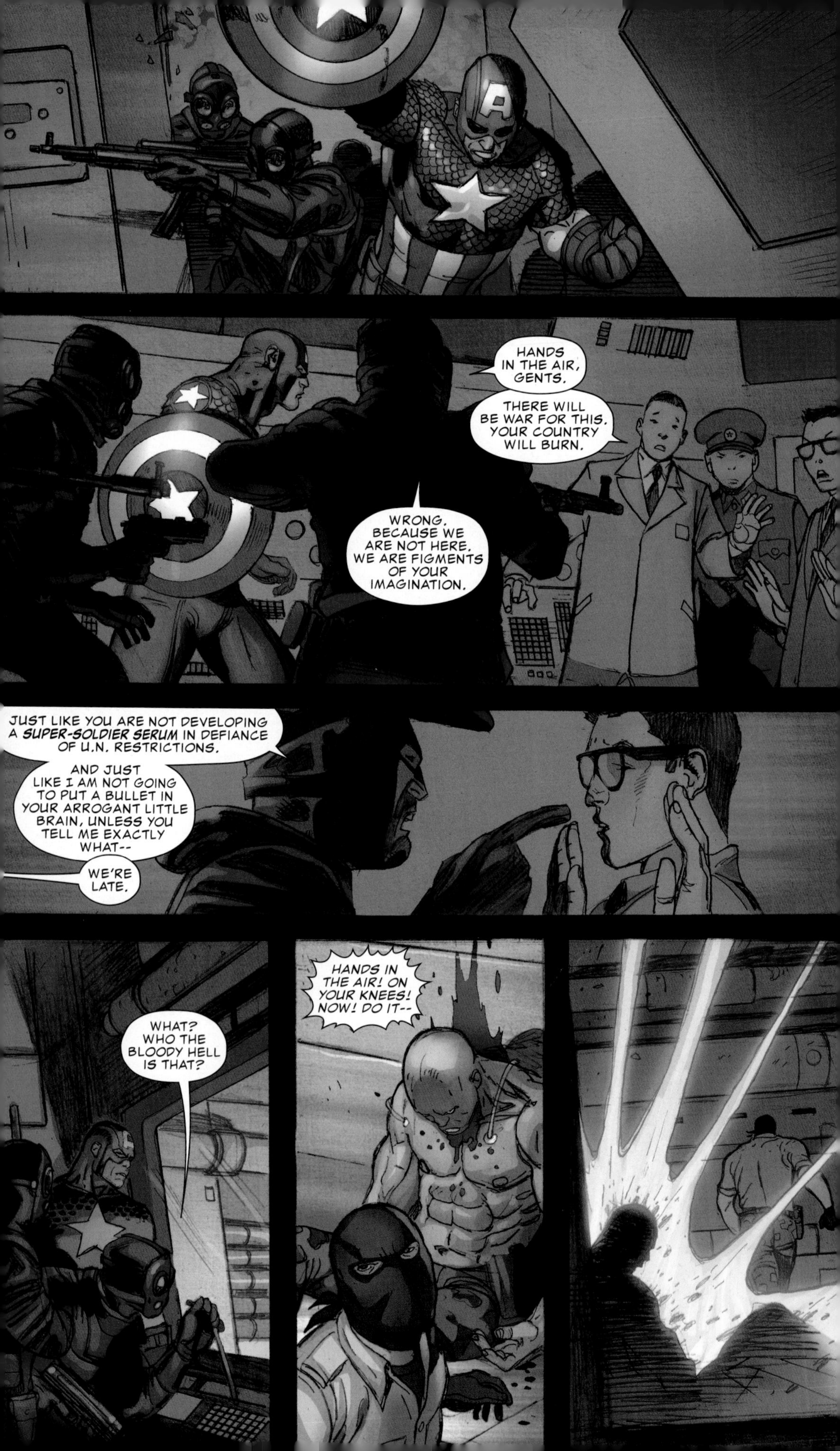

HANDS IN THE AIR, GENTS.
THERE WILL BE WAR FOR THIS. YOUR COUNTRY WILL BURN.
WRONG, BECAUSE WE ARE NOT HERE. WE ARE FIGMENTS OF YOUR IMAGINATION.
JUST LIKE YOU ARE NOT DEVELOPING A SUPER-SOLDIER SERUM IN DEFIANCE OF U.N. RESTRICTIONS.
AND JUST LIKE I AM NOT GOING TO PUT A BULLET IN YOUR ARROGANT LITTLE BRAIN, UNLESS YOU TELL ME EXACTLY WHAT--
WE'RE LATE.
WHAT? WHO THE BLOODY HELL IS THAT?
HANDS IN THE AIR! ON YOUR KNEES! NOW! DO IT--

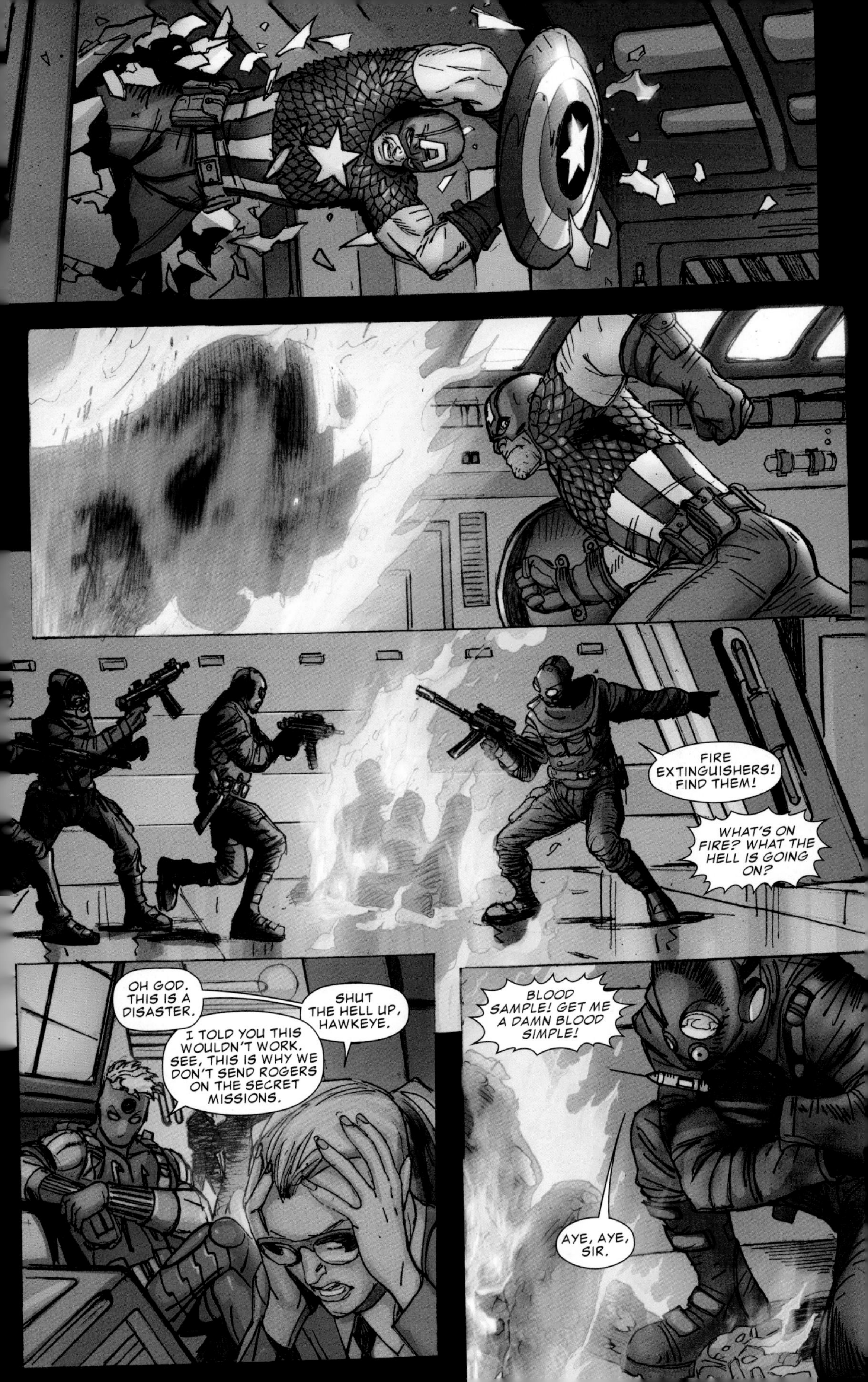

FIRE EXTINGUISHERS! FIND THEM!
WHAT'S ON FIRE? WHAT THE HELL IS GOING ON?
OH GOD. THIS IS A DISASTER.
SHUT THE HELL UP, HAWKEYE.
I TOLD YOU THIS WOULDN'T WORK. SEE, THIS IS WHY WE DON'T SEND ROGERS ON THE SECRET MISSIONS.
BLOOD SAMPLE! GET ME A DAMN BLOOD SIMPLE!
AYE, AYE, SIR.

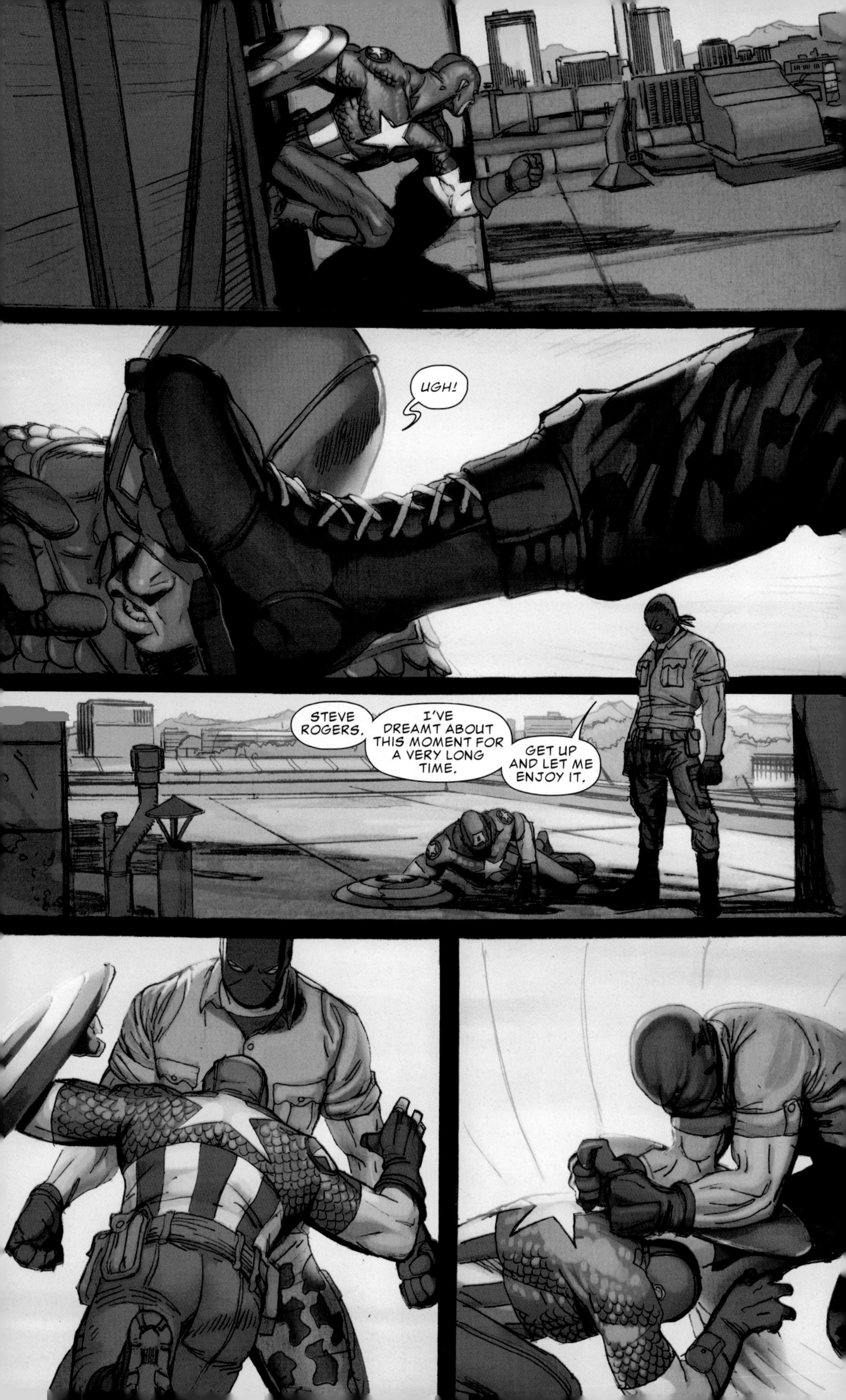
UGH!
STEVE ROGERS.
I'VE DREAMT ABOUT THIS MOMENT FOR A VERY LONG TIME.
GET UP AND LET ME ENJOY IT.

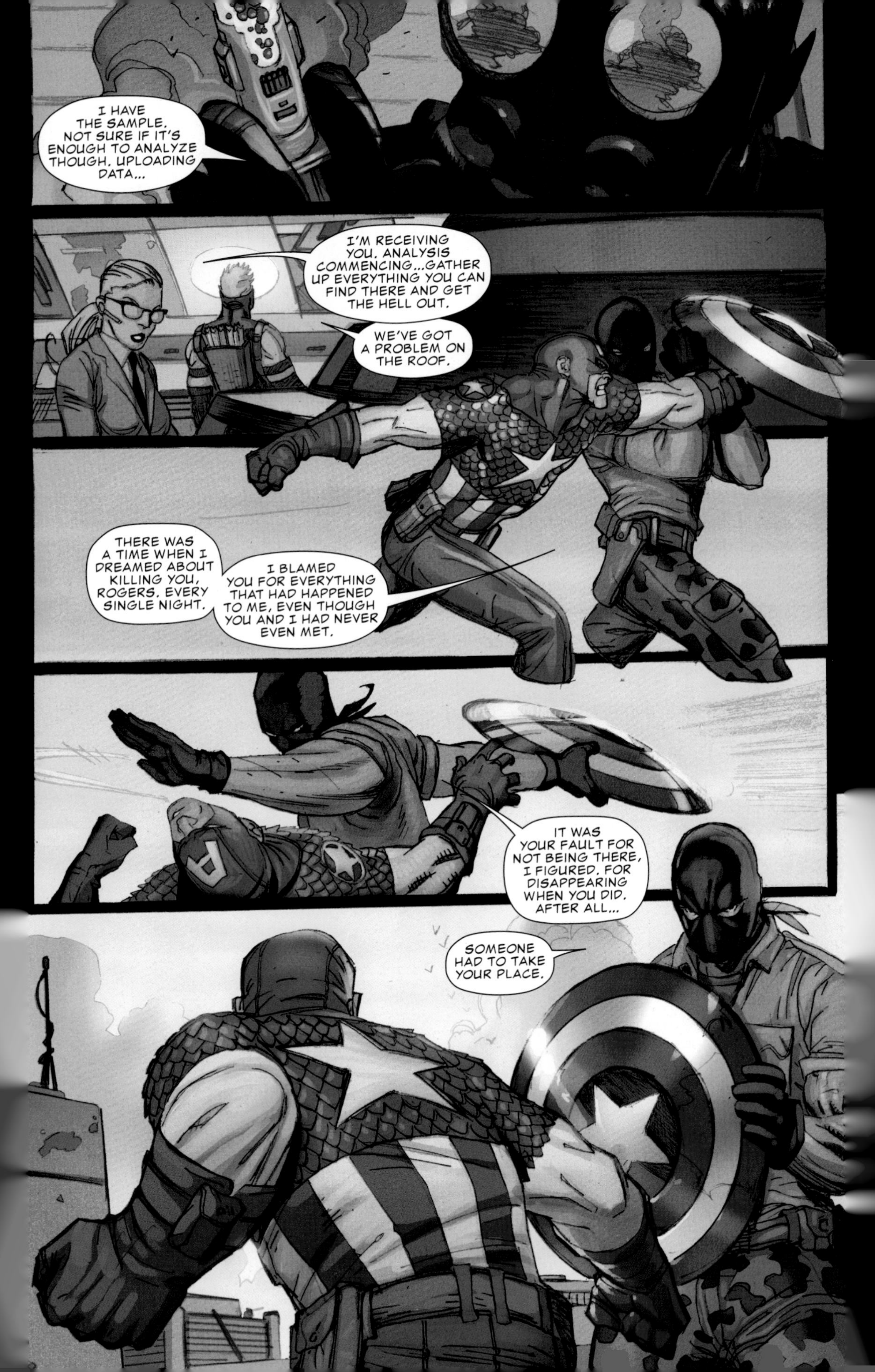
I HAVE THE SAMPLE. NOT SURE IF IT'S ENOUGH TO ANALYZE THOUGH. UPLOADING DATA...
I'M RECEIVING YOU. ANALYSIS COMMENCING...GATHER UP EVERYTHING YOU CAN FIND THERE AND GET THE HELL OUT.
WE'VE GOT A PROBLEM ON THE ROOF.
THERE WAS A TIME WHEN I DREAMED ABOUT KILLING YOU, ROGERS. EVERY SINGLE NIGHT.
I BLAMED YOU FOR EVERYTHING THAT HAD HAPPENED TO ME, EVEN THOUGH YOU AND I HAD NEVER EVEN MET.
IT WAS YOUR FAULT FOR NOT BEING THERE, I FIGURED. FOR DISAPPEARING WHEN YOU DID. AFTER ALL...
SOMEONE HAD TO TAKE YOUR PLACE.

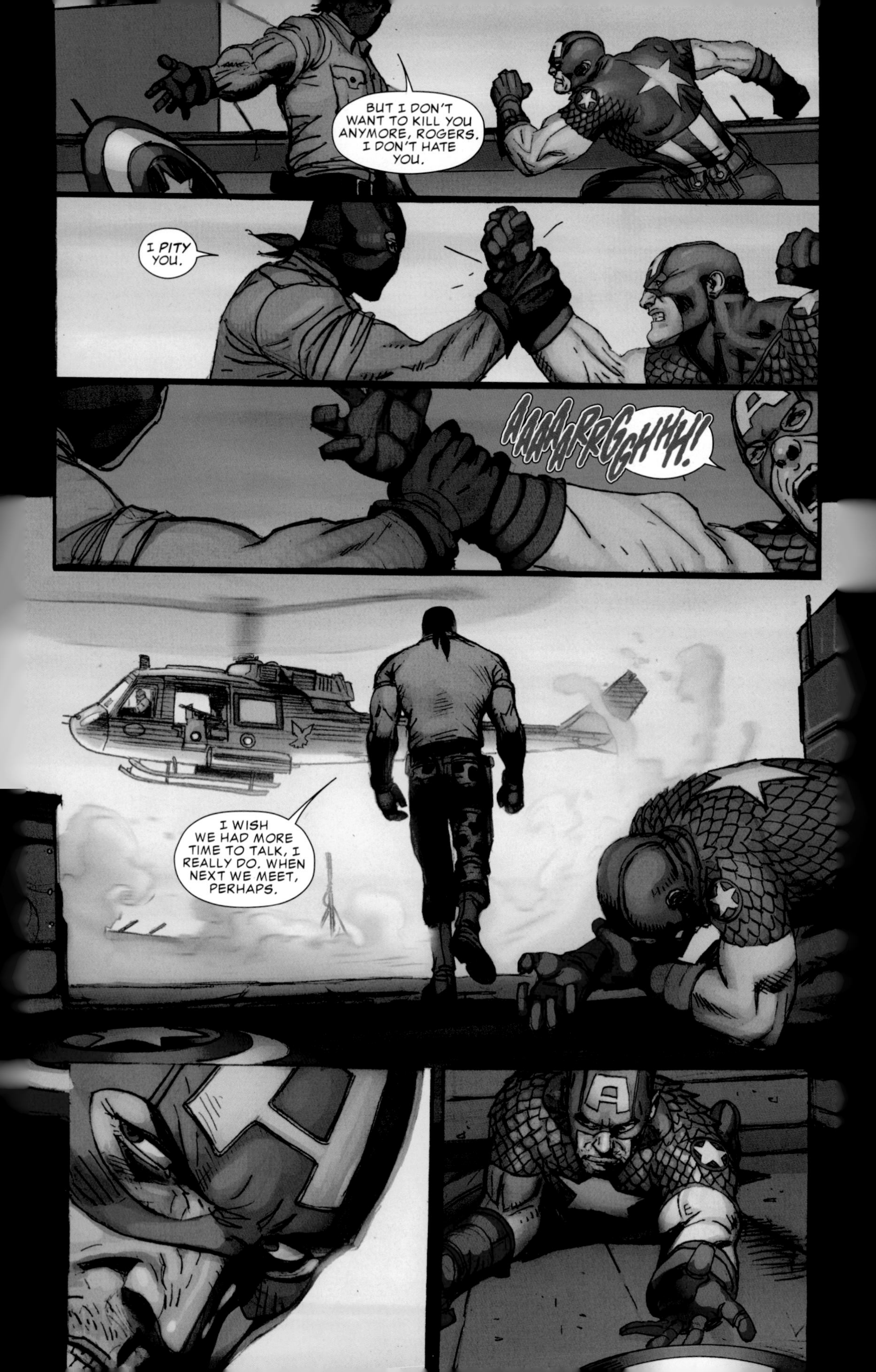
BUT I DON'T WANT TO KILL YOU ANYMORE, ROGERS. I DON'T HATE YOU.
I PITY YOU.
AAAAARRGGHHH!
I WISH WE HAD MORE TIME TO TALK, I REALLY DO. WHEN NEXT WE MEET, PERHAPS.

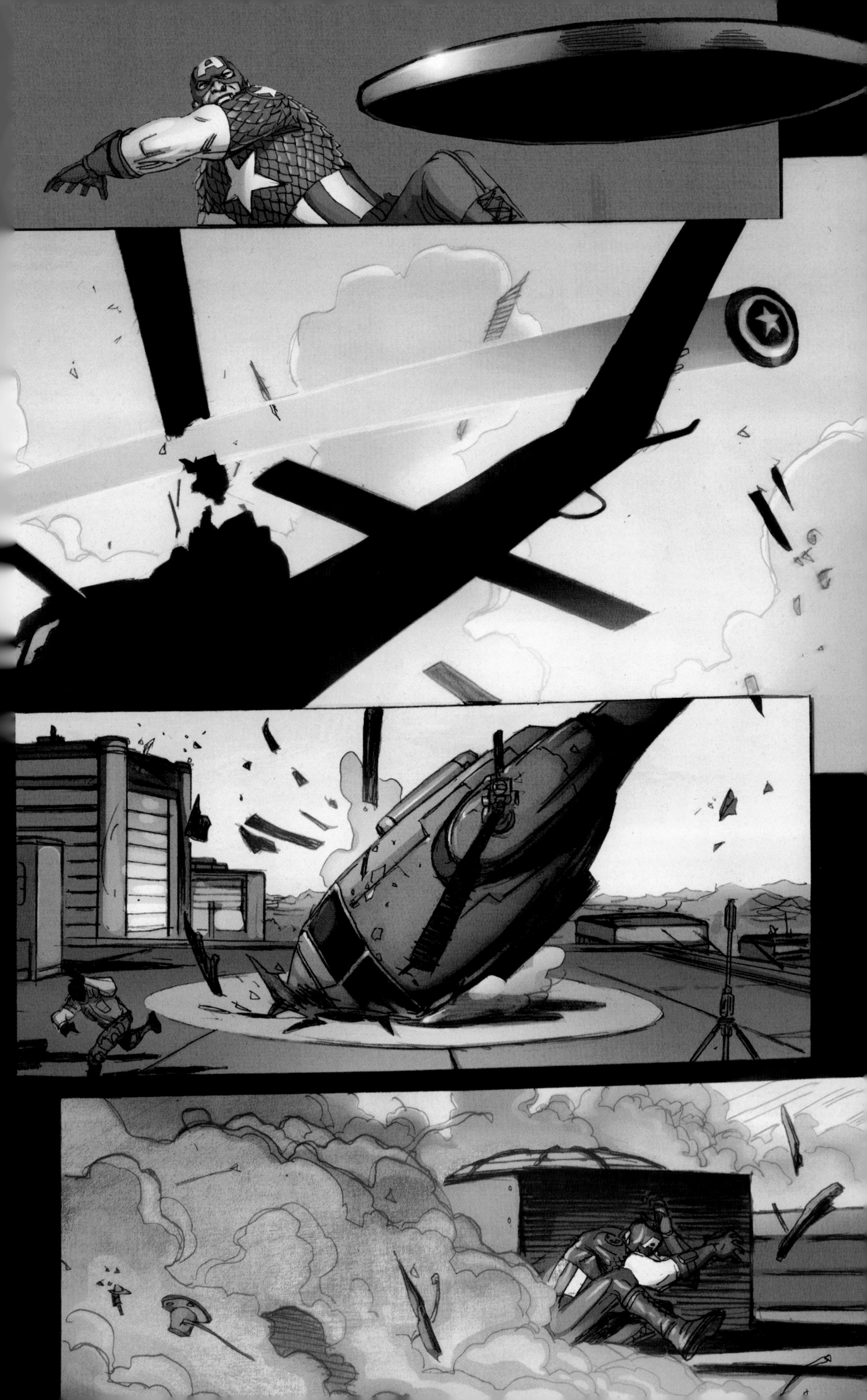

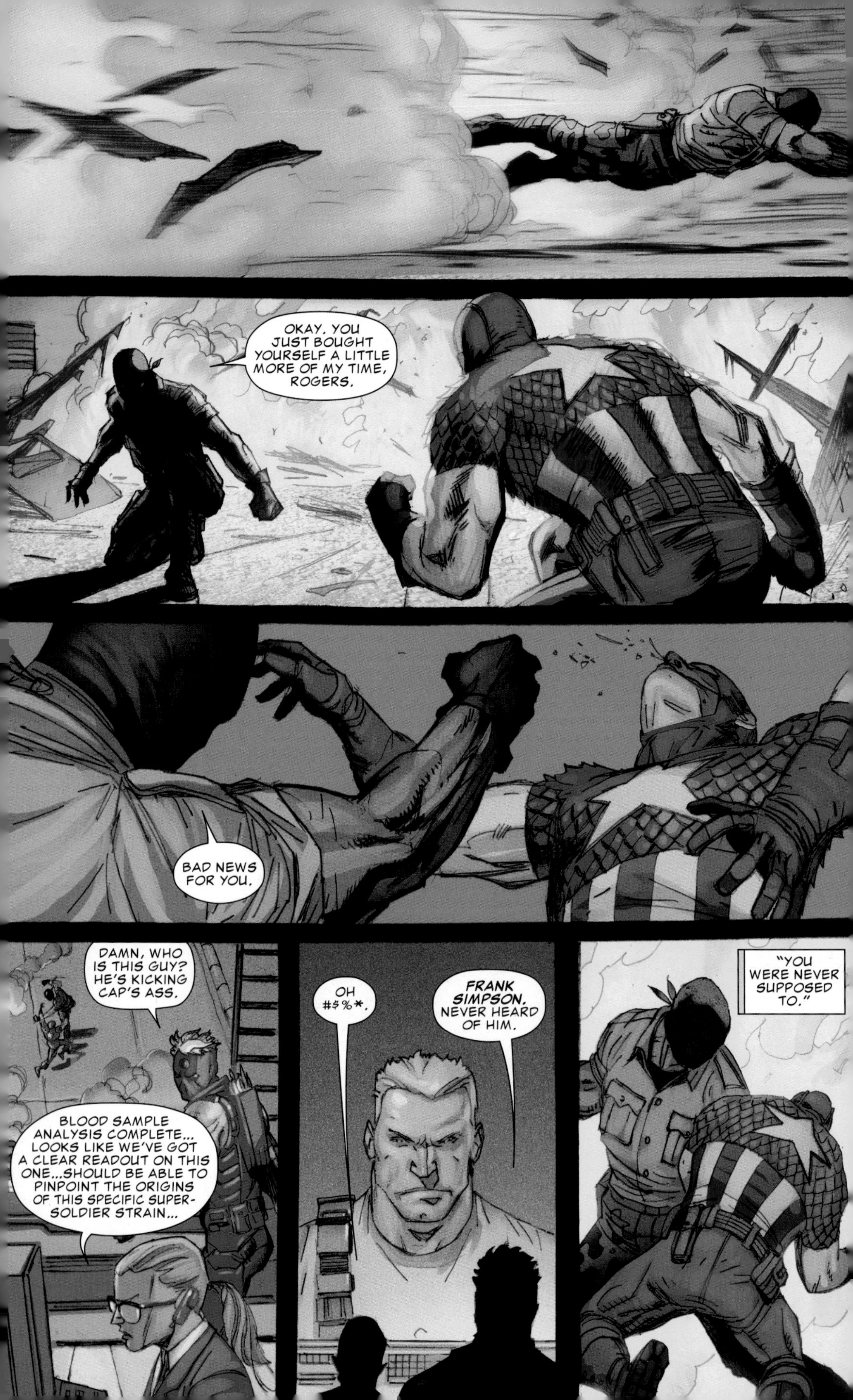
OKAY. YOU JUST BOUGHT YOURSELF A LITTLE MORE OF MY TIME, ROGERS.
BAD NEWS FOR YOU.
DAMN, WHO IS THIS GUY? HE'S KICKING CAP'S ASS.
BLOOD SAMPLE ANALYSIS COMPLETE... LOOKS LIKE WE'VE GOT A CLEAR READOUT ON THIS ONE...SHOULD BE ABLE TO PINPOINT THE ORIGINS OF THIS SPECIFIC SUPER-SOLDIER STRAIN...
OH #$%*.
FRANK SIMPSON. NEVER HEARD OF HIM.
"YOU WERE NEVER SUPPOSED TO."

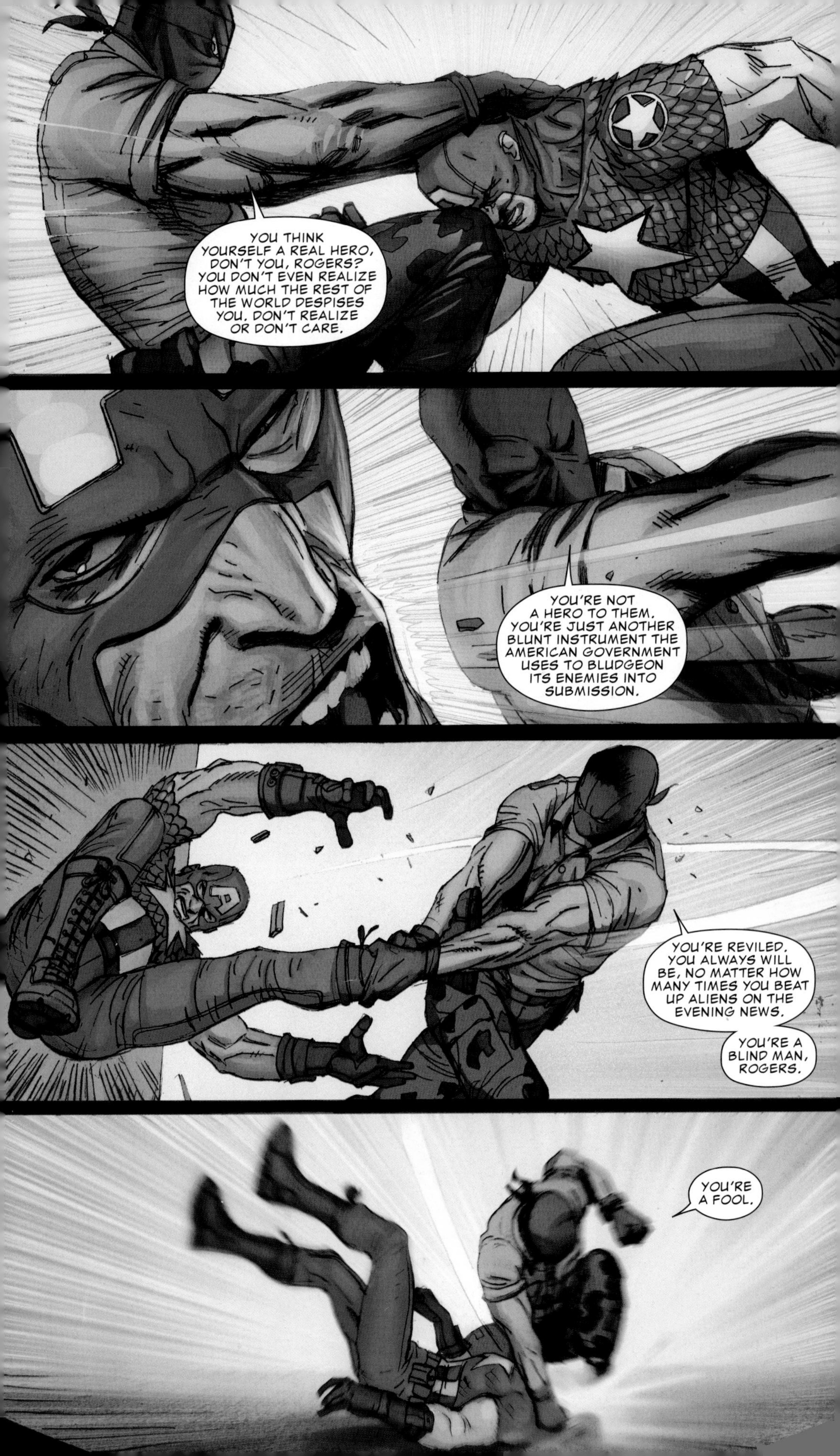
YOU THINK YOURSELF A REAL HERO, DON'T YOU, ROGERS? YOU DON'T EVEN REALIZE HOW MUCH THE REST OF THE WORLD DESPISES YOU. DON'T REALIZE OR DON'T CARE.
YOU'RE NOT A HERO TO THEM. YOU'RE JUST ANOTHER BLUNT INSTRUMENT THE AMERICAN GOVERNMENT USES TO BLUDGEON ITS ENEMIES INTO SUBMISSION.
YOU'RE REVILED. YOU ALWAYS WILL BE, NO MATTER HOW MANY TIMES YOU BEAT UP ALIENS ON THE EVENING NEWS.
YOU'RE A BLIND MAN, ROGERS.
YOU'RE A FOOL.

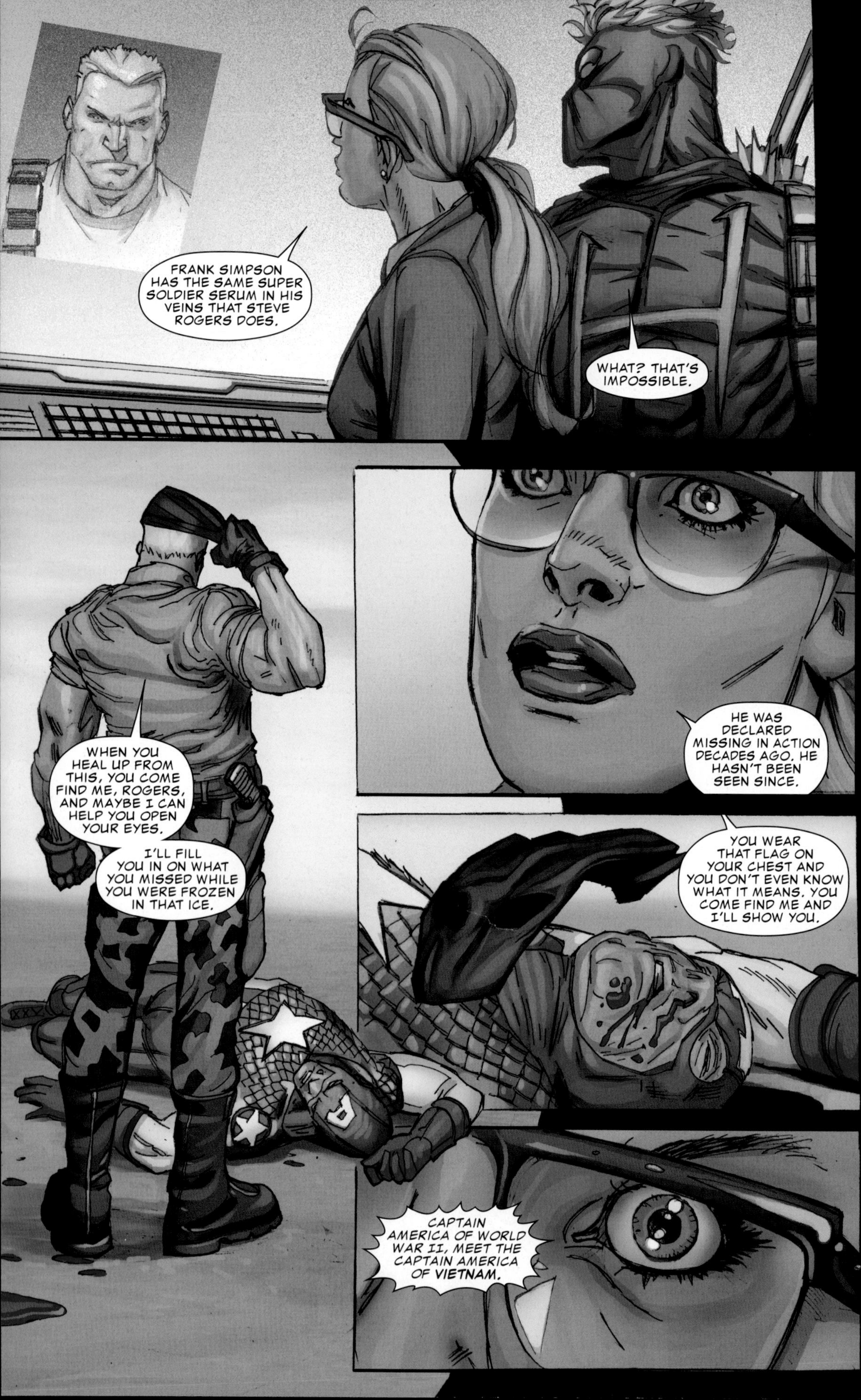
FRANK SIMPSON HAS THE SAME SUPER SOLDIER SERUM IN HIS VEINS THAT STEVE ROGERS DOES.
WHAT? THAT'S IMPOSSIBLE.
HE WAS DECLARED MISSING IN ACTION DECADES AGO. HE HASN'T BEEN SEEN SINCE.
WHEN YOU HEAL UP FROM THIS, YOU COME FIND ME, ROGERS, AND MAYBE I CAN HELP YOU OPEN YOUR EYES.
I'LL FILL YOU IN ON WHAT YOU MISSED WHILE YOU WERE FROZEN IN THAT ICE.
YOU WEAR THAT FLAG ON YOUR CHEST AND YOU DON'T EVEN KNOW WHAT IT MEANS. YOU COME FIND ME AND I'LL SHOW YOU.
CAPTAIN AMERICA OF WORLD WAR II, MEET THE CAPTAIN AMERICA OF VIETNAM.

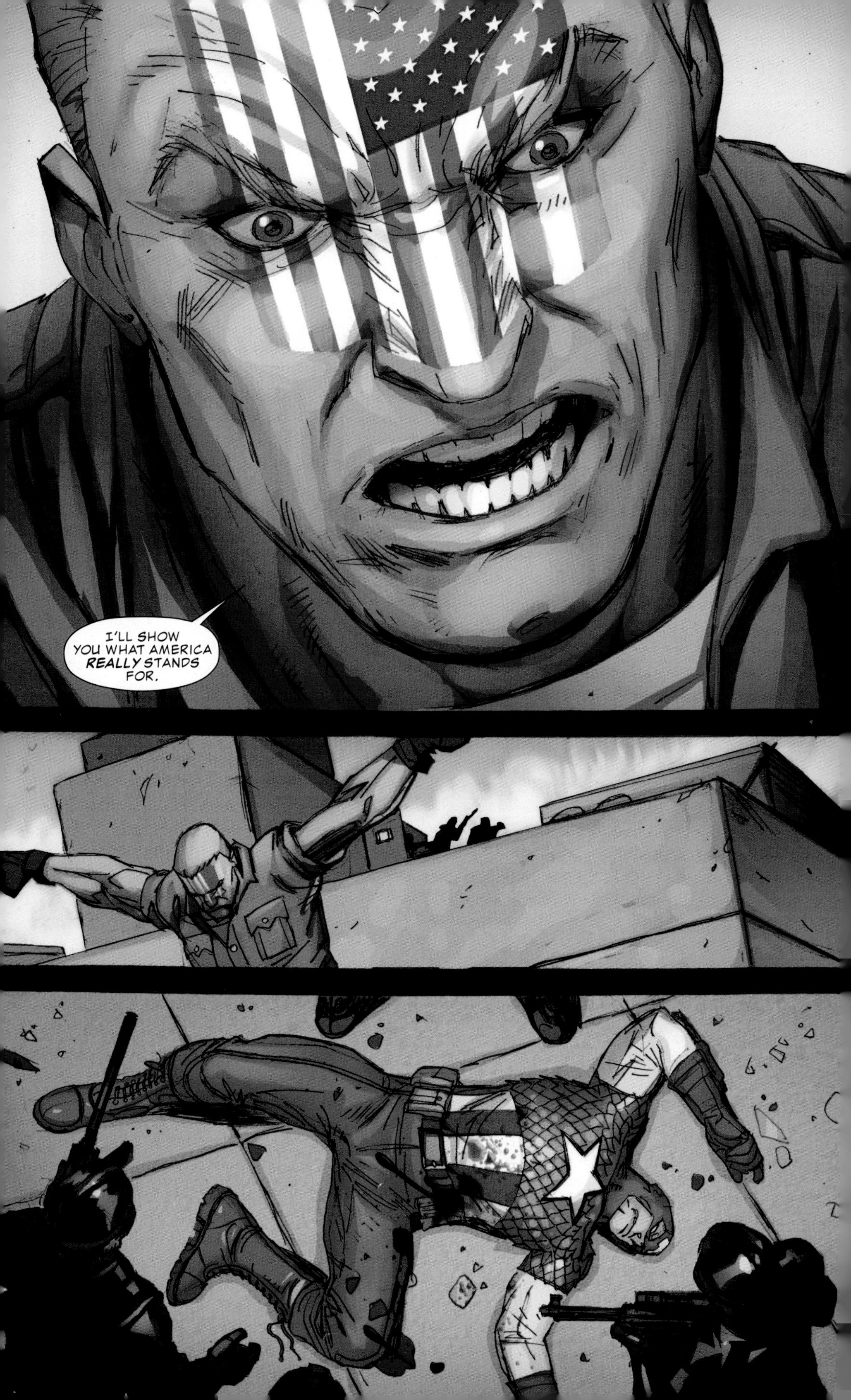
I'LL SHOW YOU WHAT AMERICA REALLY STANDS FOR.

2

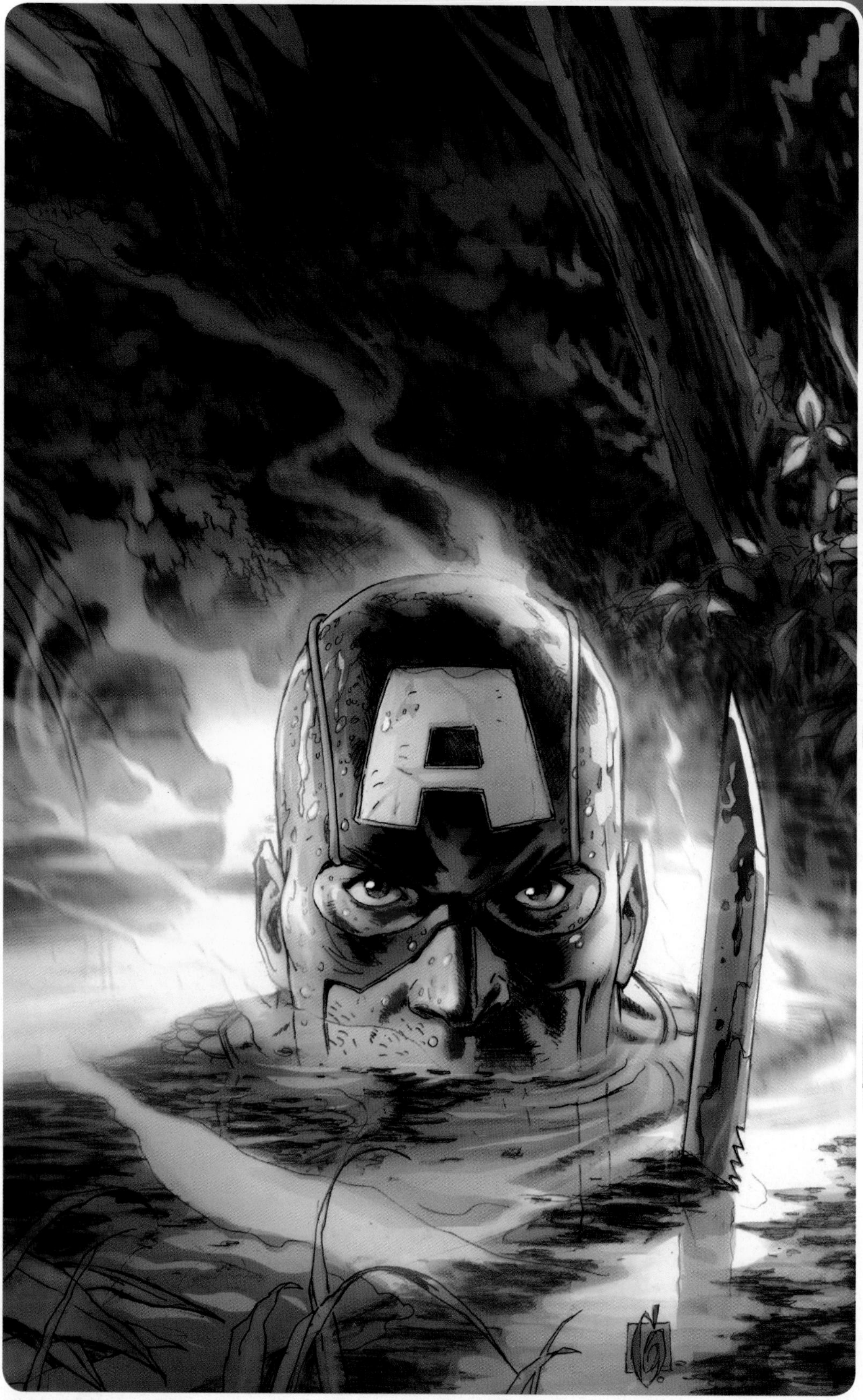

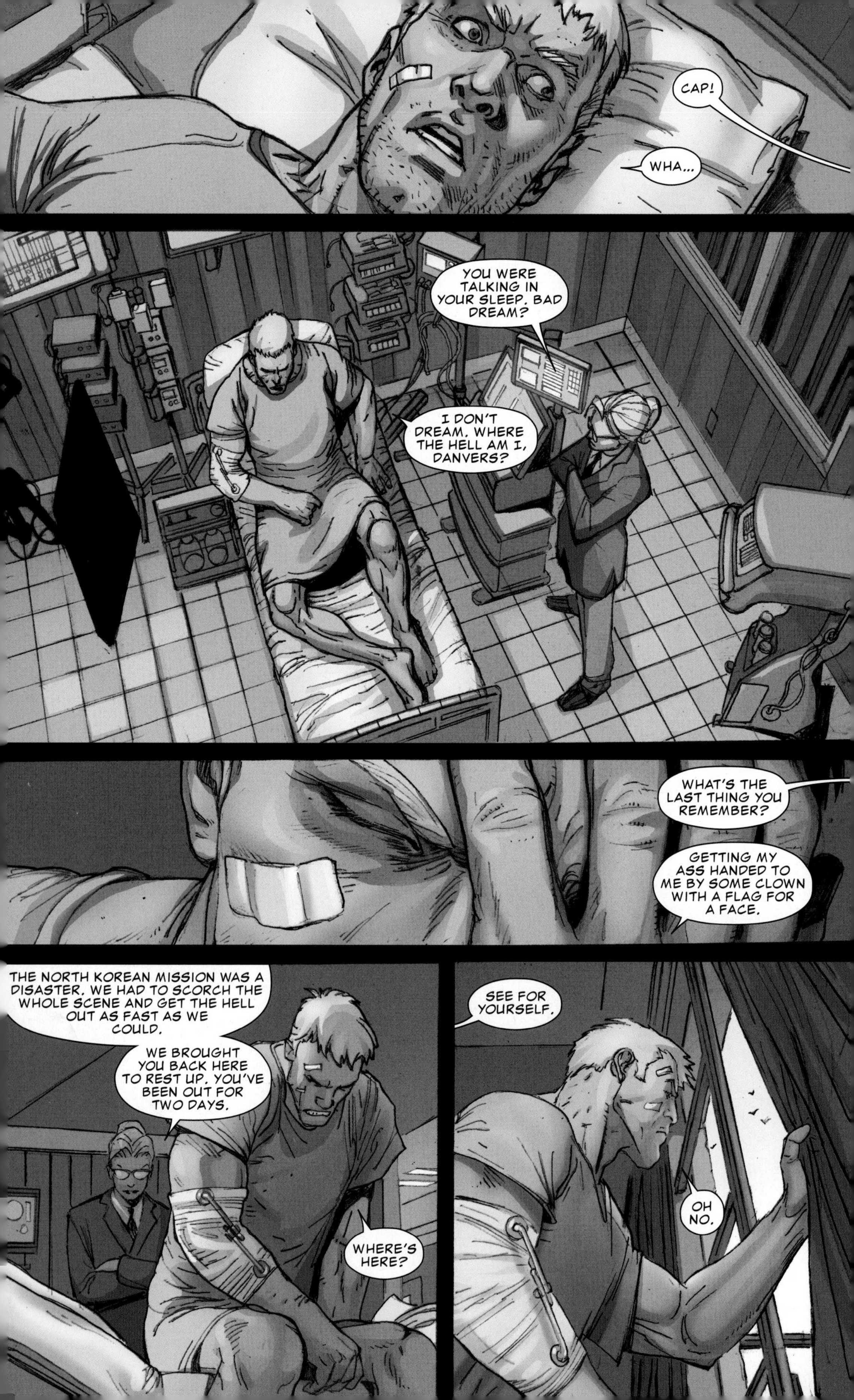
CAP!
WHA...
YOU WERE TALKING IN YOUR SLEEP. BAD DREAM?
I DON'T DREAM. WHERE THE HELL AM I, DANVERS?
WHAT'S THE LAST THING YOU REMEMBER?
GETTING MY ASS HANDED TO ME BY SOME CLOWN WITH A FLAG FOR A FACE.
THE NORTH KOREAN MISSION WAS A DISASTER. WE HAD TO SCORCH THE WHOLE SCENE AND GET THE HELL OUT AS FAST AS WE COULD.
WE BROUGHT YOU BACK HERE TO REST UP. YOU'VE BEEN OUT FOR TWO DAYS.
WHERE'S HERE?
SEE FOR YOURSELF.
OH NO.

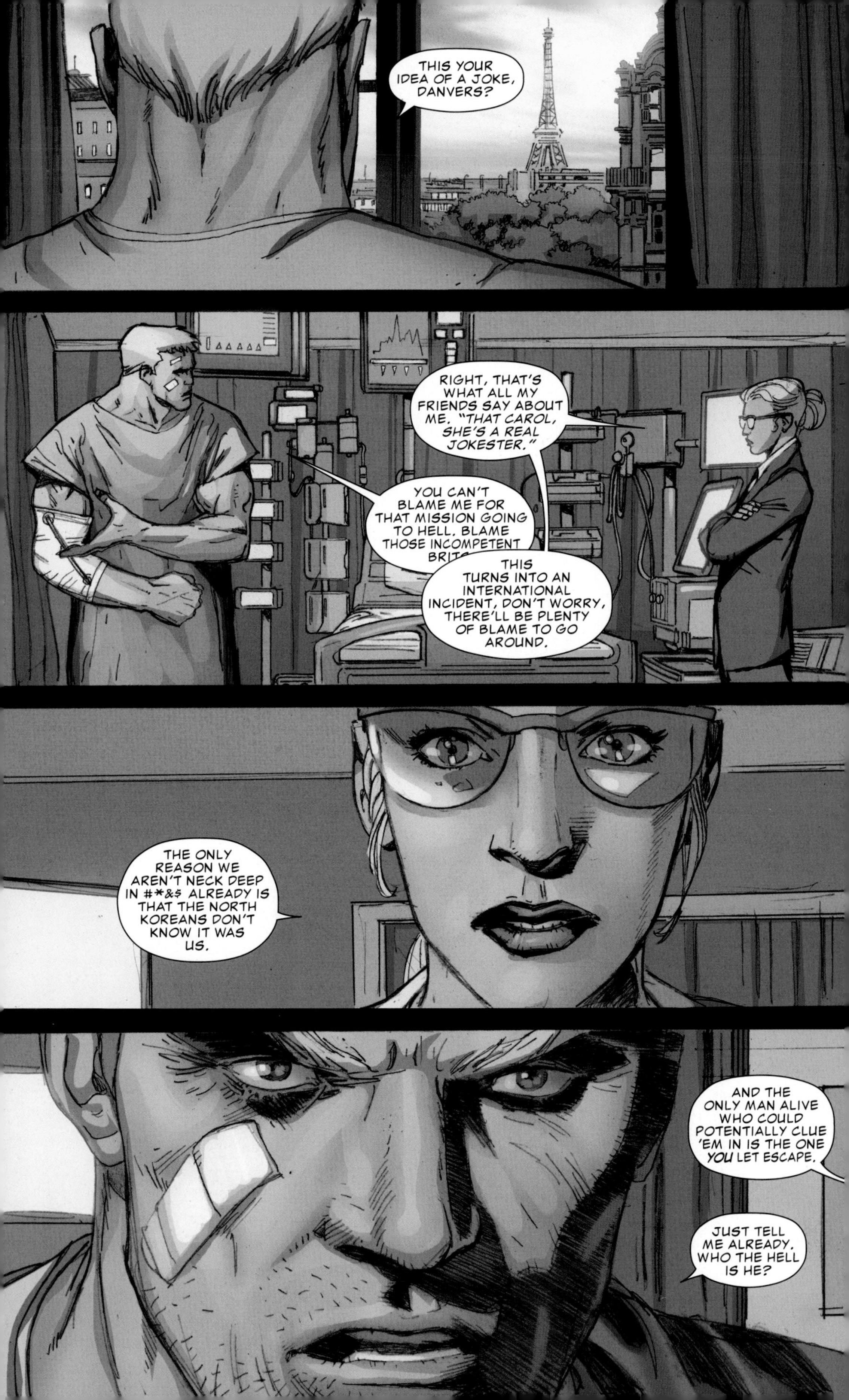
THIS YOUR IDEA OF A JOKE, DANVERS?
RIGHT, THAT'S WHAT ALL MY FRIENDS SAY ABOUT ME. "THAT CAROL, SHE'S A REAL JOKESTER."
YOU CAN'T BLAME ME FOR THAT MISSION GOING TO HELL. BLAME THOSE INCOMPETENT BRIT--
THIS TURNS INTO AN INTERNATIONAL INCIDENT, DON'T WORRY, THERE'LL BE PLENTY OF BLAME TO GO AROUND.
THE ONLY REASON WE AREN'T NECK DEEP IN #*&$ ALREADY IS THAT THE NORTH KOREANS DON'T KNOW IT WAS US.
AND THE ONLY MAN ALIVE WHO COULD POTENTIALLY CLUE 'EM IN IS THE ONE *YOU* LET ESCAPE.
JUST TELL ME ALREADY. WHO THE HELL IS HE?

FRANK SIMPSON.

WHO THE HELL'S FRANK SIMPSON?

ONCE UPON A TIME, A GUY A LOT LIKE YOU, A KID RAISED ON APPLE PIE WHO LOVED HIS COUNTRY AND WANTED TO DO HIS PART.

"IN THE YEARS AFTER YOU DISAPPEARED, THE GOVERNMENT KEPT LOOKING FOR SOMEONE TO TAKE YOUR PLACE.

"FRANK SIMPSON ANSWERED THAT CALL."

YOU MEAN PROJECT REBIRTH. THEY GAVE HIM THE SAME INJECTIONS THEY GAVE ME?

NOT EXACTLY.

WITH YOU GONE AND DR. ERSKINE DEAD, REBIRTH HAD TO START OVER FROM SCRATCH. IT TOOK YEARS OF FAILURE BEFORE THEY DEVELOPED A SERUM THAT SHOWED ANY SORT OF PROMISE.

"SIMPSON WAS THEIR GREATEST SUCCESS.

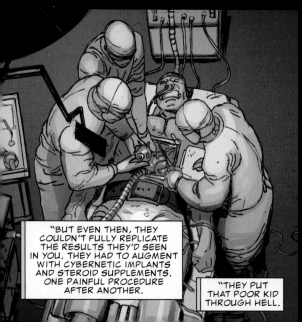

"BUT EVEN THEN, THEY COULDN'T FULLY REPLICATE THE RESULTS THEY'D SEEN IN YOU. THEY HAD TO AUGMENT WITH CYBERNETIC IMPLANTS AND STEROID SUPPLEMENTS. ONE PAINFUL PROCEDURE AFTER ANOTHER.

"THEY PUT THAT POOR KID THROUGH HELL.

"IT'S NO WONDER HE EVENTUALLY SNAPPED."

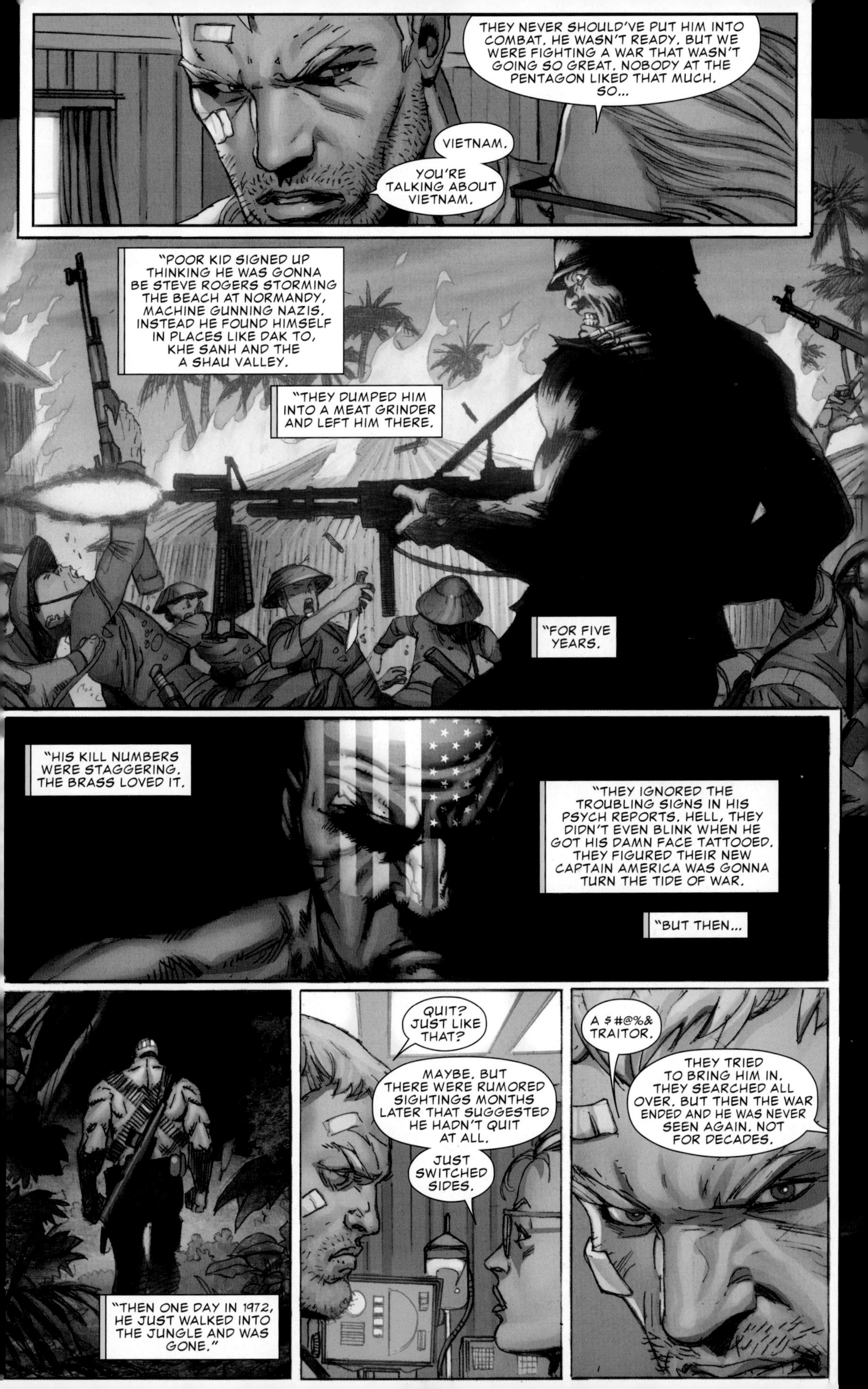

THEY NEVER SHOULD'VE PUT HIM INTO COMBAT. HE WASN'T READY. BUT WE WERE FIGHTING A WAR THAT WASN'T GOING SO GREAT. NOBODY AT THE PENTAGON LIKED THAT MUCH. SO...
VIETNAM.
YOU'RE TALKING ABOUT VIETNAM.
"POOR KID SIGNED UP THINKING HE WAS GONNA BE STEVE ROGERS STORMING THE BEACH AT NORMANDY, MACHINE GUNNING NAZIS. INSTEAD HE FOUND HIMSELF IN PLACES LIKE DAK TO, KHE SANH AND THE A SHAU VALLEY.
"THEY DUMPED HIM INTO A MEAT GRINDER AND LEFT HIM THERE.
"FOR FIVE YEARS.
"HIS KILL NUMBERS WERE STAGGERING. THE BRASS LOVED IT.
"THEY IGNORED THE TROUBLING SIGNS IN HIS PSYCH REPORTS. HELL, THEY DIDN'T EVEN BLINK WHEN HE GOT HIS DAMN FACE TATTOOED. THEY FIGURED THEIR NEW CAPTAIN AMERICA WAS GONNA TURN THE TIDE OF WAR.
"BUT THEN...
"THEN ONE DAY IN 1972, HE JUST WALKED INTO THE JUNGLE AND WAS GONE."
QUIT? JUST LIKE THAT?
MAYBE. BUT THERE WERE RUMORED SIGHTINGS MONTHS LATER THAT SUGGESTED HE HADN'T QUIT AT ALL.
JUST SWITCHED SIDES.
A $#@%& TRAITOR.
THEY TRIED TO BRING HIM IN. THEY SEARCHED ALL OVER. BUT THEN THE WAR ENDED AND HE WAS NEVER SEEN AGAIN. NOT FOR DECADES.

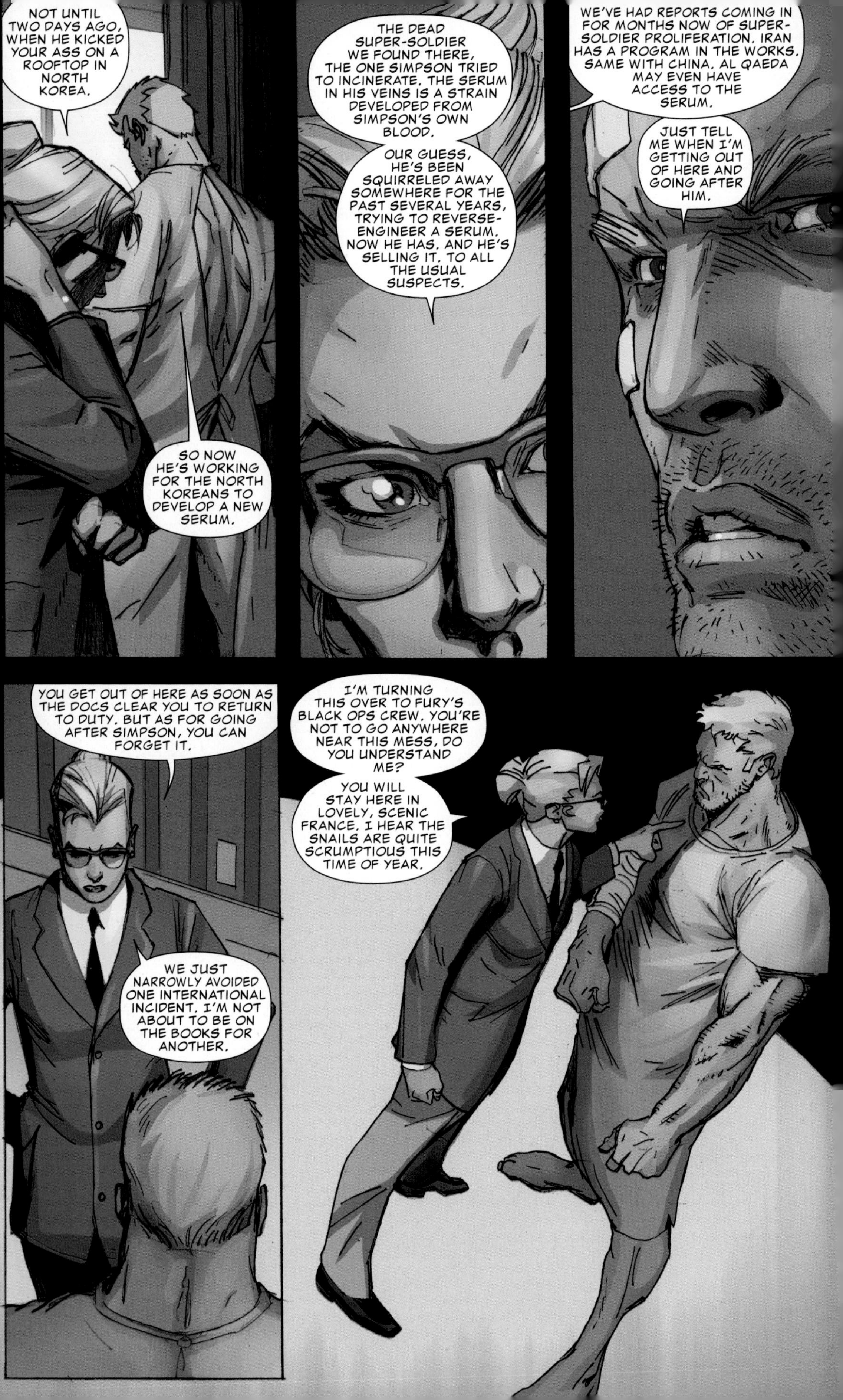
NOT UNTIL TWO DAYS AGO, WHEN HE KICKED YOUR ASS ON A ROOFTOP IN NORTH KOREA.
SO NOW HE'S WORKING FOR THE NORTH KOREANS TO DEVELOP A NEW SERUM.
THE DEAD SUPER-SOLDIER WE FOUND THERE, THE ONE SIMPSON TRIED TO INCINERATE. THE SERUM IN HIS VEINS IS A STRAIN DEVELOPED FROM SIMPSON'S OWN BLOOD.
OUR GUESS, HE'S BEEN SQUIRRELED AWAY SOMEWHERE FOR THE PAST SEVERAL YEARS, TRYING TO REVERSE-ENGINEER A SERUM. NOW HE HAS, AND HE'S SELLING IT. TO ALL THE USUAL SUSPECTS.
WE'VE HAD REPORTS COMING IN FOR MONTHS NOW OF SUPER-SOLDIER PROLIFERATION. IRAN HAS A PROGRAM IN THE WORKS. SAME WITH CHINA. AL QAEDA MAY EVEN HAVE ACCESS TO THE SERUM.
JUST TELL ME WHEN I'M GETTING OUT OF HERE AND GOING AFTER HIM.
YOU GET OUT OF HERE AS SOON AS THE DOCS CLEAR YOU TO RETURN TO DUTY. BUT AS FOR GOING AFTER SIMPSON, YOU CAN FORGET IT.
WE JUST NARROWLY AVOIDED ONE INTERNATIONAL INCIDENT. I'M NOT ABOUT TO BE ON THE BOOKS FOR ANOTHER.
I'M TURNING THIS OVER TO FURY'S BLACK OPS CREW. YOU'RE NOT TO GO ANYWHERE NEAR THIS MESS, DO YOU UNDERSTAND ME?
YOU WILL STAY HERE IN LOVELY, SCENIC FRANCE. I HEAR THE SNAILS ARE QUITE SCRUMPTIOUS THIS TIME OF YEAR.

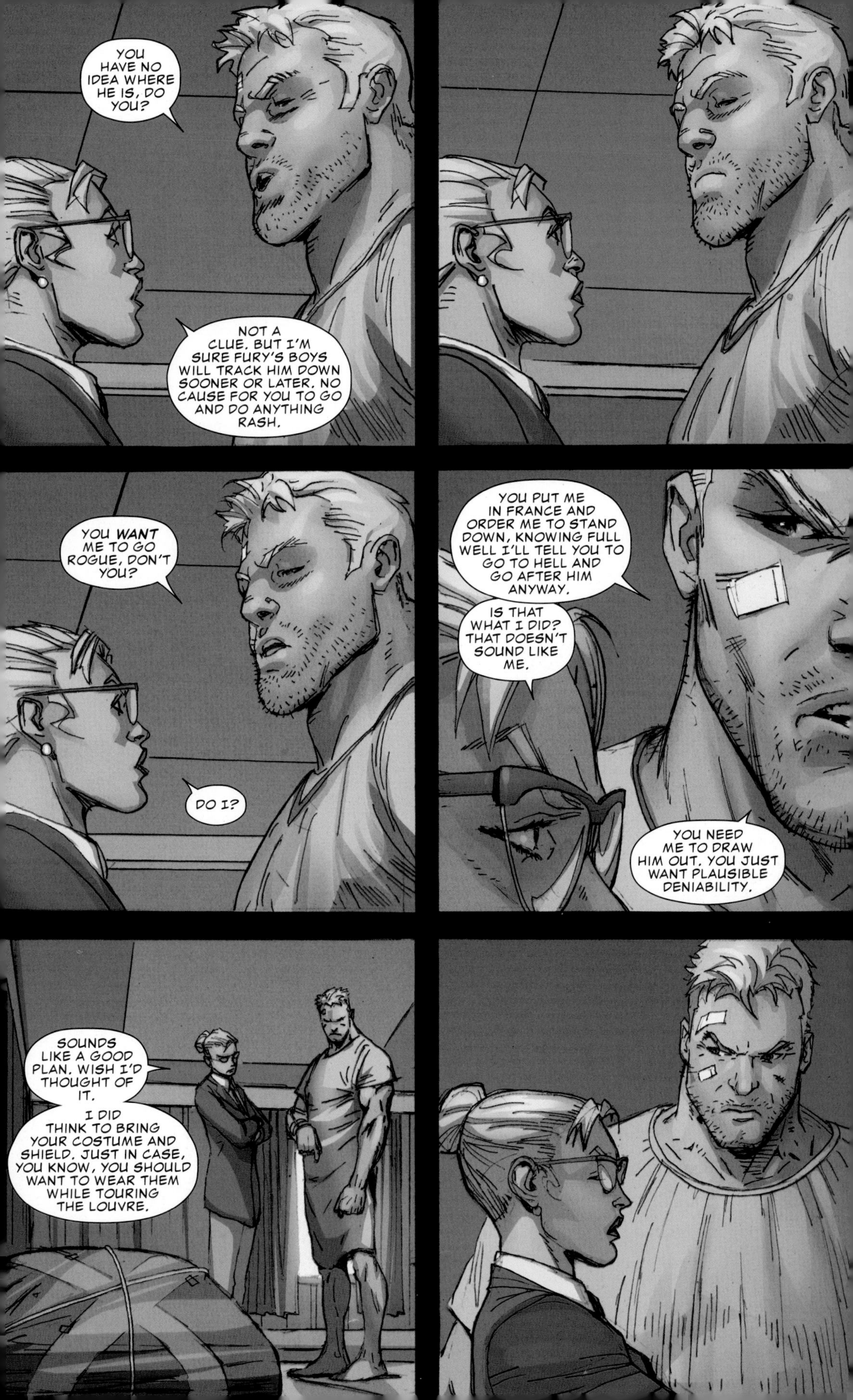
YOU HAVE NO IDEA WHERE HE IS, DO YOU?
NOT A CLUE. BUT I'M SURE FURY'S BOYS WILL TRACK HIM DOWN SOONER OR LATER. NO CAUSE FOR YOU TO GO AND DO ANYTHING RASH.
YOU WANT ME TO GO ROGUE, DON'T YOU?
DO I?
YOU PUT ME IN FRANCE AND ORDER ME TO STAND DOWN, KNOWING FULL WELL I'LL TELL YOU TO GO TO HELL AND GO AFTER HIM ANYWAY.
IS THAT WHAT I DID? THAT DOESN'T SOUND LIKE ME.
YOU NEED ME TO DRAW HIM OUT. YOU JUST WANT PLAUSIBLE DENIABILITY.
SOUNDS LIKE A GOOD PLAN. WISH I'D THOUGHT OF IT.
I DID THINK TO BRING YOUR COSTUME AND SHIELD. JUST IN CASE, YOU KNOW, YOU SHOULD WANT TO WEAR THEM WHILE TOURING THE LOUVRE.

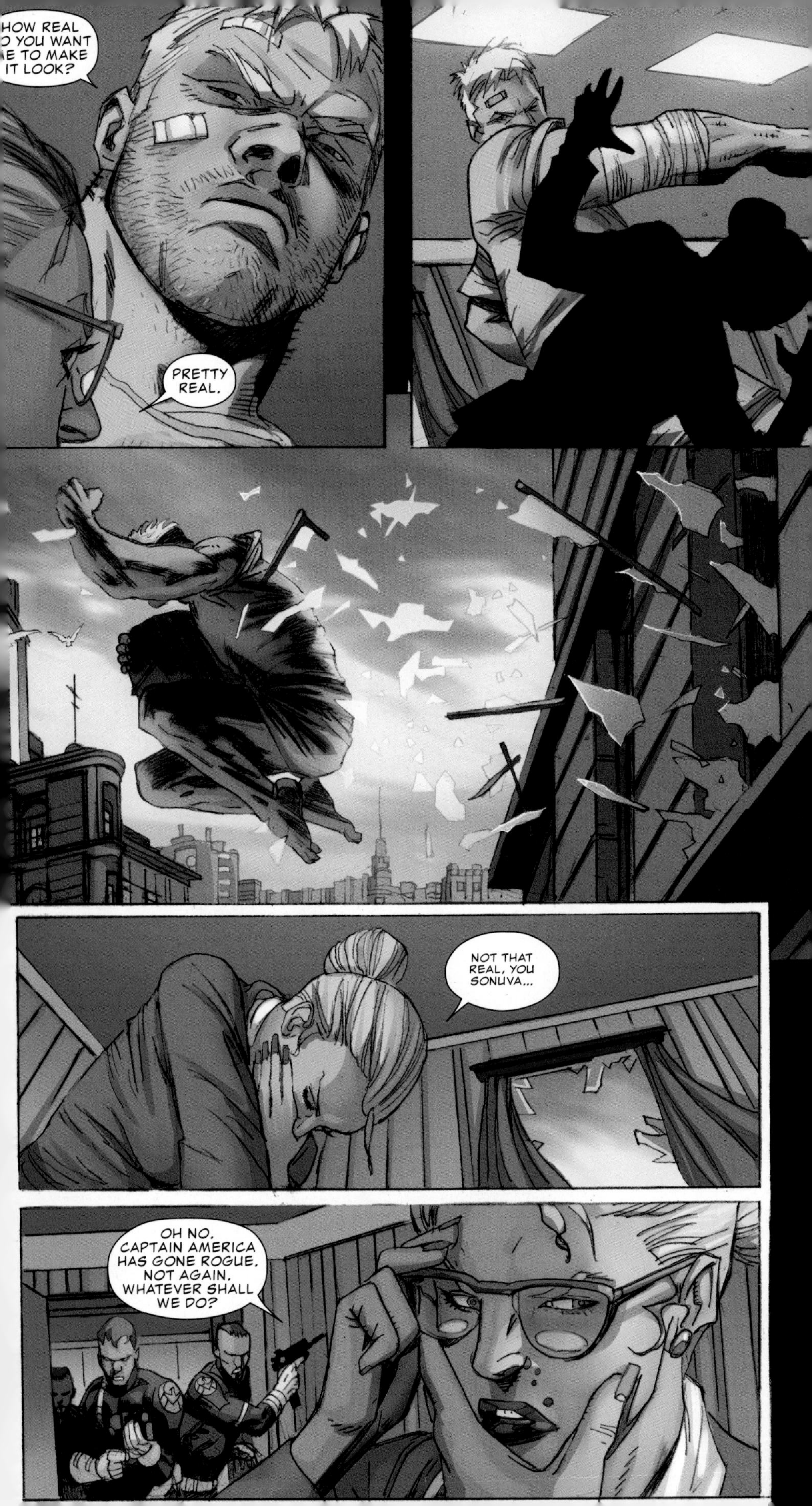
HOW REAL DO YOU WANT ME TO MAKE IT LOOK?
PRETTY REAL.
NOT THAT REAL, YOU SONUVA...
OH NO. CAPTAIN AMERICA HAS GONE ROGUE. NOT AGAIN. WHATEVER SHALL WE DO?

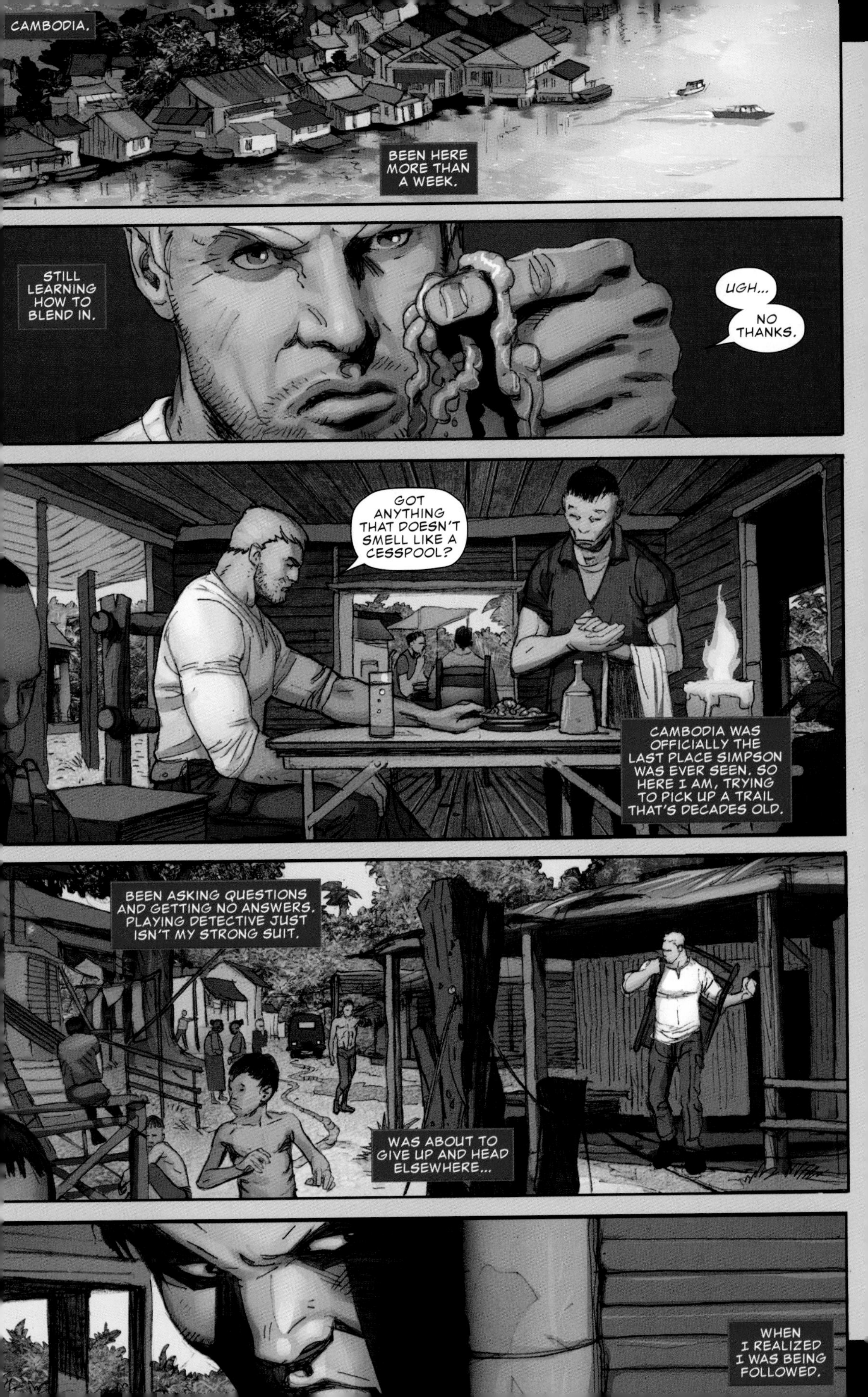
CAMBODIA.
BEEN HERE MORE THAN A WEEK.
STILL LEARNING HOW TO BLEND IN.
UGH...
NO THANKS.
GOT ANYTHING THAT DOESN'T SMELL LIKE A CESSPOOL?
CAMBODIA WAS OFFICIALLY THE LAST PLACE SIMPSON WAS EVER SEEN. SO HERE I AM, TRYING TO PICK UP A TRAIL THAT'S DECADES OLD.
BEEN ASKING QUESTIONS AND GETTING NO ANSWERS. PLAYING DETECTIVE JUST ISN'T MY STRONG SUIT.
WAS ABOUT TO GIVE UP AND HEAD ELSEWHERE...
WHEN I REALIZED I WAS BEING FOLLOWED.

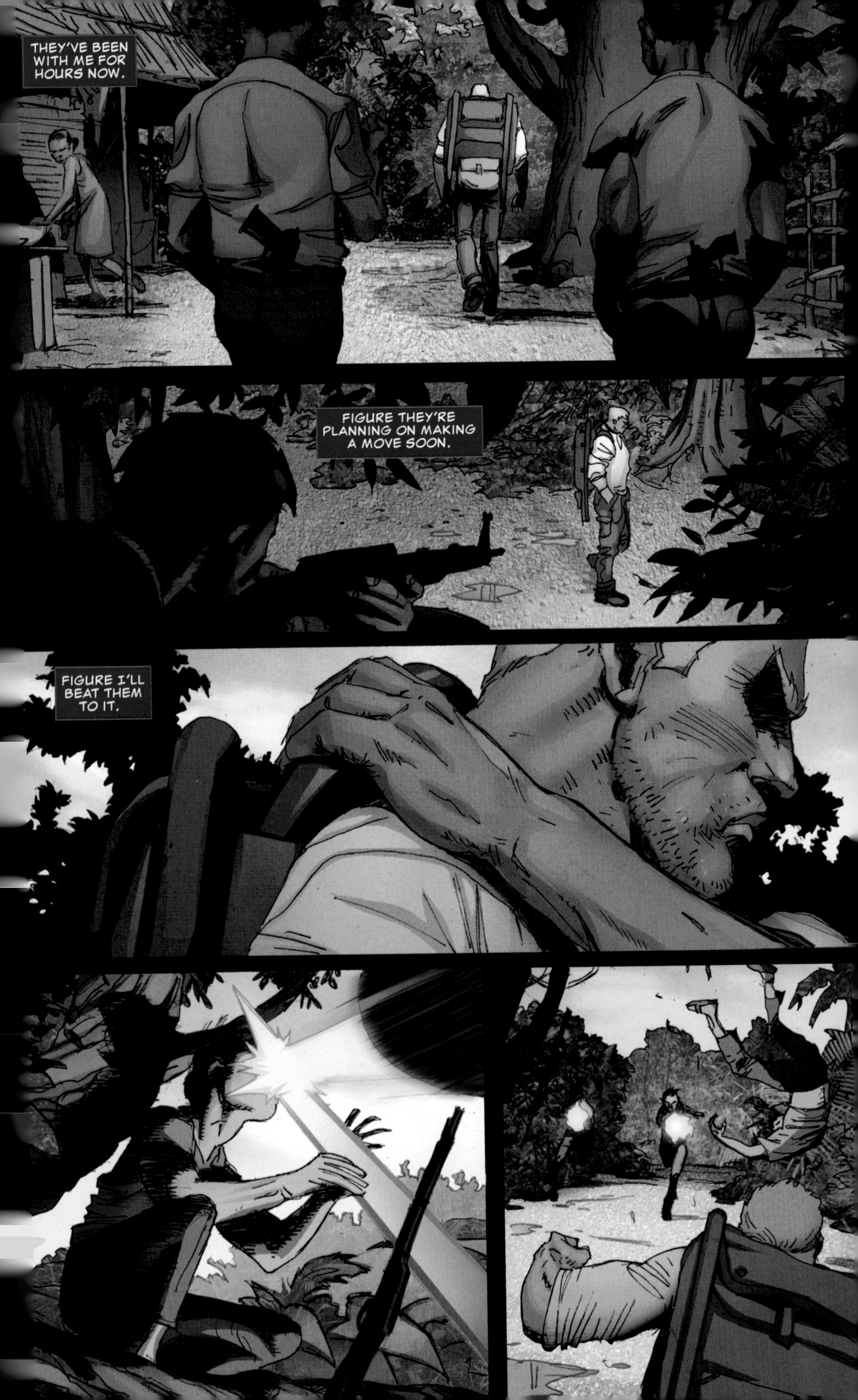
THEY'VE BEEN WITH ME FOR HOURS NOW.
FIGURE THEY'RE PLANNING ON MAKING A MOVE SOON.
FIGURE I'LL BEAT THEM TO IT.

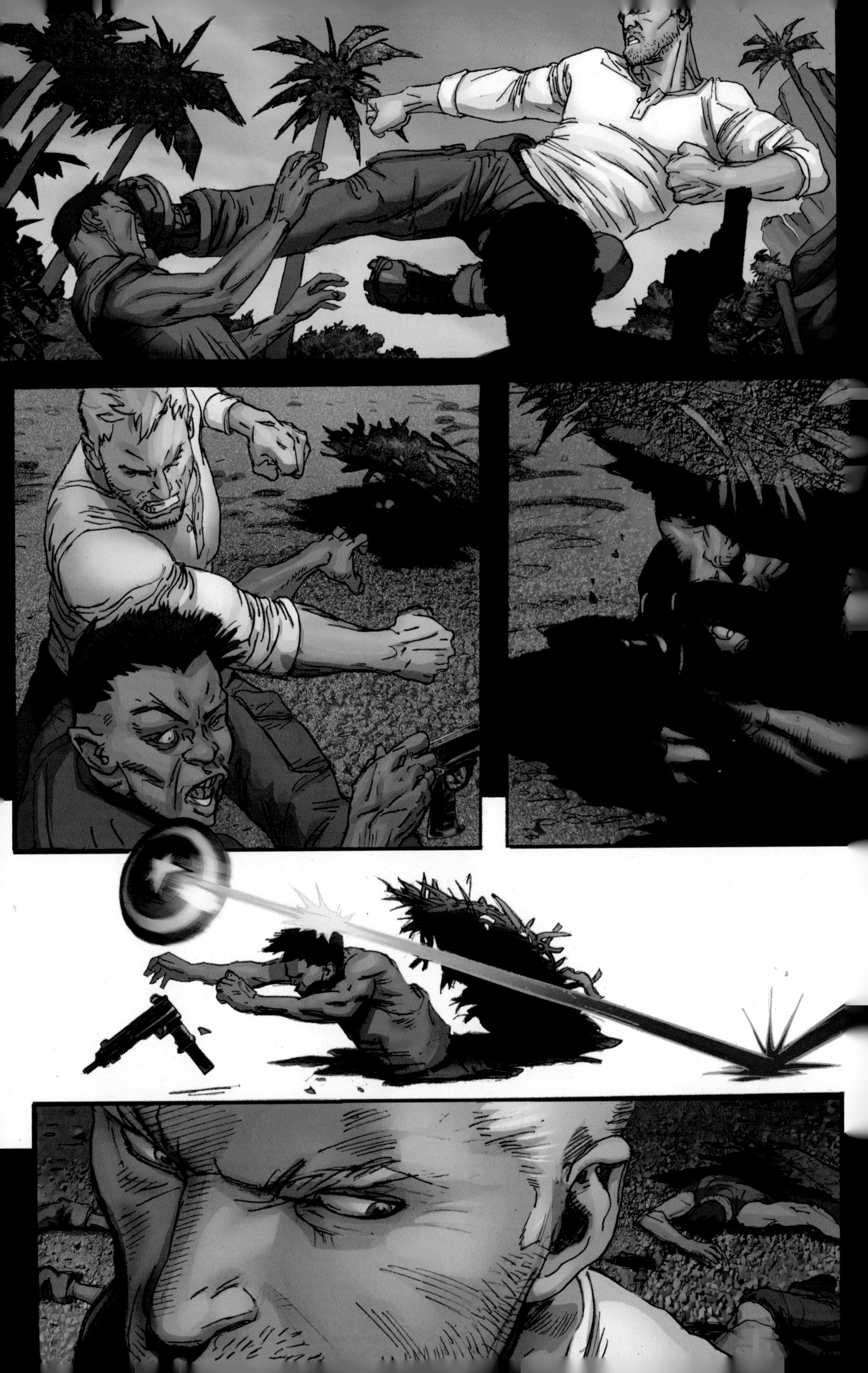

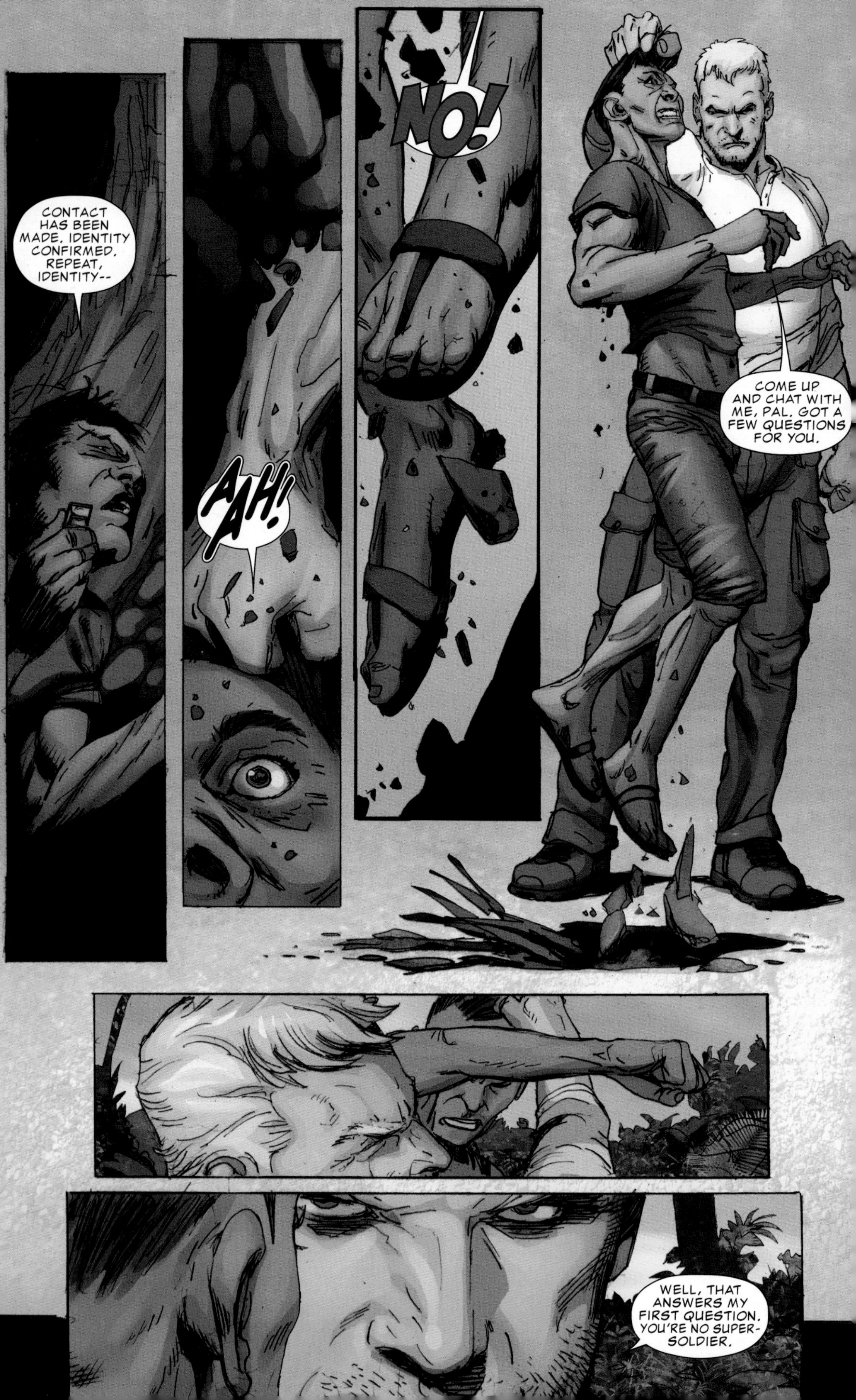
CONTACT HAS BEEN MADE. IDENTITY CONFIRMED. REPEAT, IDENTITY--
AAH!
NO!
COME UP AND CHAT WITH ME, PAL. GOT A FEW QUESTIONS FOR YOU.
WELL, THAT ANSWERS MY FIRST QUESTION. YOU'RE NO SUPER-SOLDIER.

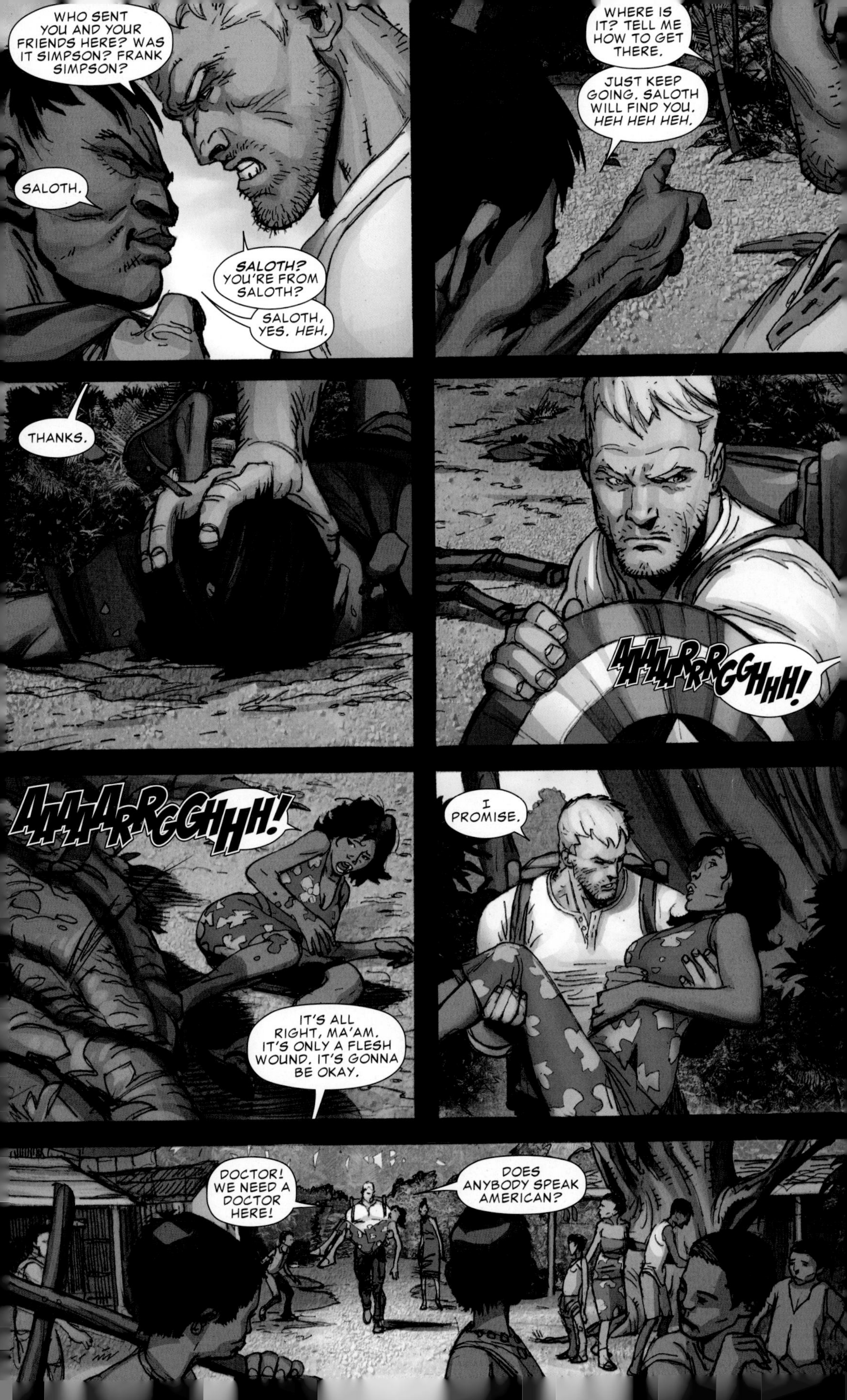
WHO SENT YOU AND YOUR FRIENDS HERE? WAS IT SIMPSON? FRANK SIMPSON?
SALOTH.
SALOTH? YOU'RE FROM SALOTH?
SALOTH, YES. HEH.
WHERE IS IT? TELL ME HOW TO GET THERE.
JUST KEEP GOING. SALOTH WILL FIND YOU. HEH HEH HEH.
THANKS.
AAAARRGGHHH!
AAAARRGGHHH!
IT'S ALL RIGHT, MA'AM. IT'S ONLY A FLESH WOUND. IT'S GONNA BE OKAY.
I PROMISE.
DOCTOR! WE NEED A DOCTOR HERE!
DOES ANYBODY SPEAK AMERICAN?

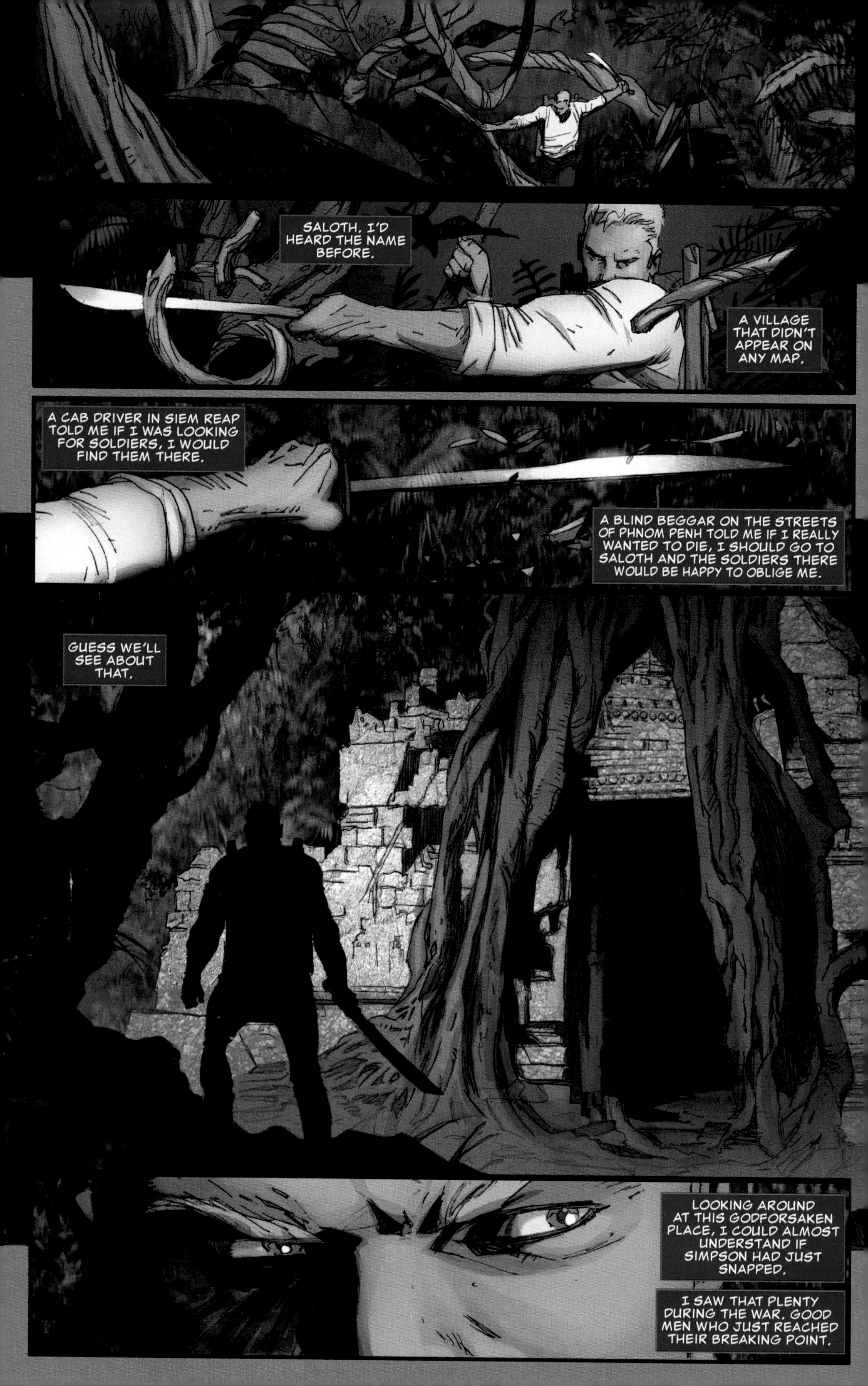
SALOTH. I'D HEARD THE NAME BEFORE.
A VILLAGE THAT DIDN'T APPEAR ON ANY MAP.
A CAB DRIVER IN SIEM REAP TOLD ME IF I WAS LOOKING FOR SOLDIERS, I WOULD FIND THEM THERE.
A BLIND BEGGAR ON THE STREETS OF PHNOM PENH TOLD ME IF I REALLY WANTED TO DIE, I SHOULD GO TO SALOTH AND THE SOLDIERS THERE WOULD BE HAPPY TO OBLIGE ME.
GUESS WE'LL SEE ABOUT THAT.
LOOKING AROUND AT THIS GODFORSAKEN PLACE, I COULD ALMOST UNDERSTAND IF SIMPSON HAD JUST SNAPPED.
I SAW THAT PLENTY DURING THE WAR. GOOD MEN WHO JUST REACHED THEIR BREAKING POINT.

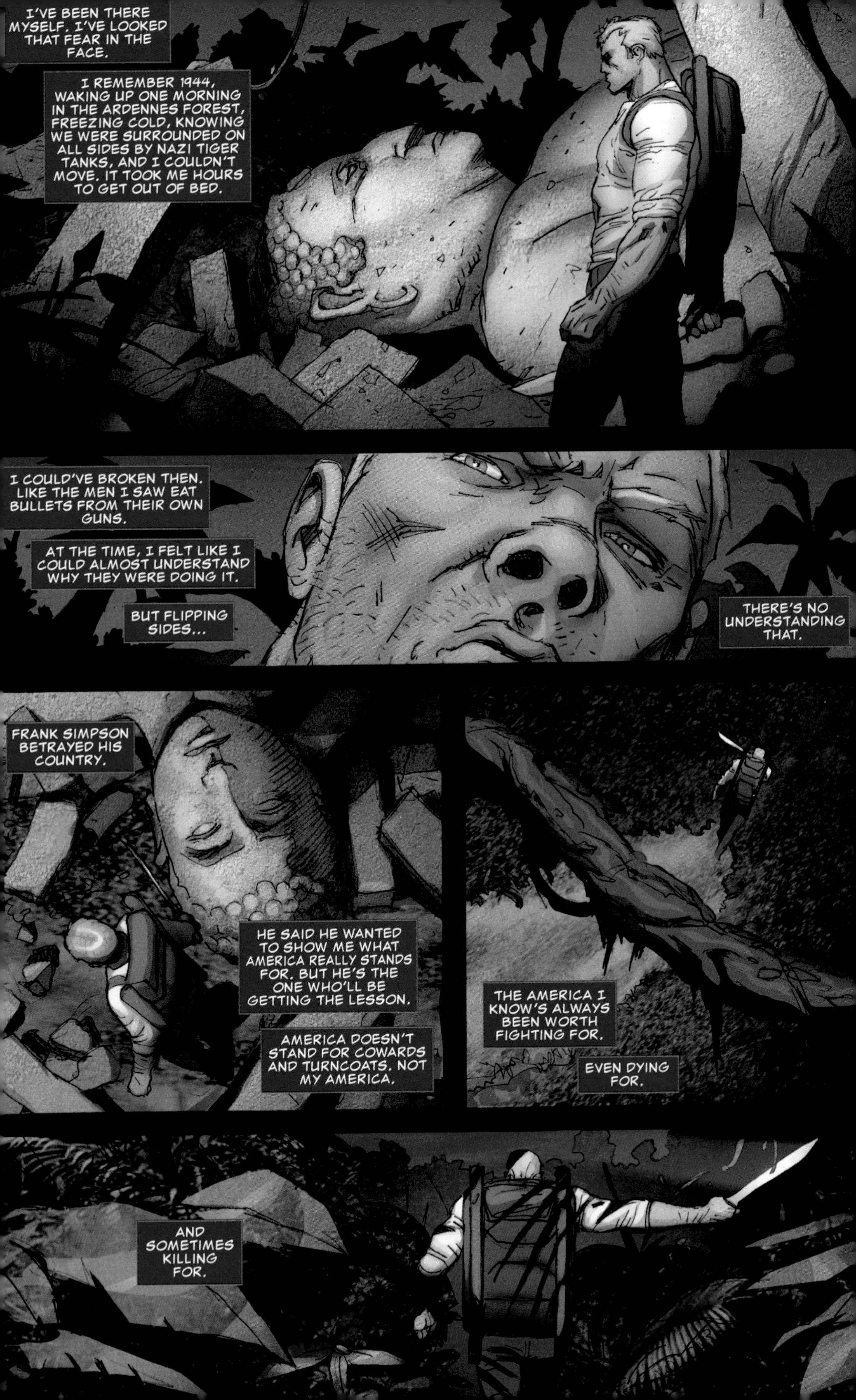
I'VE BEEN THERE MYSELF. I'VE LOOKED THAT FEAR IN THE FACE.
I REMEMBER 1944, WAKING UP ONE MORNING IN THE ARDENNES FOREST, FREEZING COLD, KNOWING WE WERE SURROUNDED ON ALL SIDES BY NAZI TIGER TANKS, AND I COULDN'T MOVE. IT TOOK ME HOURS TO GET OUT OF BED.
I COULD'VE BROKEN THEN. LIKE THE MEN I SAW EAT BULLETS FROM THEIR OWN GUNS.
AT THE TIME, I FELT LIKE I COULD ALMOST UNDERSTAND WHY THEY WERE DOING IT.
BUT FLIPPING SIDES...
THERE'S NO UNDERSTANDING THAT.
FRANK SIMPSON BETRAYED HIS COUNTRY.
HE SAID HE WANTED TO SHOW ME WHAT AMERICA REALLY STANDS FOR. BUT HE'S THE ONE WHO'LL BE GETTING THE LESSON.
AMERICA DOESN'T STAND FOR COWARDS AND TURNCOATS. NOT MY AMERICA.
THE AMERICA I KNOW'S ALWAYS BEEN WORTH FIGHTING FOR.
EVEN DYING FOR.
AND SOMETIMES KILLING FOR.

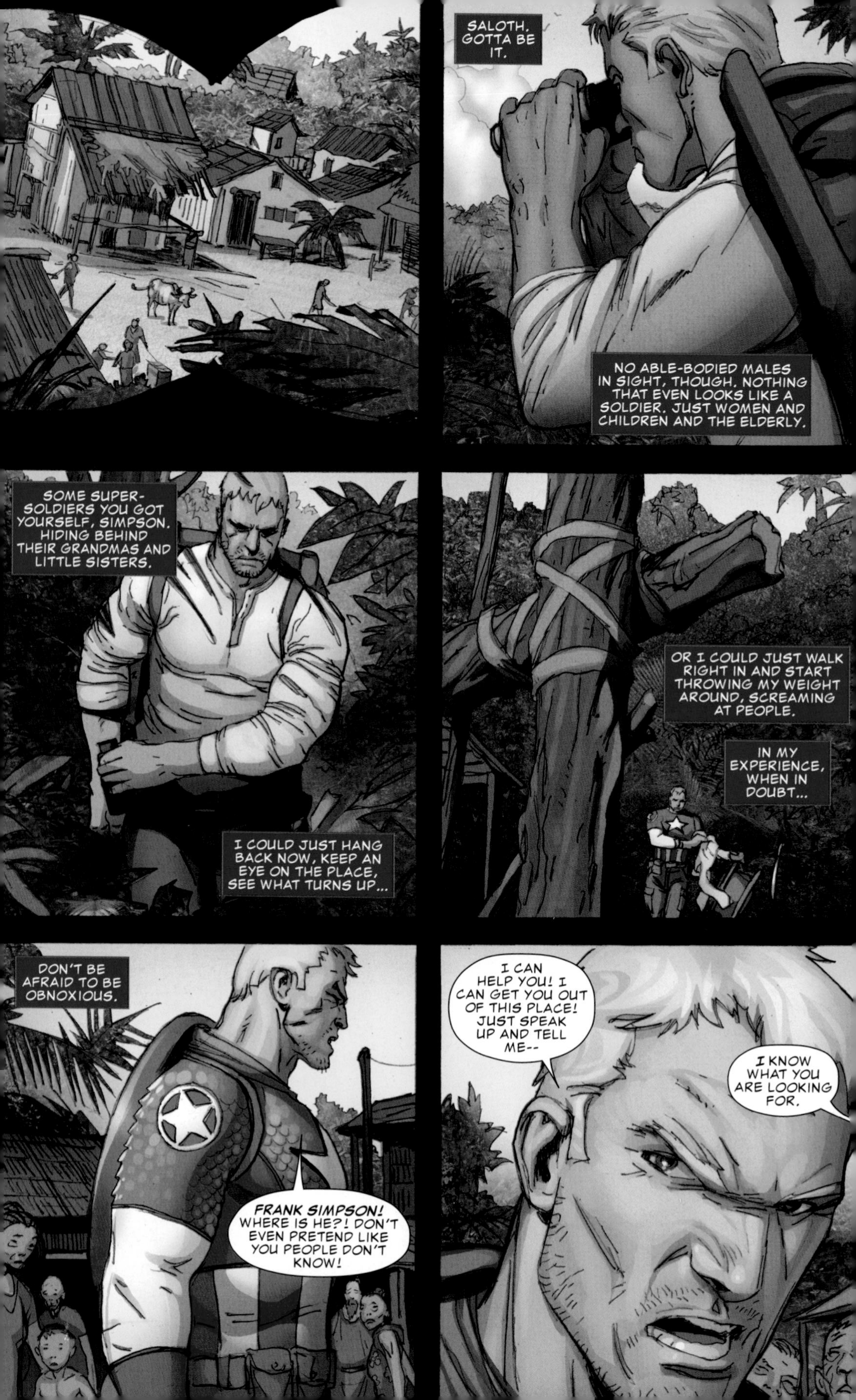
SALOTH. GOTTA BE IT.
NO ABLE-BODIED MALES IN SIGHT, THOUGH. NOTHING THAT EVEN LOOKS LIKE A SOLDIER. JUST WOMEN AND CHILDREN AND THE ELDERLY.
SOME SUPER-SOLDIERS YOU GOT YOURSELF, SIMPSON. HIDING BEHIND THEIR GRANDMAS AND LITTLE SISTERS.
I COULD JUST HANG BACK NOW, KEEP AN EYE ON THE PLACE, SEE WHAT TURNS UP...
OR I COULD JUST WALK RIGHT IN AND START THROWING MY WEIGHT AROUND, SCREAMING AT PEOPLE.
IN MY EXPERIENCE, WHEN IN DOUBT...
DON'T BE AFRAID TO BE OBNOXIOUS.
FRANK SIMPSON! WHERE IS HE?! DON'T EVEN PRETEND LIKE YOU PEOPLE DON'T KNOW!
I CAN HELP YOU! I CAN GET YOU OUT OF THIS PLACE! JUST SPEAK UP AND TELL ME--
I KNOW WHAT YOU ARE LOOKING FOR.

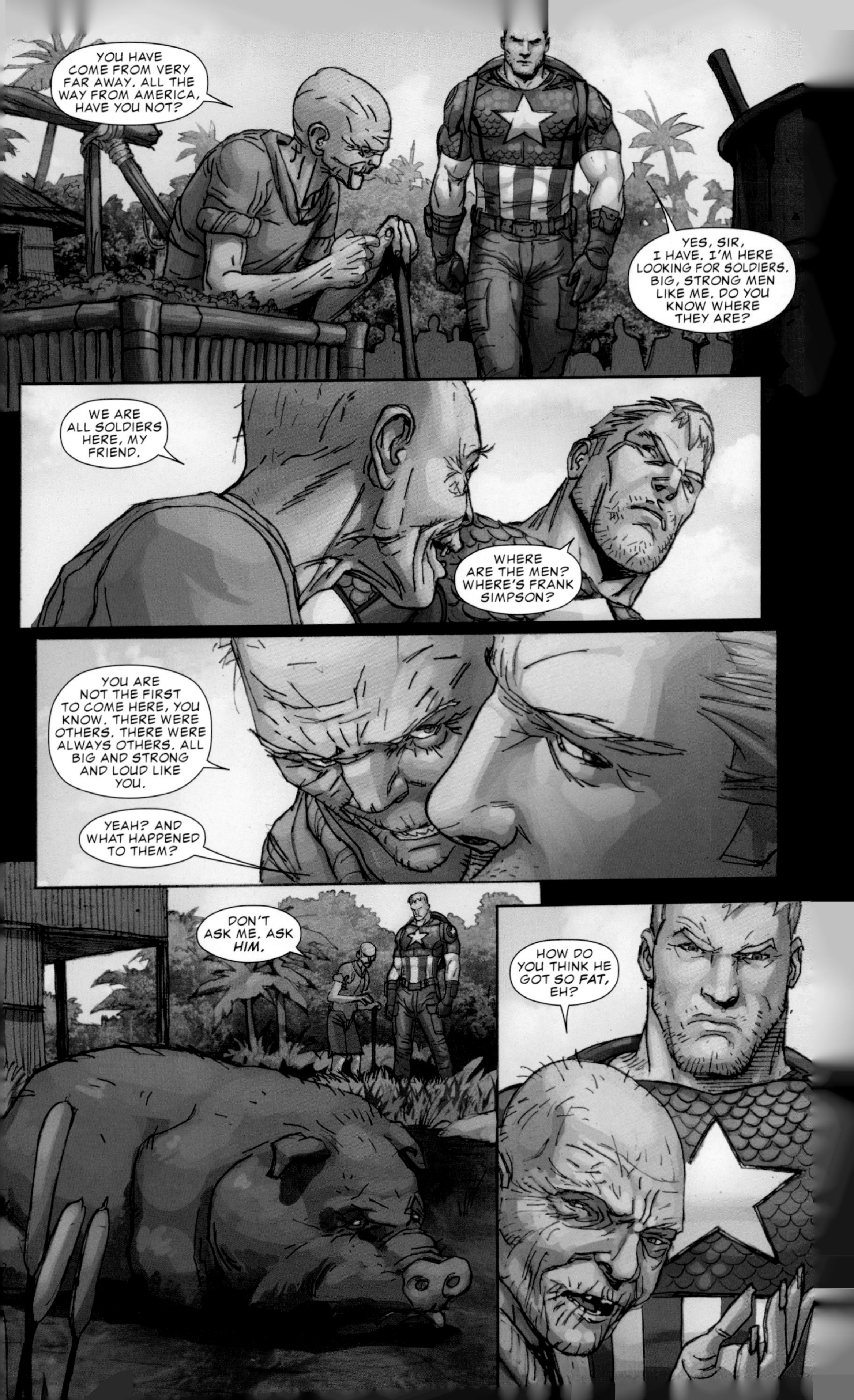
YOU HAVE COME FROM VERY FAR AWAY. ALL THE WAY FROM AMERICA, HAVE YOU NOT?
YES, SIR, I HAVE. I'M HERE LOOKING FOR SOLDIERS. BIG, STRONG MEN LIKE ME. DO YOU KNOW WHERE THEY ARE?
WE ARE ALL SOLDIERS HERE, MY FRIEND.
WHERE ARE THE MEN? WHERE'S FRANK SIMPSON?
YOU ARE NOT THE FIRST TO COME HERE, YOU KNOW. THERE WERE OTHERS. THERE WERE ALWAYS OTHERS. ALL BIG AND STRONG AND LOUD LIKE YOU.
YEAH? AND WHAT HAPPENED TO THEM?
DON'T ASK ME. ASK *HIM.*
HOW DO YOU THINK HE GOT SO *FAT,* EH?

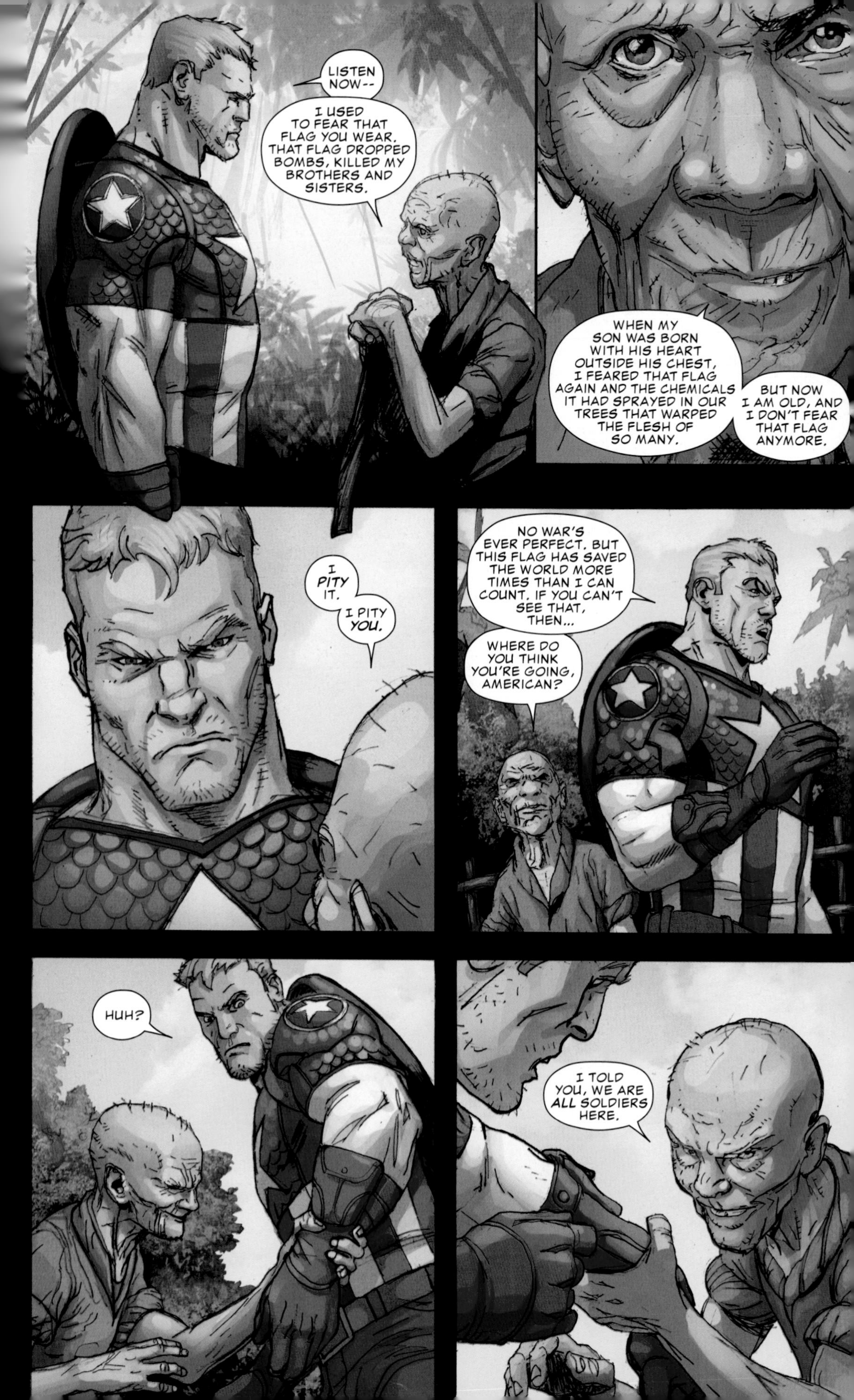
LISTEN NOW--
I USED TO FEAR THAT FLAG YOU WEAR. THAT FLAG DROPPED BOMBS, KILLED MY BROTHERS AND SISTERS.
WHEN MY SON WAS BORN WITH HIS HEART OUTSIDE HIS CHEST, I FEARED THAT FLAG AGAIN AND THE CHEMICALS IT HAD SPRAYED IN OUR TREES THAT WARPED THE FLESH OF SO MANY.
BUT NOW I AM OLD, AND I DON'T FEAR THAT FLAG ANYMORE.
I PITY IT.
I PITY YOU.
NO WAR'S EVER PERFECT. BUT THIS FLAG HAS SAVED THE WORLD MORE TIMES THAN I CAN COUNT. IF YOU CAN'T SEE THAT, THEN...
WHERE DO YOU THINK YOU'RE GOING, AMERICAN?
HUH?
I TOLD YOU, WE ARE ALL SOLDIERS HERE.

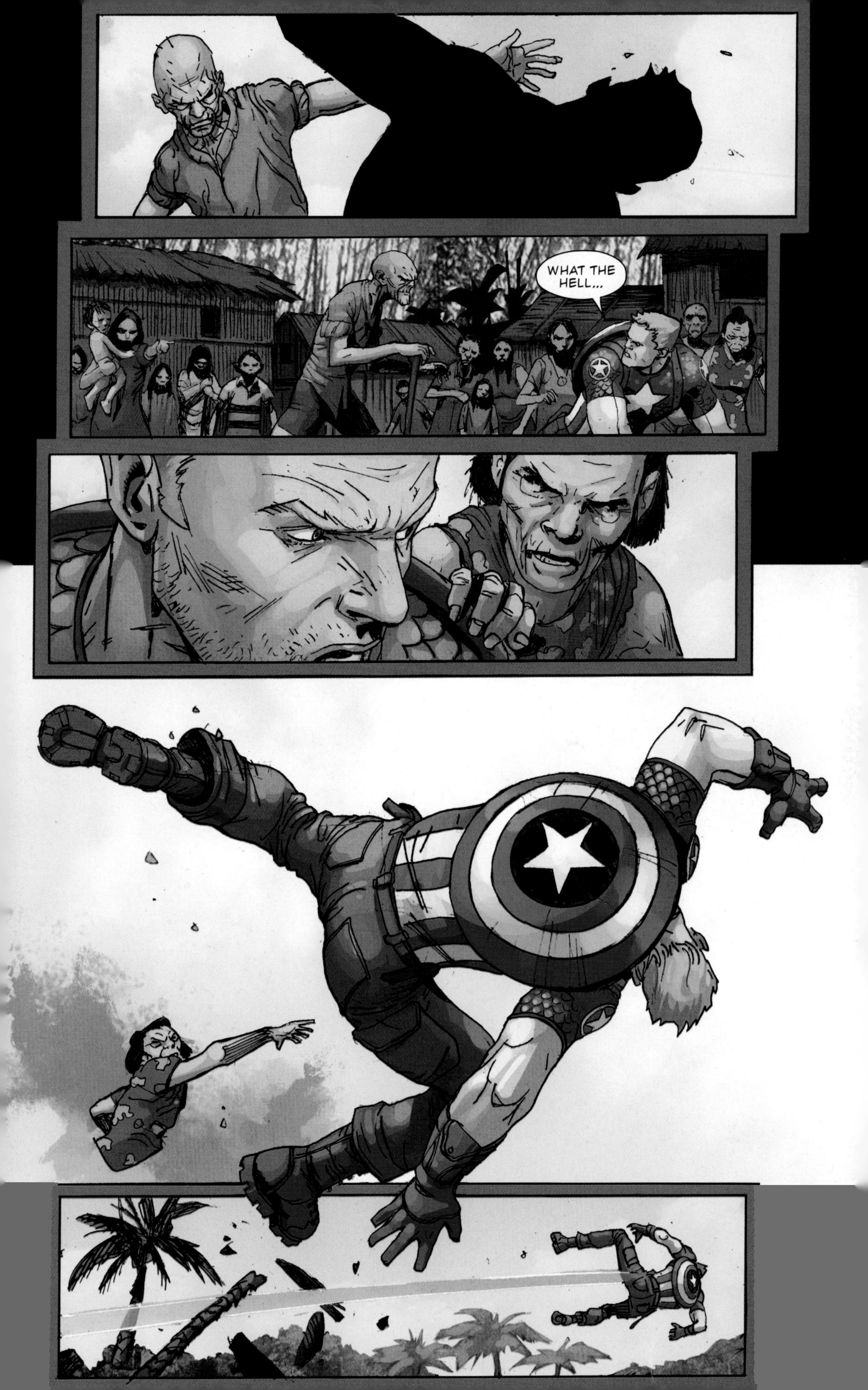
WHAT THE HELL...

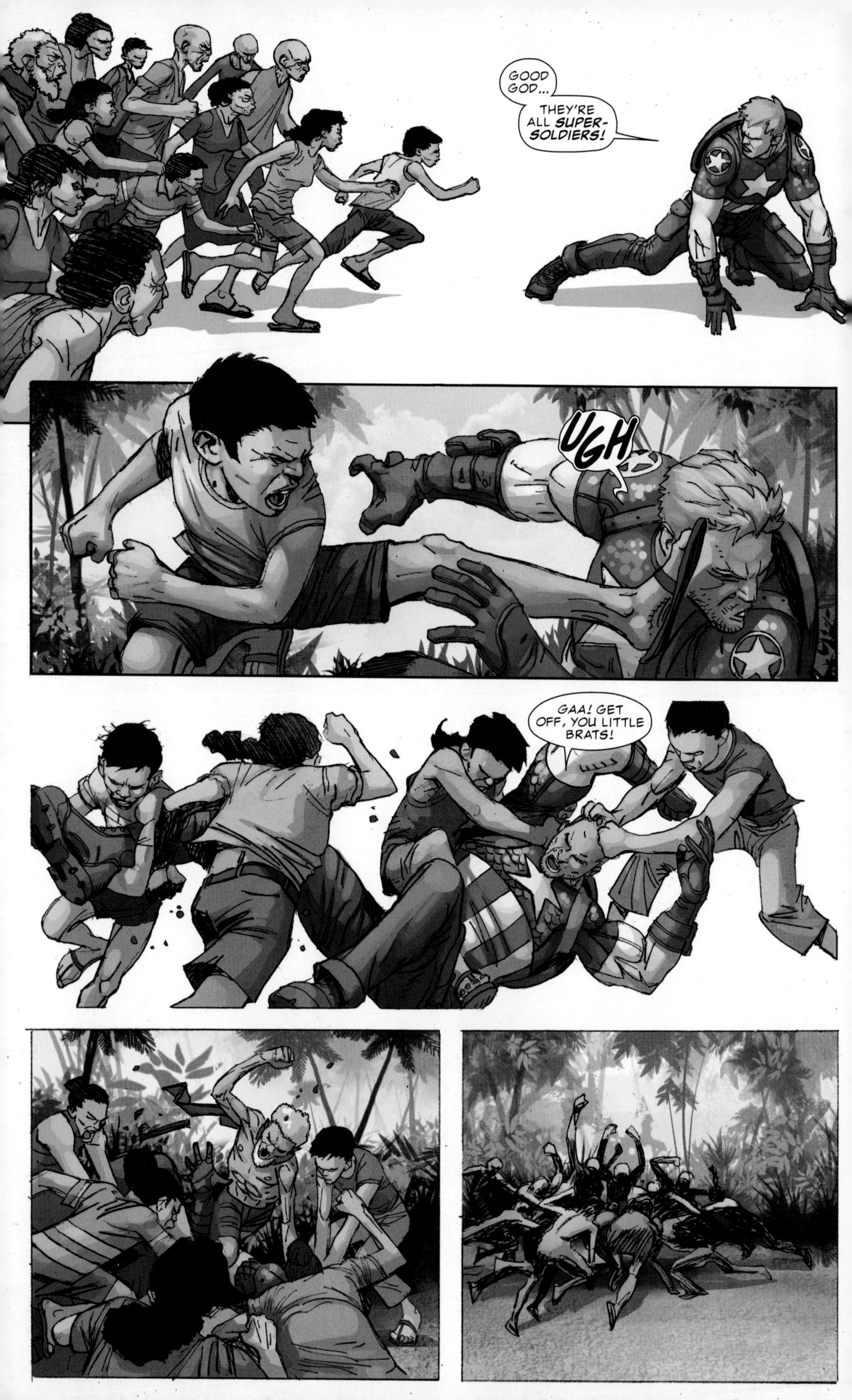
GOOD GOD...
THEY'RE ALL SUPER-SOLDIERS!
UGH
GAA! GET OFF, YOU LITTLE BRATS!

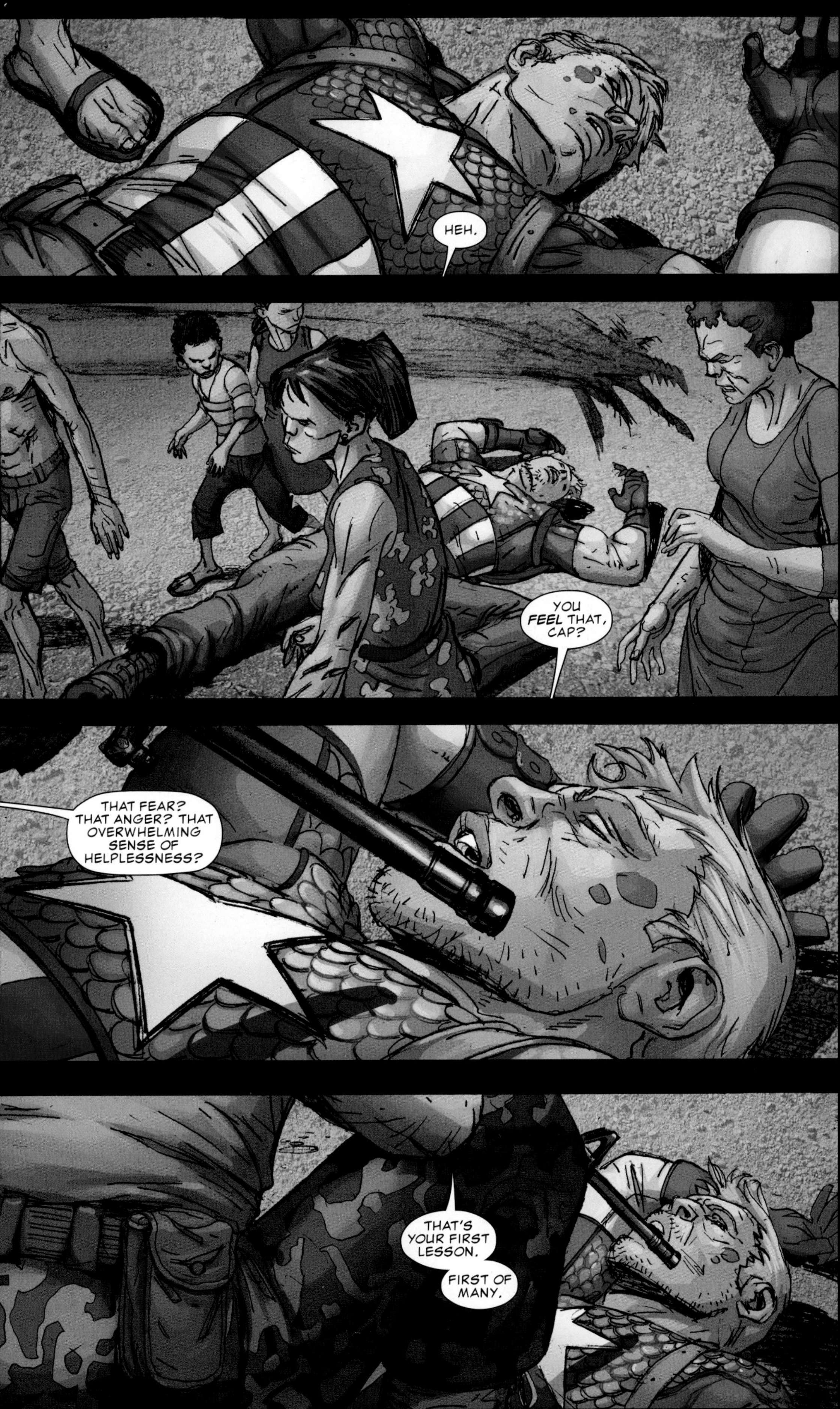
HEH.
YOU FEEL THAT, CAP?
THAT FEAR? THAT ANGER? THAT OVERWHELMING SENSE OF HELPLESSNESS?
THAT'S YOUR FIRST LESSON.
FIRST OF MANY.

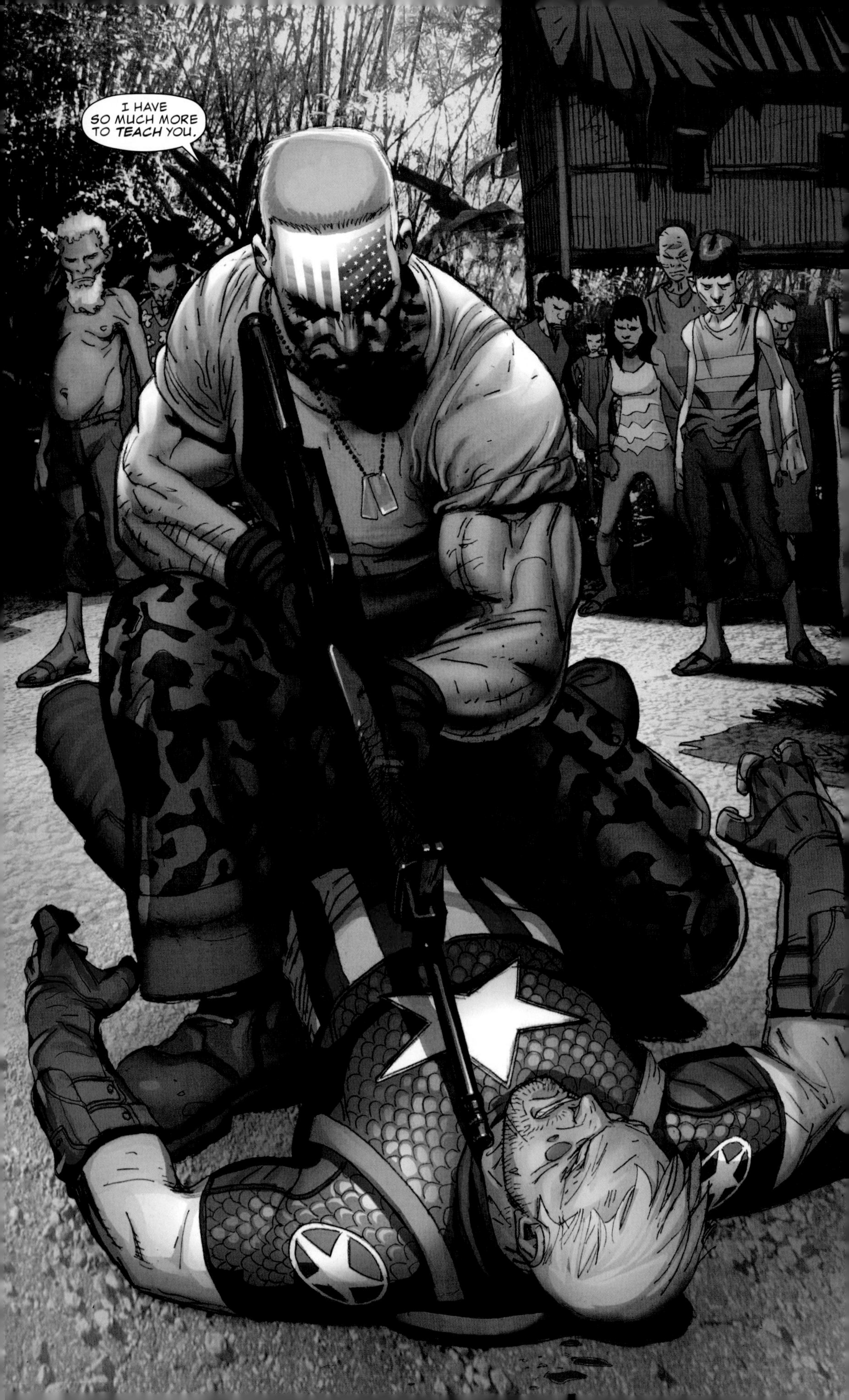
I HAVE SO MUCH MORE TO TEACH YOU.

3

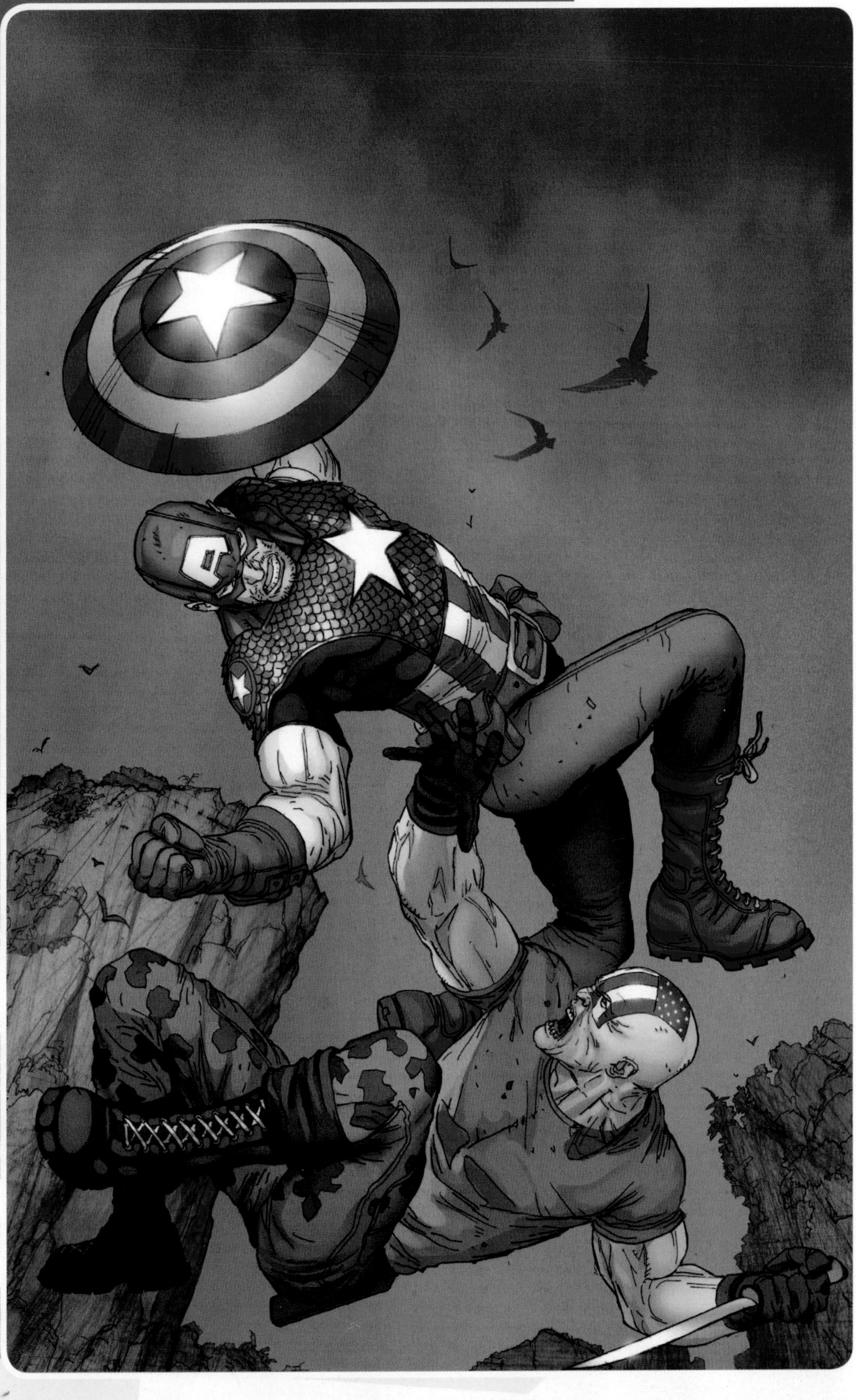

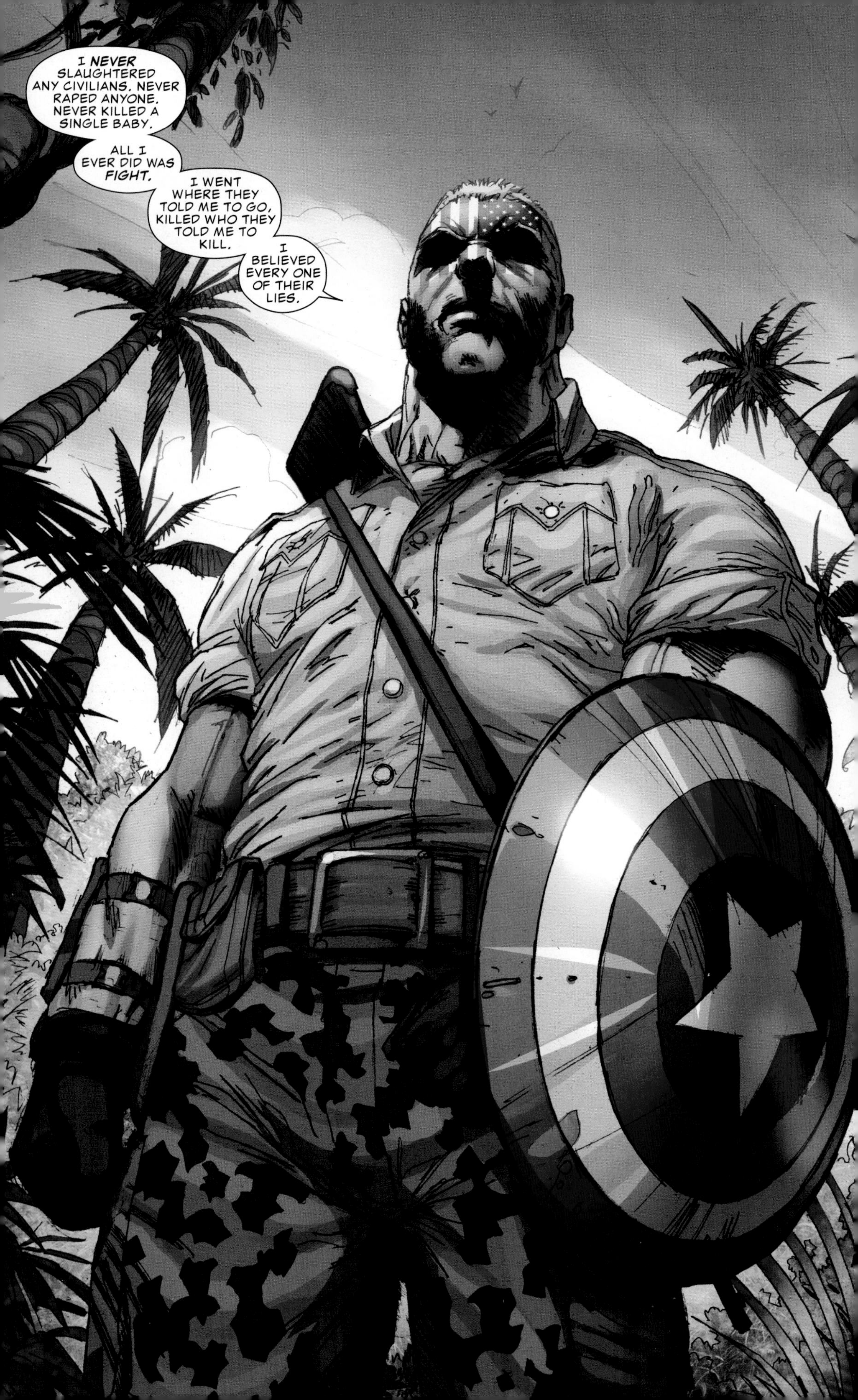
I **NEVER** SLAUGHTERED ANY CIVILIANS. NEVER RAPED ANYONE. NEVER KILLED A SINGLE BABY.
ALL I EVER DID WAS **FIGHT.**
I WENT WHERE THEY TOLD ME TO GO, KILLED WHO THEY TOLD ME TO KILL.
I BELIEVED EVERY ONE OF THEIR LIES.

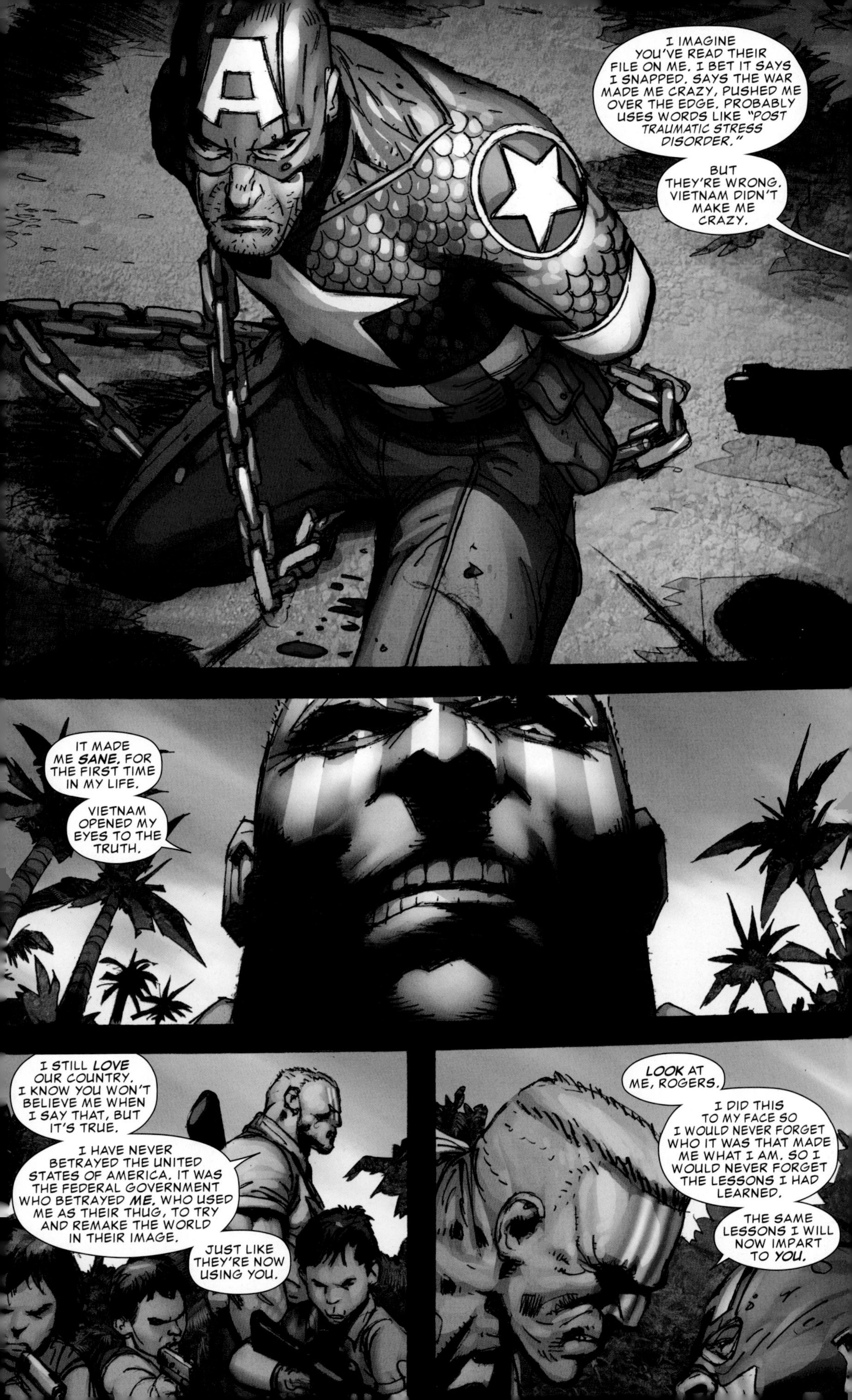
I IMAGINE YOU'VE READ THEIR FILE ON ME. I BET IT SAYS I SNAPPED. SAYS THE WAR MADE ME CRAZY, PUSHED ME OVER THE EDGE. PROBABLY USES WORDS LIKE "POST TRAUMATIC STRESS DISORDER."
BUT THEY'RE WRONG. VIETNAM DIDN'T MAKE ME CRAZY.
IT MADE ME SANE. FOR THE FIRST TIME IN MY LIFE.
VIETNAM OPENED MY EYES TO THE TRUTH.
I STILL LOVE OUR COUNTRY. I KNOW YOU WON'T BELIEVE ME WHEN I SAY THAT, BUT IT'S TRUE.
I HAVE NEVER BETRAYED THE UNITED STATES OF AMERICA. IT WAS THE FEDERAL GOVERNMENT WHO BETRAYED ME. WHO USED ME AS THEIR THUG, TO TRY AND REMAKE THE WORLD IN THEIR IMAGE.
JUST LIKE THEY'RE NOW USING YOU.
LOOK AT ME, ROGERS.
I DID THIS TO MY FACE SO I WOULD NEVER FORGET WHO IT WAS THAT MADE ME WHAT I AM. SO I WOULD NEVER FORGET THE LESSONS I HAD LEARNED.
THE SAME LESSONS I WILL NOW IMPART TO YOU.

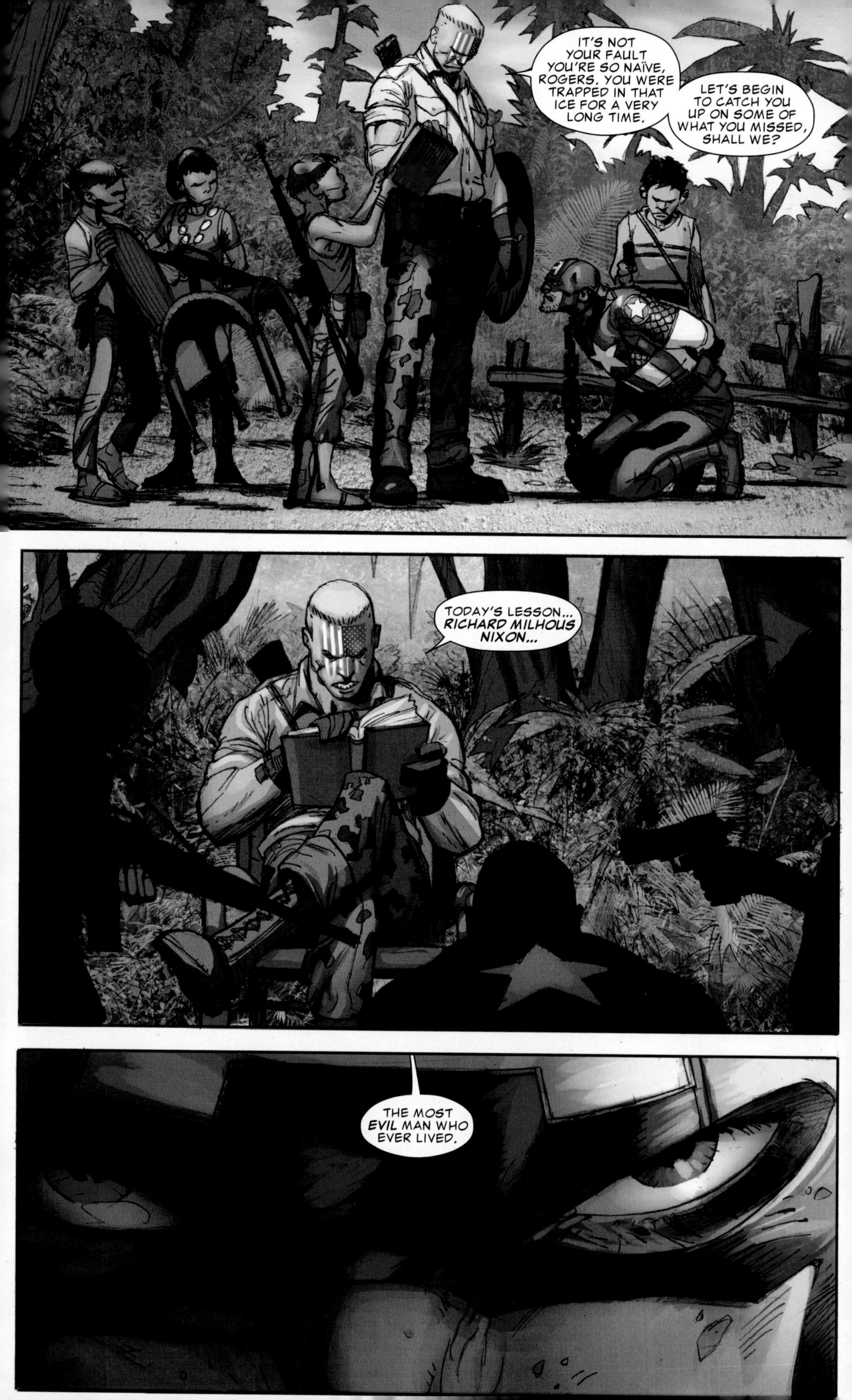
IT'S NOT YOUR FAULT YOU'RE SO NAÏVE, ROGERS. YOU WERE TRAPPED IN THAT ICE FOR A VERY LONG TIME.
LET'S BEGIN TO CATCH YOU UP ON SOME OF WHAT YOU MISSED, SHALL WE?
TODAY'S LESSON... RICHARD MILHOUS NIXON...
THE MOST EVIL MAN WHO EVER LIVED.

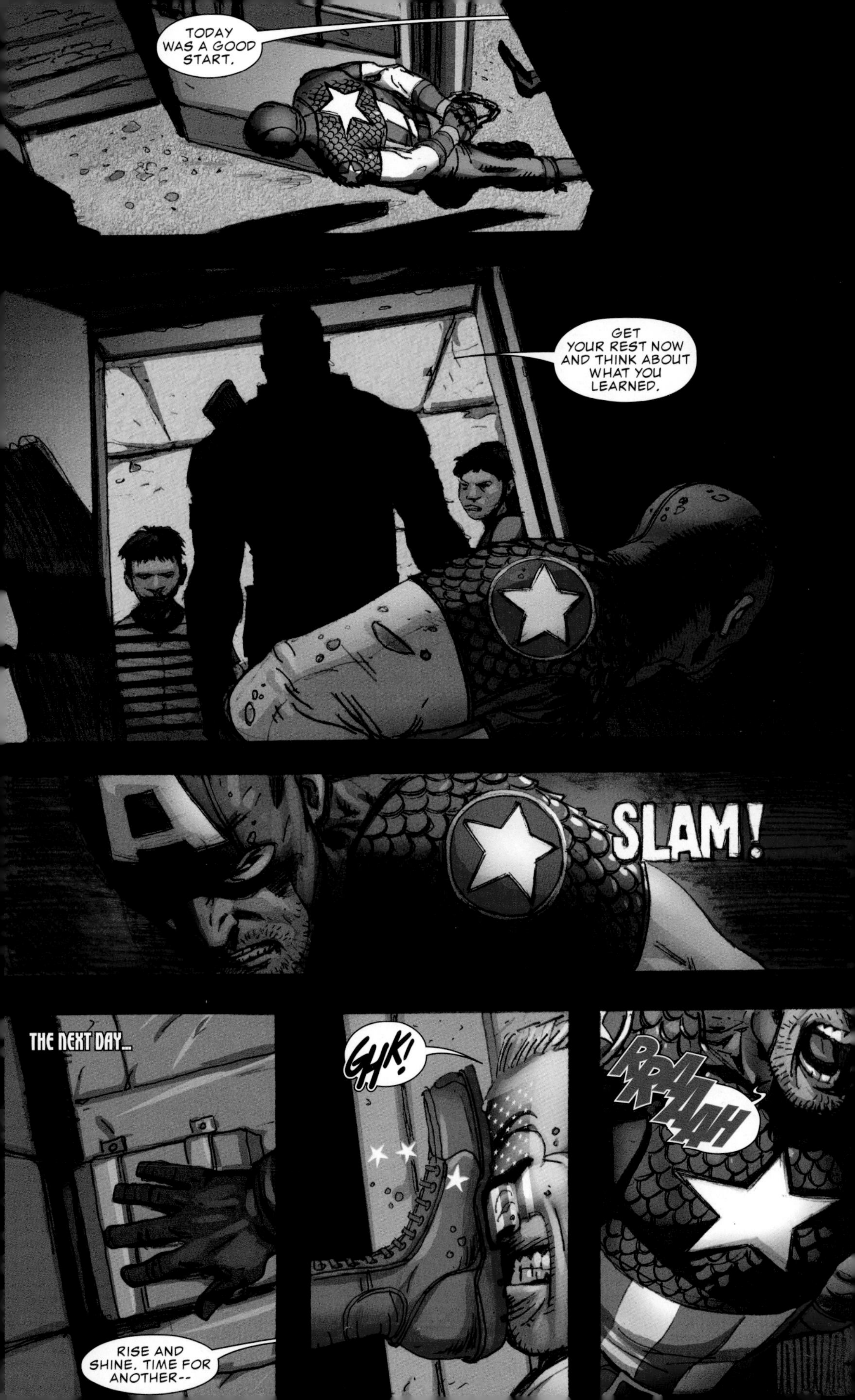
TODAY WAS A GOOD START.
GET YOUR REST NOW AND THINK ABOUT WHAT YOU LEARNED.
SLAM!
THE NEXT DAY...
RISE AND SHINE. TIME FOR ANOTHER--
GHK!
RRAAAAH

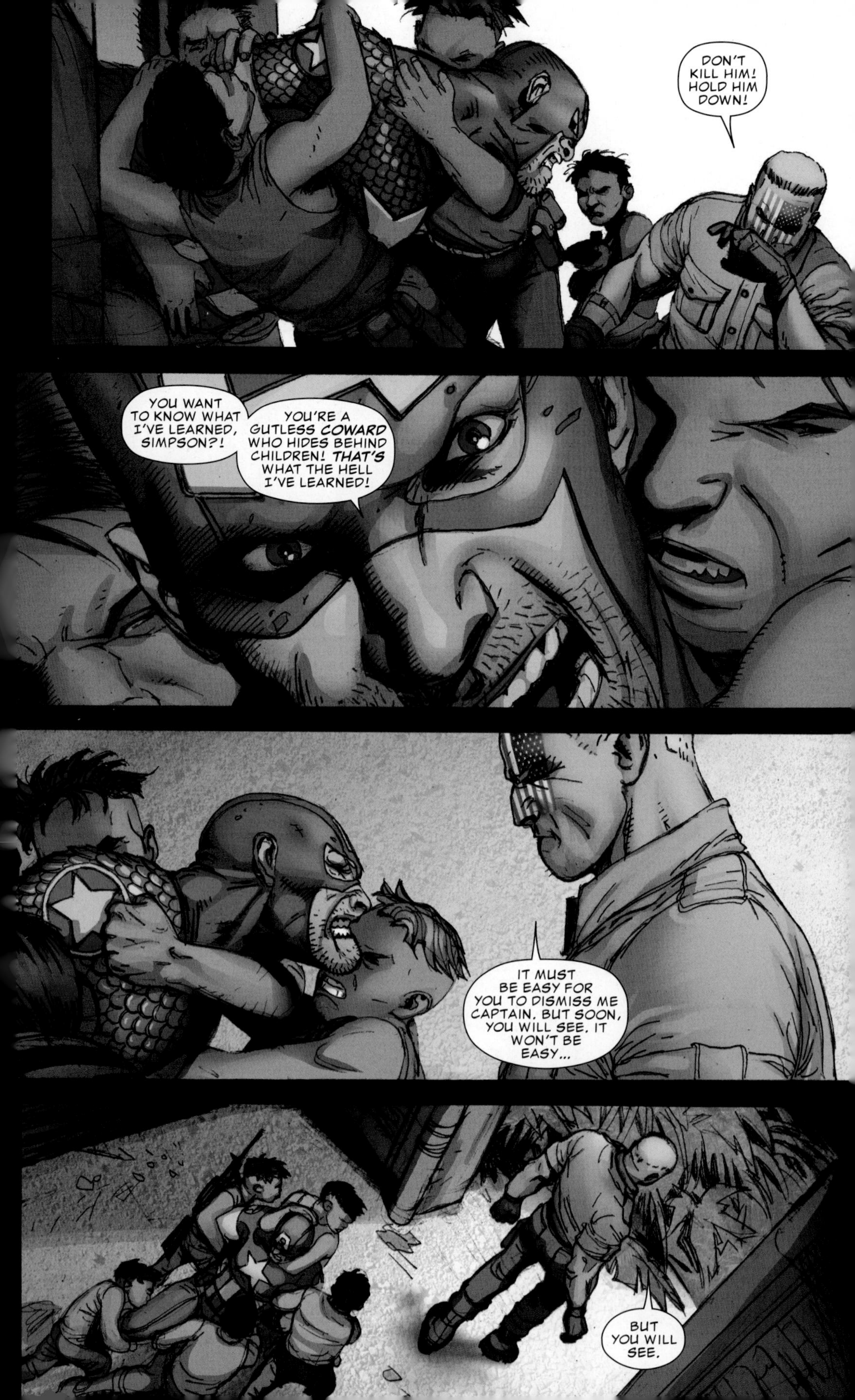
DON'T KILL HIM! HOLD HIM DOWN!
YOU WANT TO KNOW WHAT I'VE LEARNED, SIMPSON?!
YOU'RE A GUTLESS COWARD WHO HIDES BEHIND CHILDREN! THAT'S WHAT THE HELL I'VE LEARNED!
IT MUST BE EASY FOR YOU TO DISMISS ME CAPTAIN. BUT SOON, YOU WILL SEE. IT WON'T BE EASY...
BUT YOU WILL SEE.

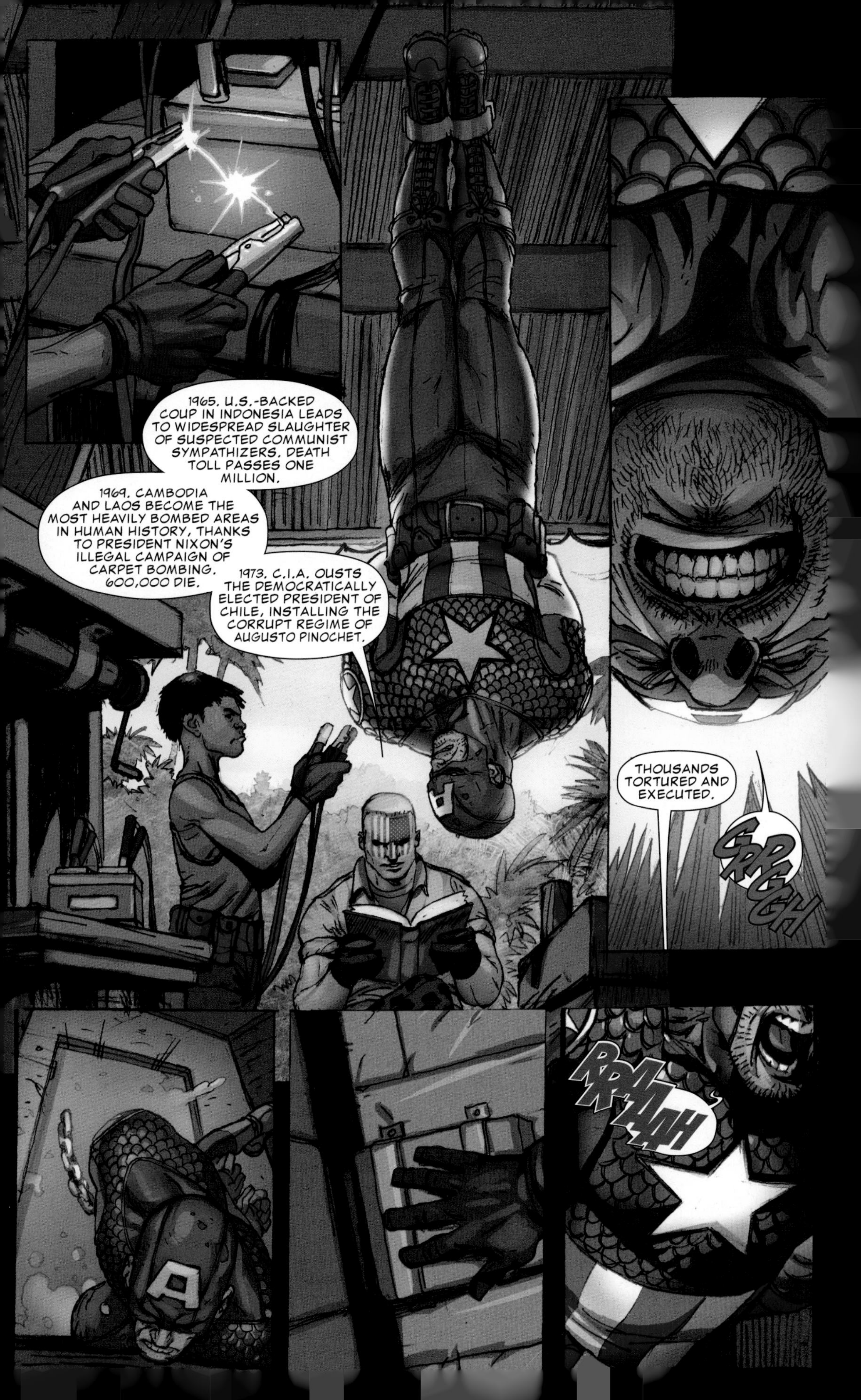
1965. U.S.-BACKED COUP IN INDONESIA LEADS TO WIDESPREAD SLAUGHTER OF SUSPECTED COMMUNIST SYMPATHIZERS. DEATH TOLL PASSES ONE MILLION.
1969. CAMBODIA AND LAOS BECOME THE MOST HEAVILY BOMBED AREAS IN HUMAN HISTORY, THANKS TO PRESIDENT NIXON'S ILLEGAL CAMPAIGN OF CARPET BOMBING. 600,000 DIE.
1973. C.I.A. OUSTS THE DEMOCRATICALLY ELECTED PRESIDENT OF CHILE, INSTALLING THE CORRUPT REGIME OF AUGUSTO PINOCHET.
THOUSANDS TORTURED AND EXECUTED.
GRRGH
RRAAAAH

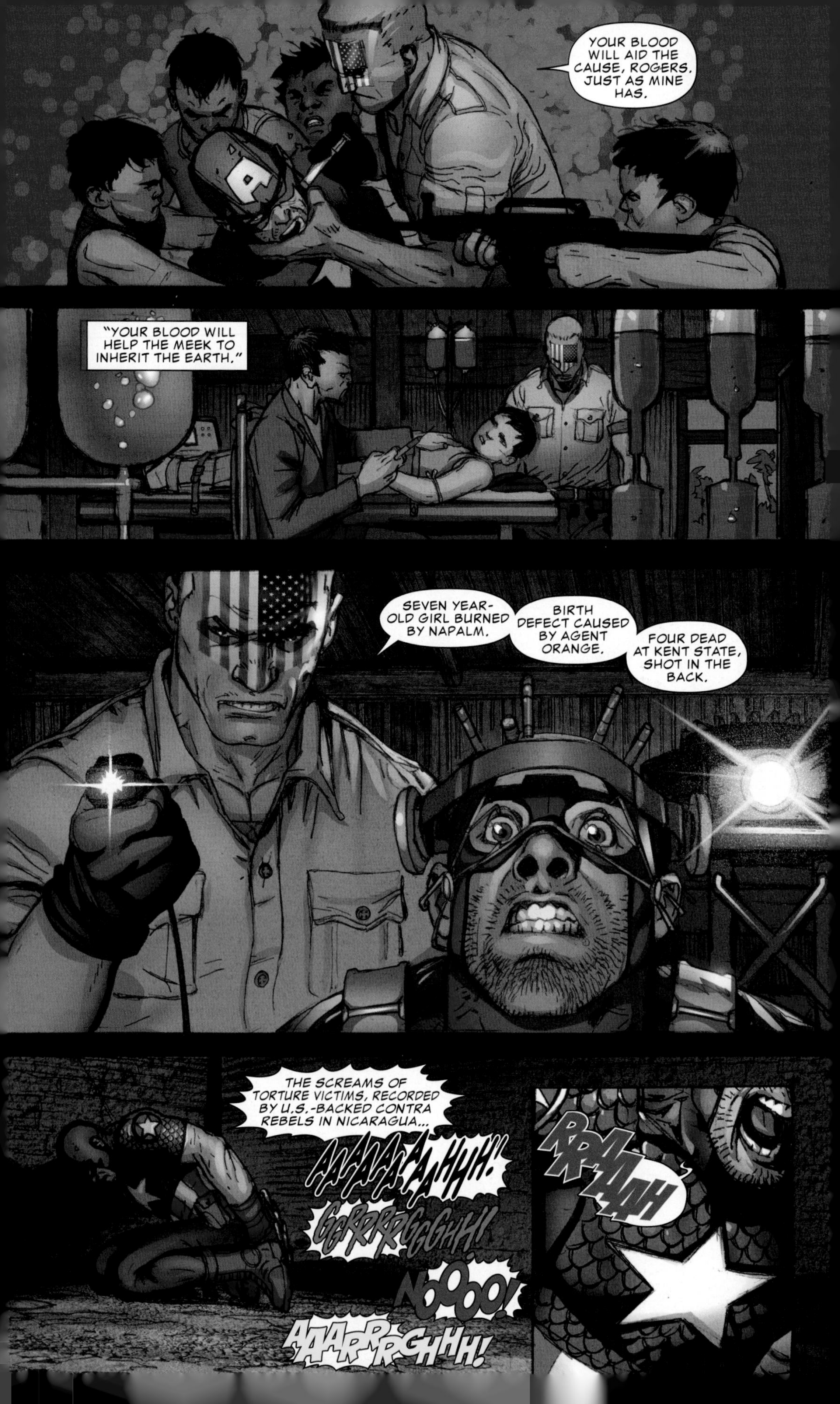

YOUR BLOOD WILL AID THE CAUSE, ROGERS. JUST AS MINE HAS.
"YOUR BLOOD WILL HELP THE MEEK TO INHERIT THE EARTH."
SEVEN YEAR-OLD GIRL BURNED BY NAPALM.
BIRTH DEFECT CAUSED BY AGENT ORANGE.
FOUR DEAD AT KENT STATE, SHOT IN THE BACK.
THE SCREAMS OF TORTURE VICTIMS, RECORDED BY U.S.-BACKED CONTRA REBELS IN NICARAGUA...
AAAAAAAAHHH!
GGRRRRGGHH!
NOOOO!
AAARRRGHHH!
RRAAAAH

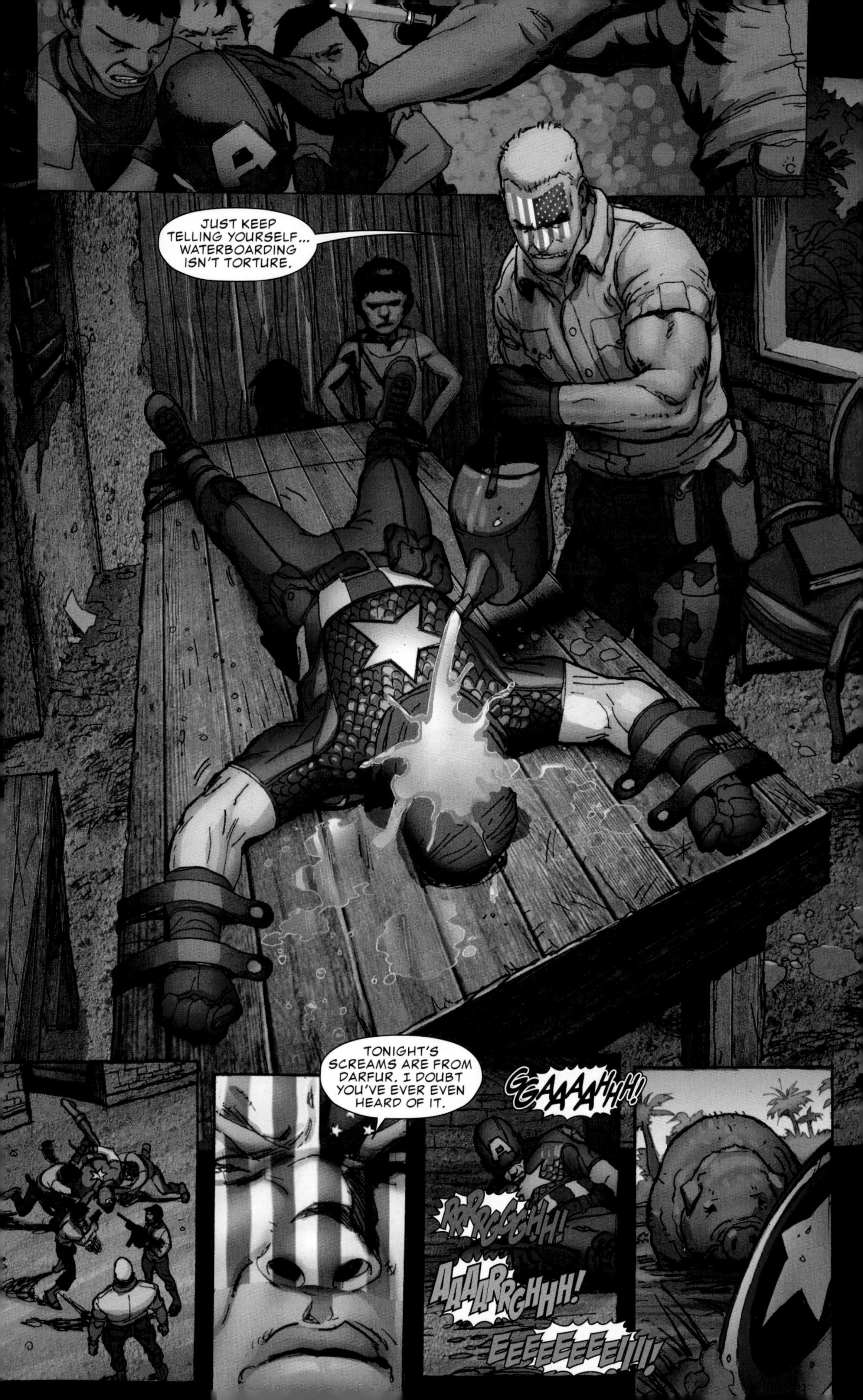
JUST KEEP TELLING YOURSELF... WATERBOARDING ISN'T TORTURE.
TONIGHT'S SCREAMS ARE FROM DARFUR. I DOUBT YOU'VE EVER EVEN HEARD OF IT.
GGAAAAHHH!
RRRRGGHH!
AAAARRGHHH!
EEEEEEEEII!!!

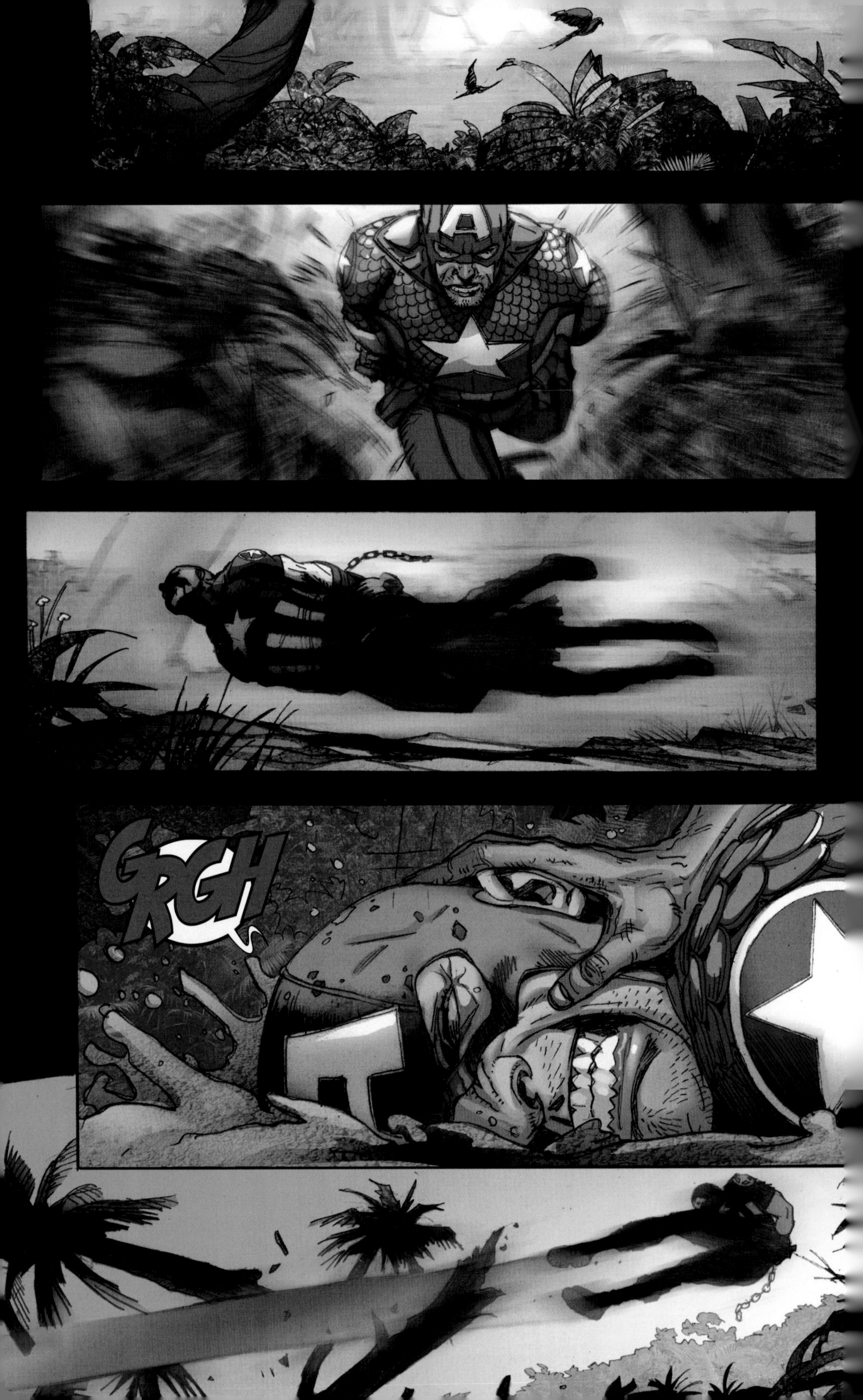
GRGH

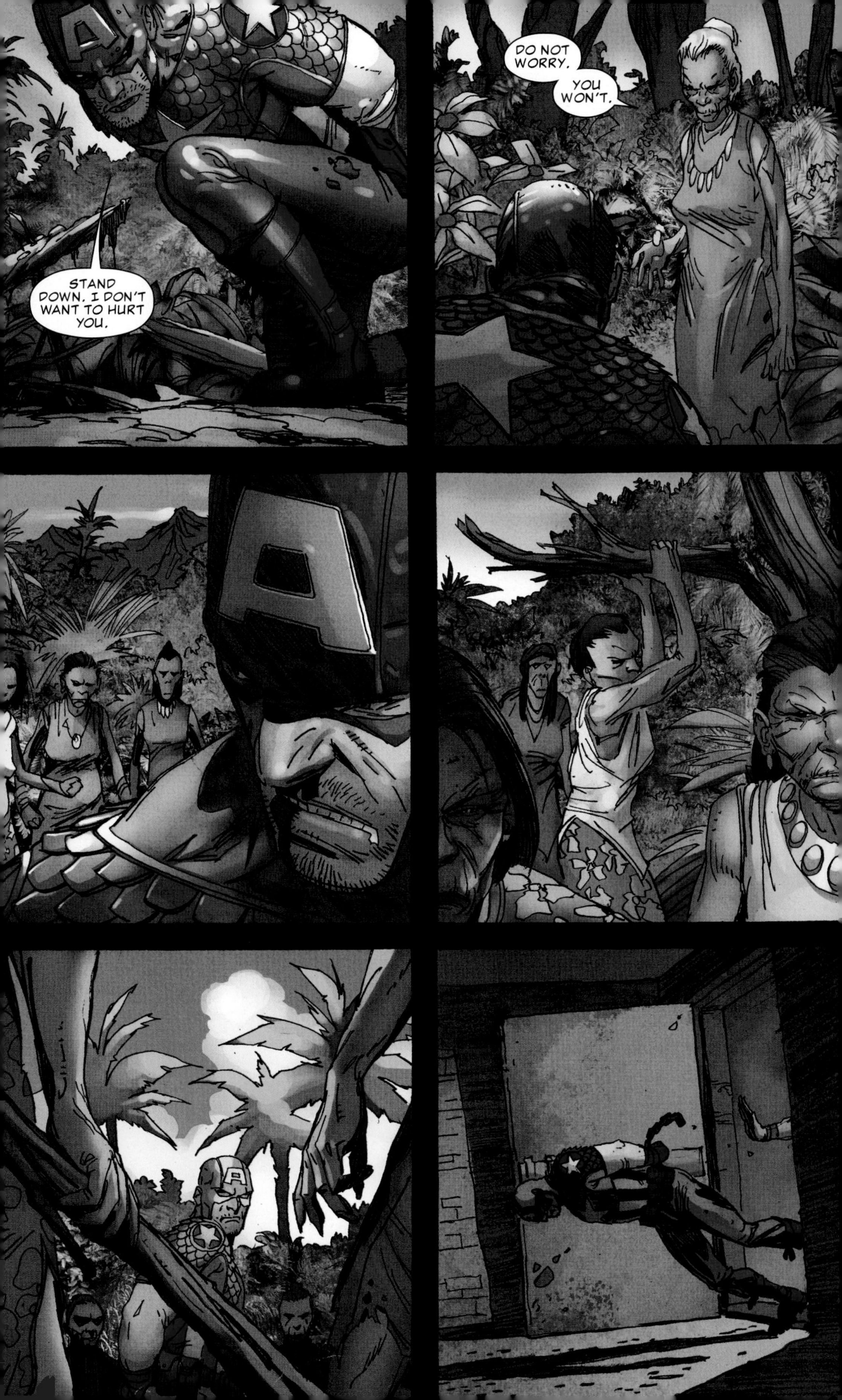
STAND DOWN. I DON'T WANT TO HURT YOU.
DO NOT WORRY.
YOU WON'T.

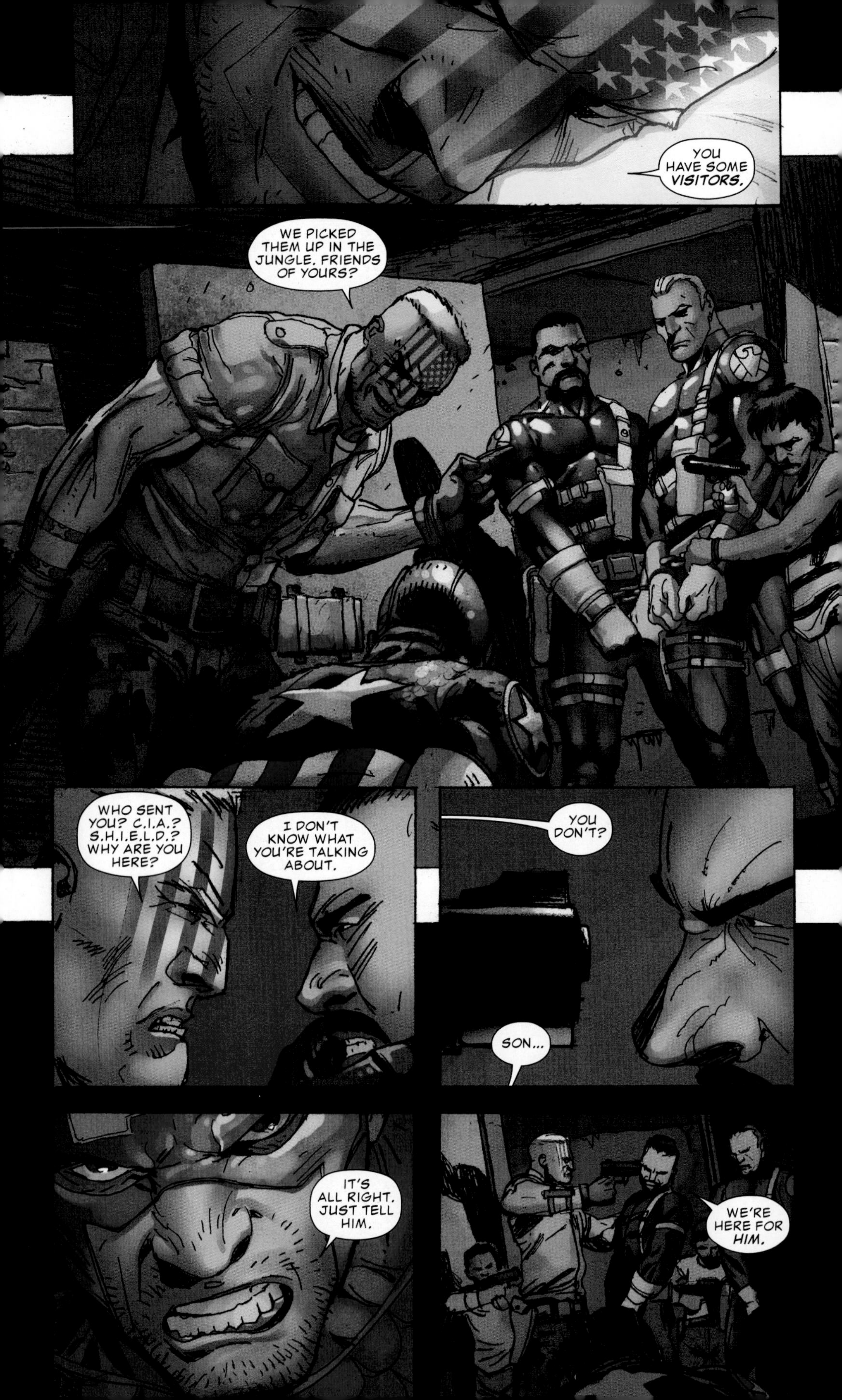
YOU HAVE SOME VISITORS.
WE PICKED THEM UP IN THE JUNGLE. FRIENDS OF YOURS?
WHO SENT YOU? C.I.A.? S.H.I.E.L.D.? WHY ARE YOU HERE?
I DON'T KNOW WHAT YOU'RE TALKING ABOUT.
YOU DON'T?
SON...
IT'S ALL RIGHT. JUST TELL HIM.
WE'RE HERE FOR HIM.

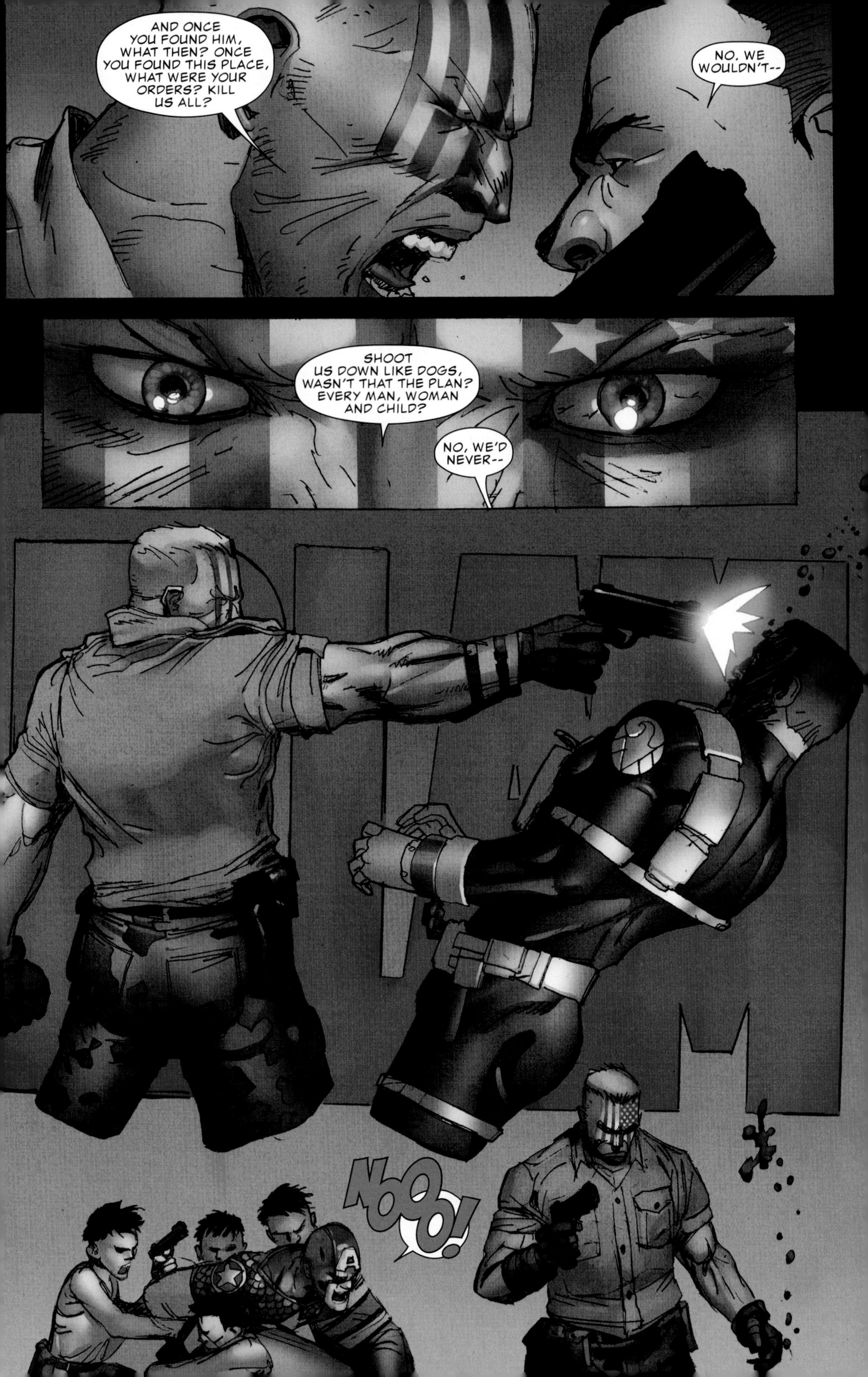
AND ONCE YOU FOUND HIM, WHAT THEN? ONCE YOU FOUND THIS PLACE, WHAT WERE YOUR ORDERS? KILL US ALL?
NO. WE WOULDN'T--
SHOOT US DOWN LIKE DOGS, WASN'T THAT THE PLAN? EVERY MAN, WOMAN AND CHILD?
NO, WE'D NEVER--
NOOO!

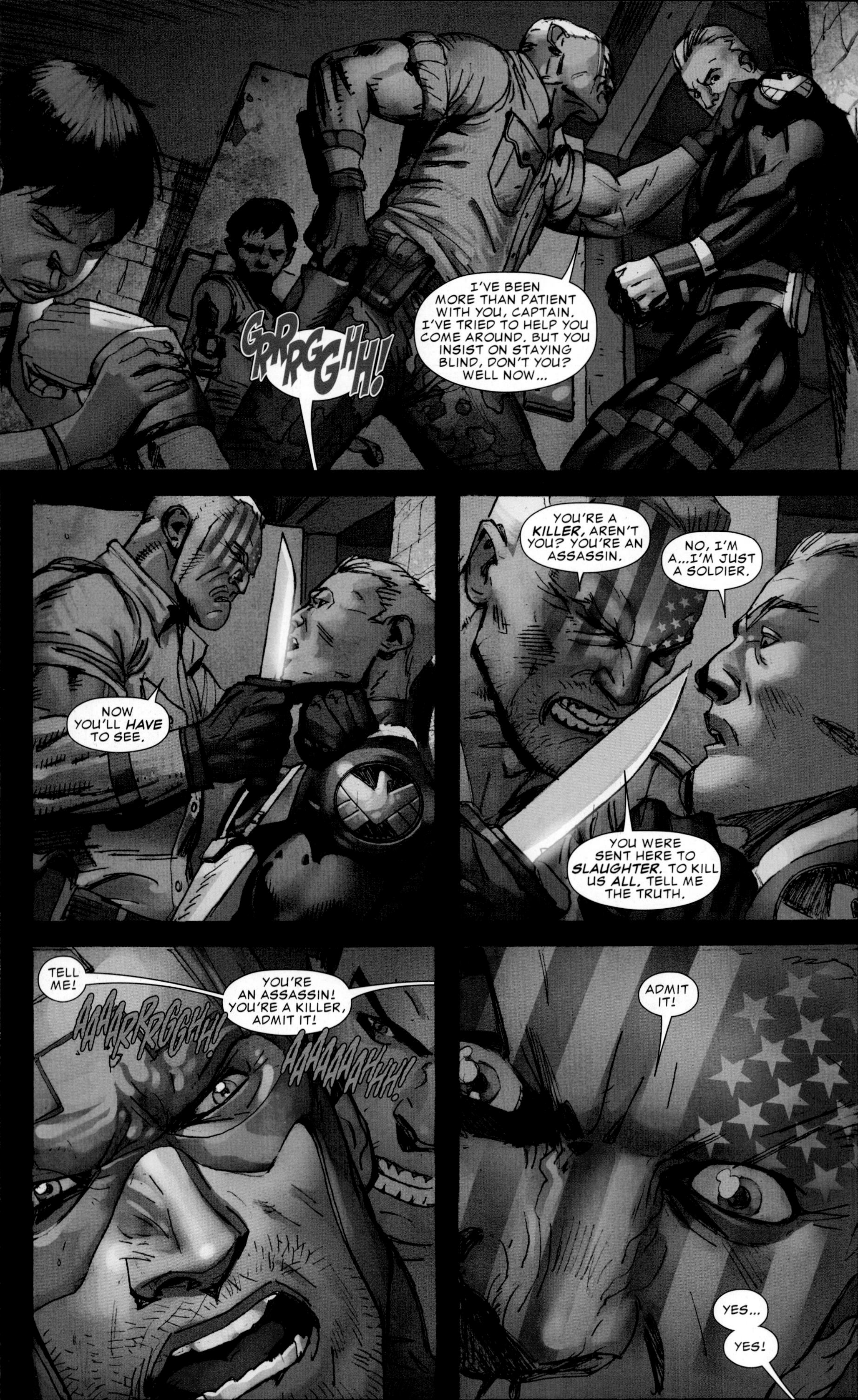
GRRRGGHH!
I'VE BEEN MORE THAN PATIENT WITH YOU, CAPTAIN. I'VE TRIED TO HELP YOU COME AROUND. BUT YOU INSIST ON STAYING BLIND, DON'T YOU? WELL NOW...
NOW YOU'LL HAVE TO SEE.
YOU'RE A KILLER, AREN'T YOU? YOU'RE AN ASSASSIN.
NO, I'M A...I'M JUST A SOLDIER.
YOU WERE SENT HERE TO SLAUGHTER. TO KILL US ALL. TELL ME THE TRUTH.
TELL ME!
AAAARRGGHH!
YOU'RE AN ASSASSIN! YOU'RE A KILLER, ADMIT IT!
AAAAAAAHHH!
ADMIT IT!
YES...
YES!

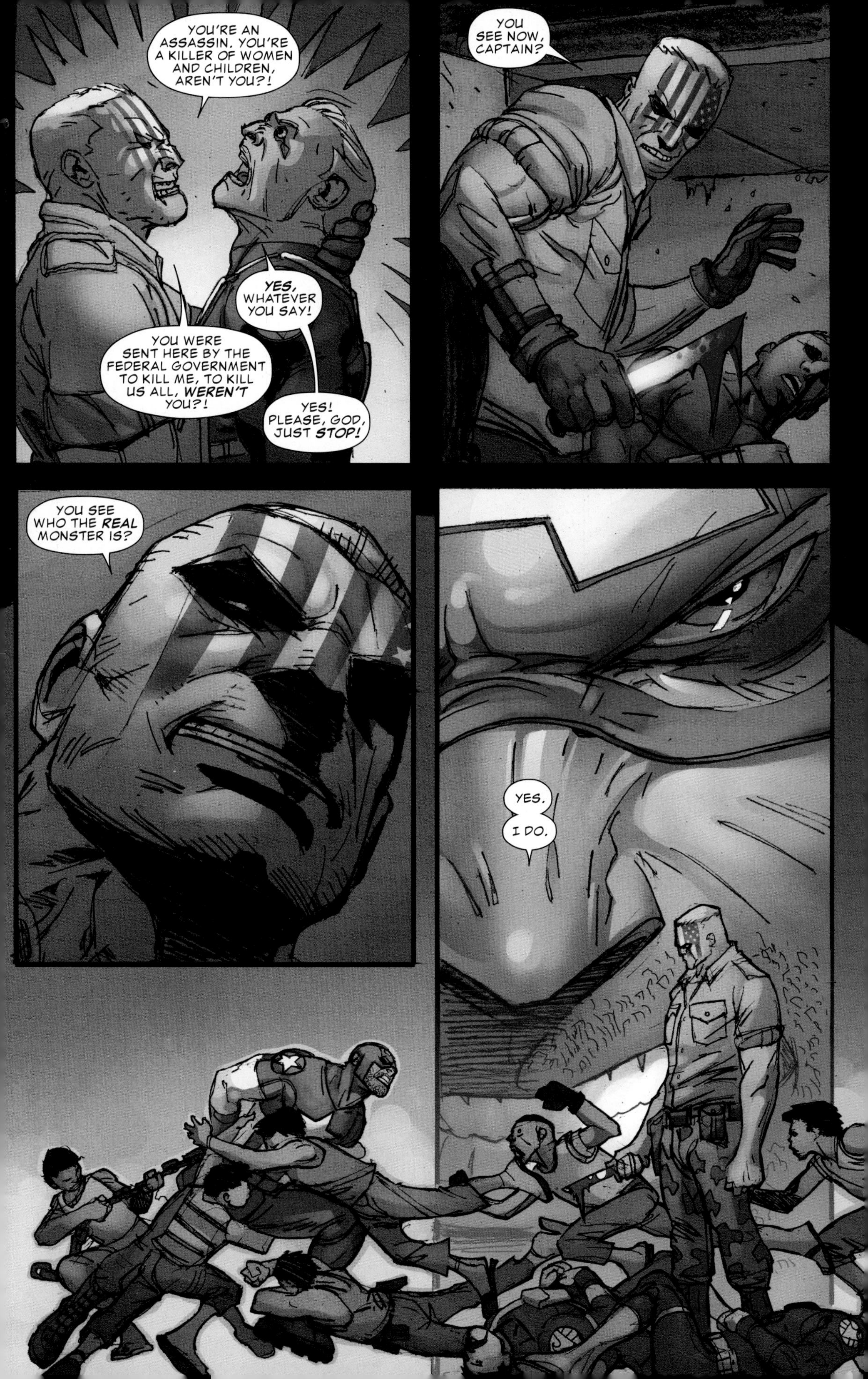
YOU'RE AN ASSASSIN. YOU'RE A KILLER OF WOMEN AND CHILDREN, AREN'T YOU?!
YES, WHATEVER YOU SAY!
YOU WERE SENT HERE BY THE FEDERAL GOVERNMENT TO KILL ME, TO KILL US ALL, WEREN'T YOU?!
YES! PLEASE, GOD, JUST STOP!
YOU SEE NOW, CAPTAIN?
YOU SEE WHO THE REAL MONSTER IS?
YES.
I DO.

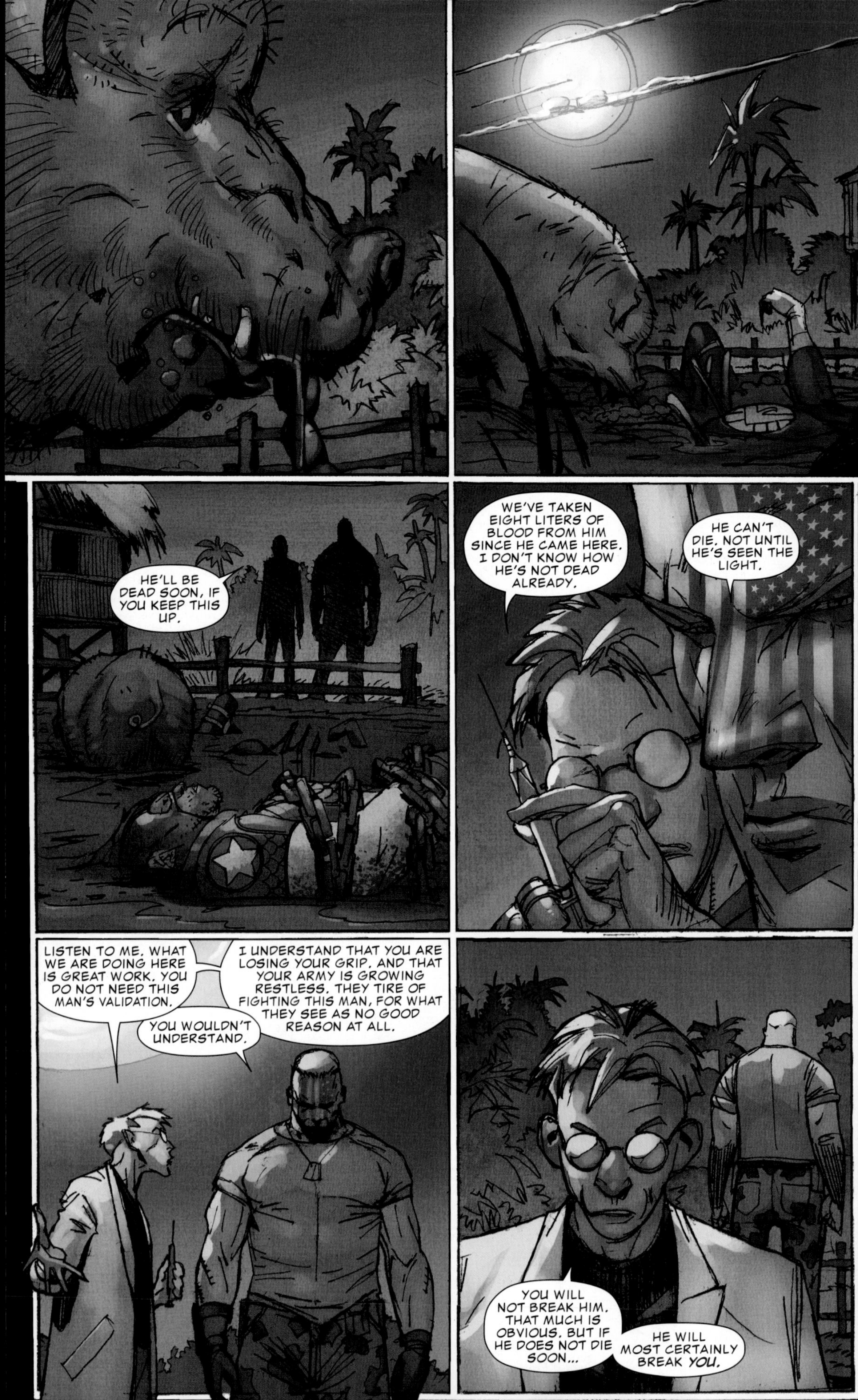
HE'LL BE DEAD SOON, IF YOU KEEP THIS UP.
WE'VE TAKEN EIGHT LITERS OF BLOOD FROM HIM SINCE HE CAME HERE. I DON'T KNOW HOW HE'S NOT DEAD ALREADY.
HE CAN'T DIE. NOT UNTIL HE'S SEEN THE LIGHT.
LISTEN TO ME. WHAT WE ARE DOING HERE IS GREAT WORK. YOU DO NOT NEED THIS MAN'S VALIDATION.
YOU WOULDN'T UNDERSTAND.
I UNDERSTAND THAT YOU ARE LOSING YOUR GRIP. AND THAT YOUR ARMY IS GROWING RESTLESS. THEY TIRE OF FIGHTING THIS MAN, FOR WHAT THEY SEE AS NO GOOD REASON AT ALL.
YOU WILL NOT BREAK HIM. THAT MUCH IS OBVIOUS. BUT IF HE DOES NOT DIE SOON...
HE WILL MOST CERTAINLY BREAK *YOU*.

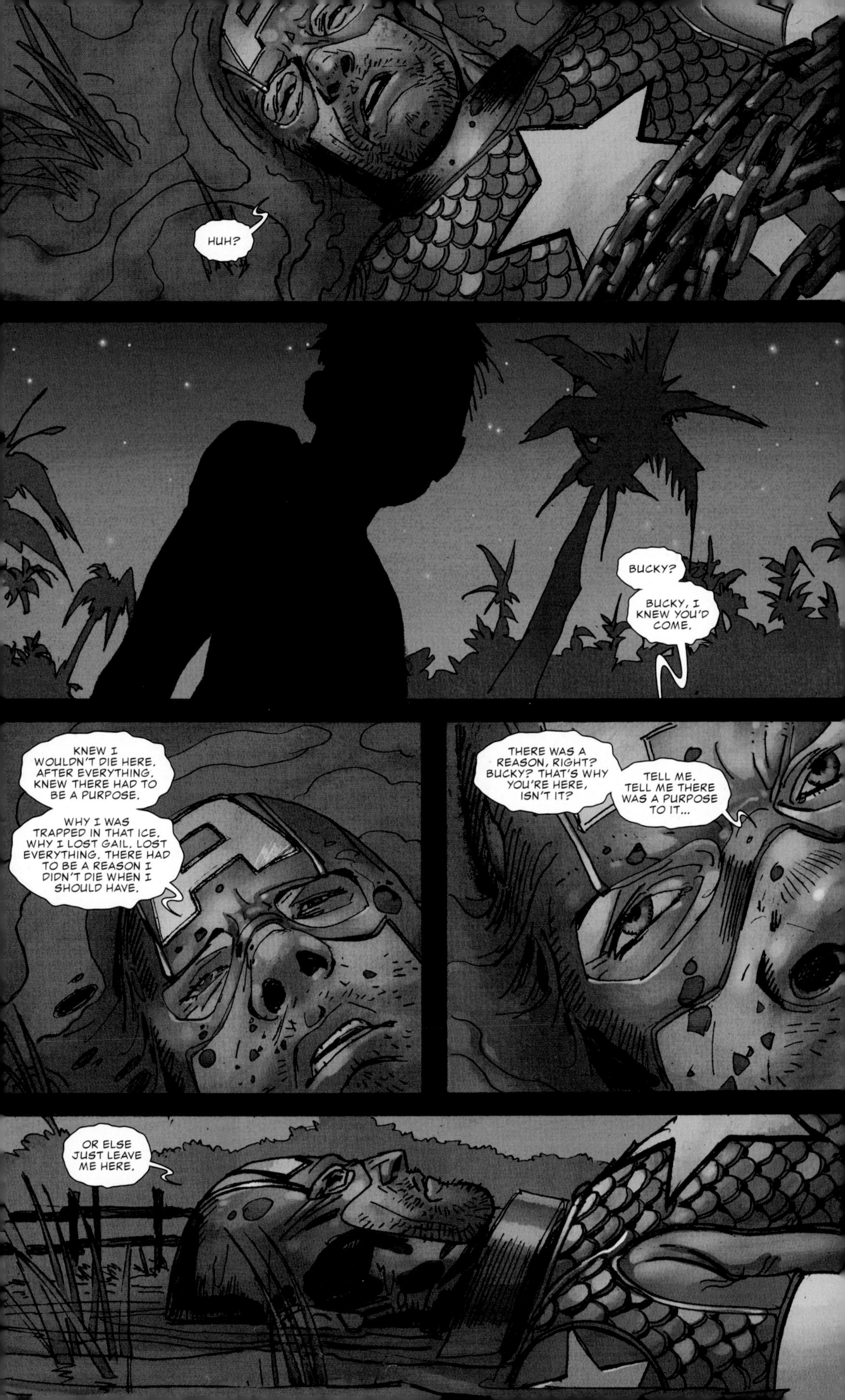
HUH?
BUCKY?
BUCKY, I KNEW YOU'D COME.
KNEW I WOULDN'T DIE HERE. AFTER EVERYTHING. KNEW THERE HAD TO BE A PURPOSE.
WHY I WAS TRAPPED IN THAT ICE. WHY I LOST GAIL. LOST EVERYTHING. THERE HAD TO BE A REASON I DIDN'T DIE WHEN I SHOULD HAVE.
THERE WAS A REASON, RIGHT? BUCKY? THAT'S WHY YOU'RE HERE, ISN'T IT?
TELL ME. TELL ME THERE WAS A PURPOSE TO IT...
OR ELSE JUST LEAVE ME HERE.

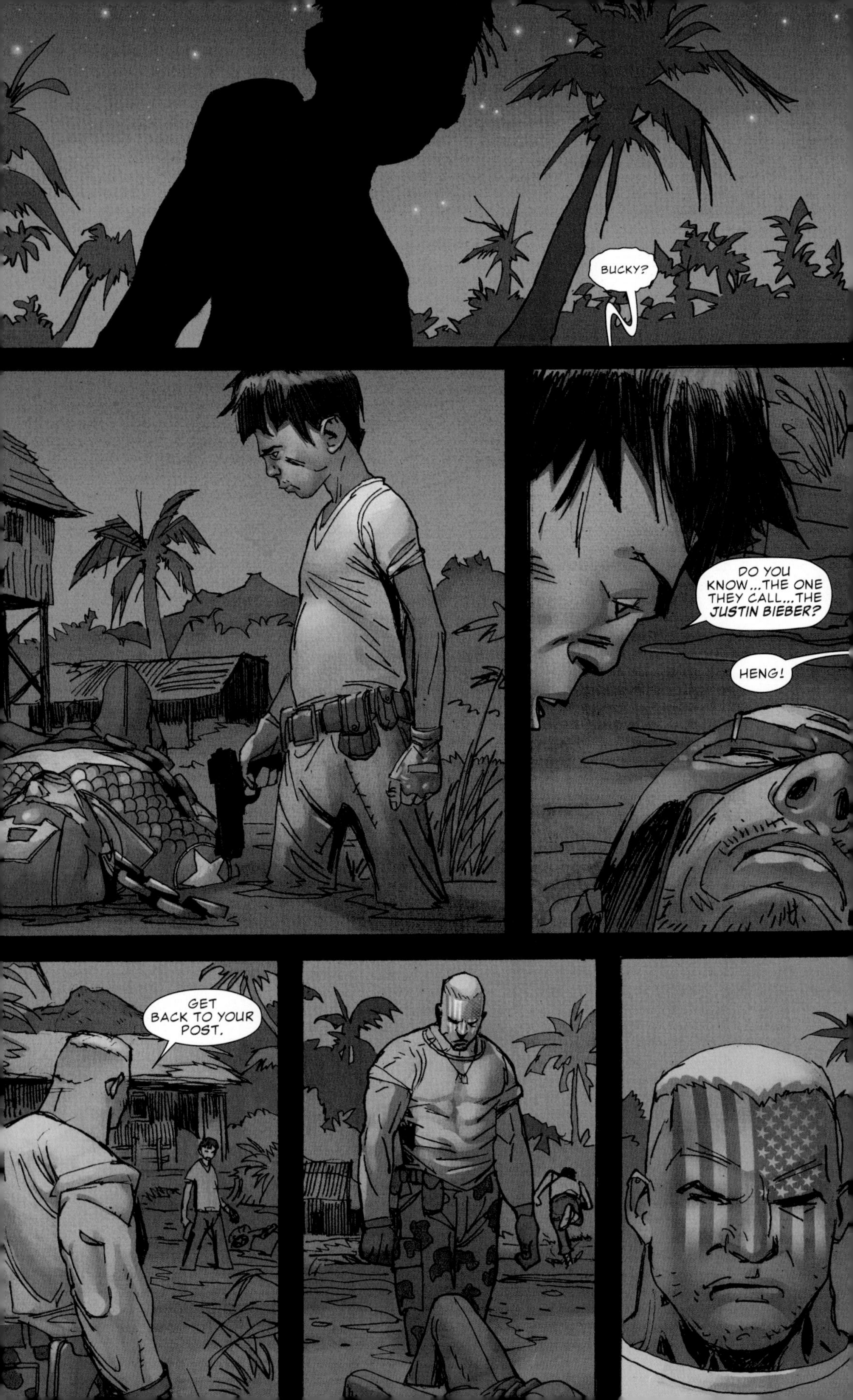
BUCKY?
DO YOU KNOW...THE ONE THEY CALL...THE JUSTIN BIEBER?
HENG!
GET BACK TO YOUR POST.

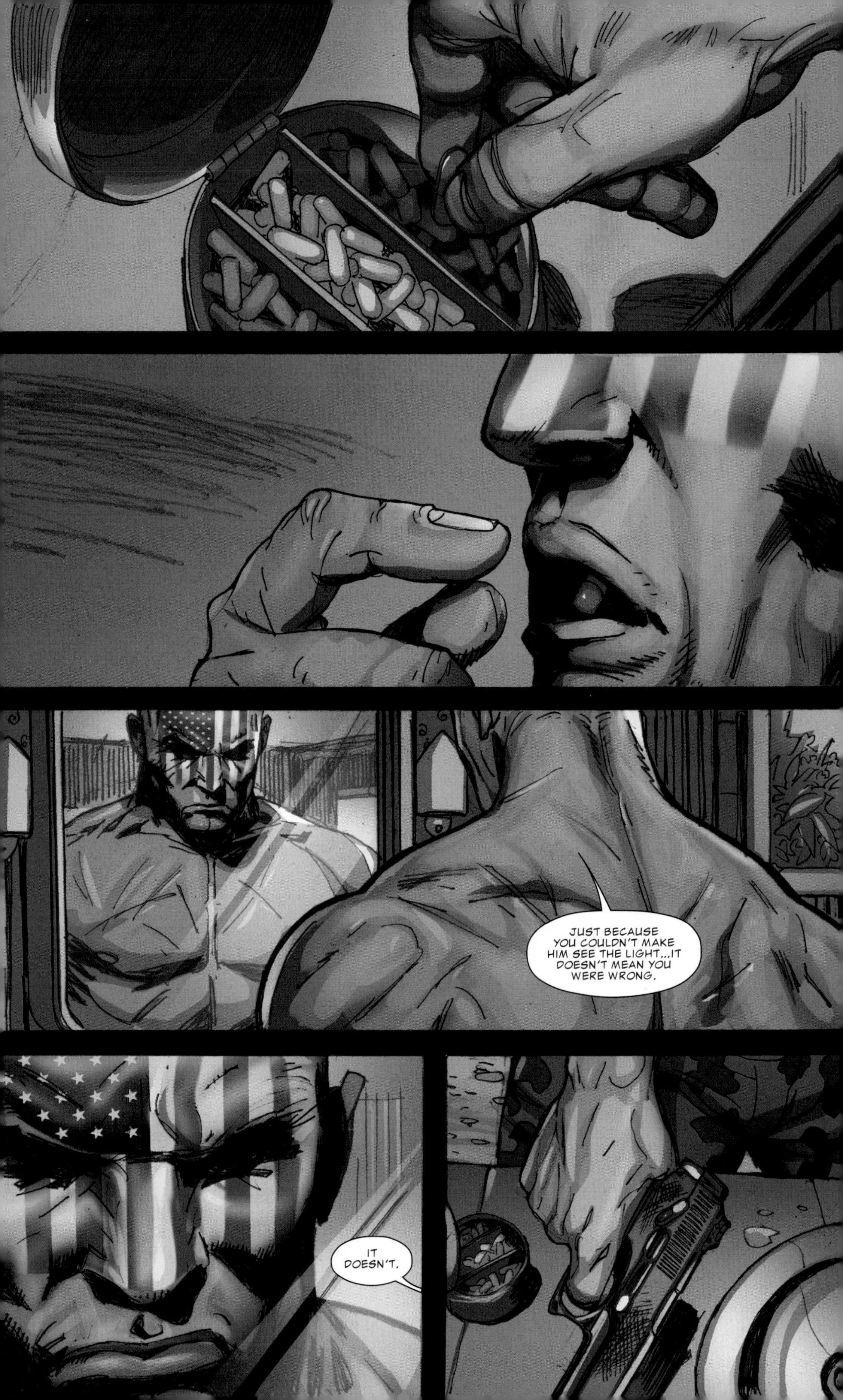
JUST BECAUSE YOU COULDN'T MAKE HIM SEE THE LIGHT...IT DOESN'T MEAN YOU WERE WRONG.
IT DOESN'T.

RRAAAH

YOU ARE NOTHING IF NOT PERSISTENT, ROGERS, I WILL GIVE YOU THAT, BUT MY PATIENCE HAS FINALLY RUN OUT. I'M SORRY I COULDN'T HELP YOU, I TRULY AM.

GOODBYE, CAPTAIN AMERICA, IT'S BEEN A PLEASURE.

GO TO HELL.

ARE YOU... PRAYING?

IN FIVE MINUTES, WHEN I COME BACK IN HERE AND YOU'RE STILL KNEELING THERE, BABBLING LIKE AN IDIOT, I'M GOING TO WALK OVER AND PUT A BULLET IN YOUR BRAIN.

AND THEN YOU'LL DIE KNOWING EVERYTHING YOU EVER BELIEVED IN WAS A LIE.

I'M NOT GONNA BEG. NOT ANYONE.

NOT EVEN YOU.

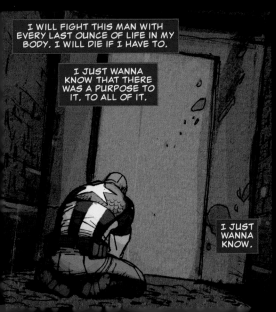

I WILL FIGHT THIS MAN WITH EVERY LAST OUNCE OF LIFE IN MY BODY. I WILL DIE IF I HAVE TO.

I JUST WANNA KNOW THAT THERE WAS A PURPOSE TO IT. TO ALL OF IT.

I JUST WANNA KNOW.

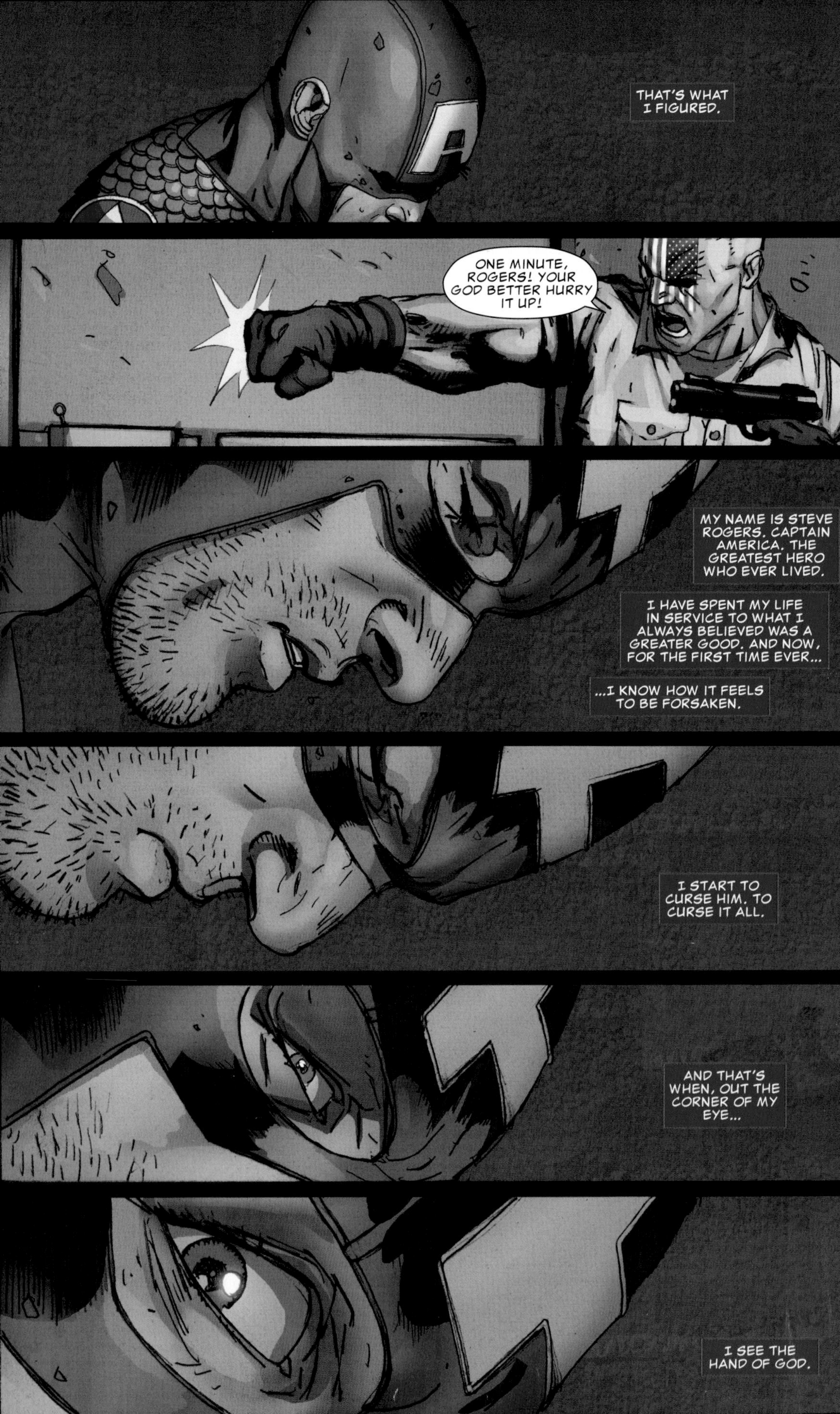
THAT'S WHAT I FIGURED.
ONE MINUTE, ROGERS! YOUR GOD BETTER HURRY IT UP!
MY NAME IS STEVE ROGERS. CAPTAIN AMERICA. THE GREATEST HERO WHO EVER LIVED.
I HAVE SPENT MY LIFE IN SERVICE TO WHAT I ALWAYS BELIEVED WAS A GREATER GOOD. AND NOW, FOR THE FIRST TIME EVER...
...I KNOW HOW IT FEELS TO BE FORSAKEN.
I START TO CURSE HIM. TO CURSE IT ALL.
AND THAT'S WHEN, OUT THE CORNER OF MY EYE...
I SEE THE HAND OF GOD.

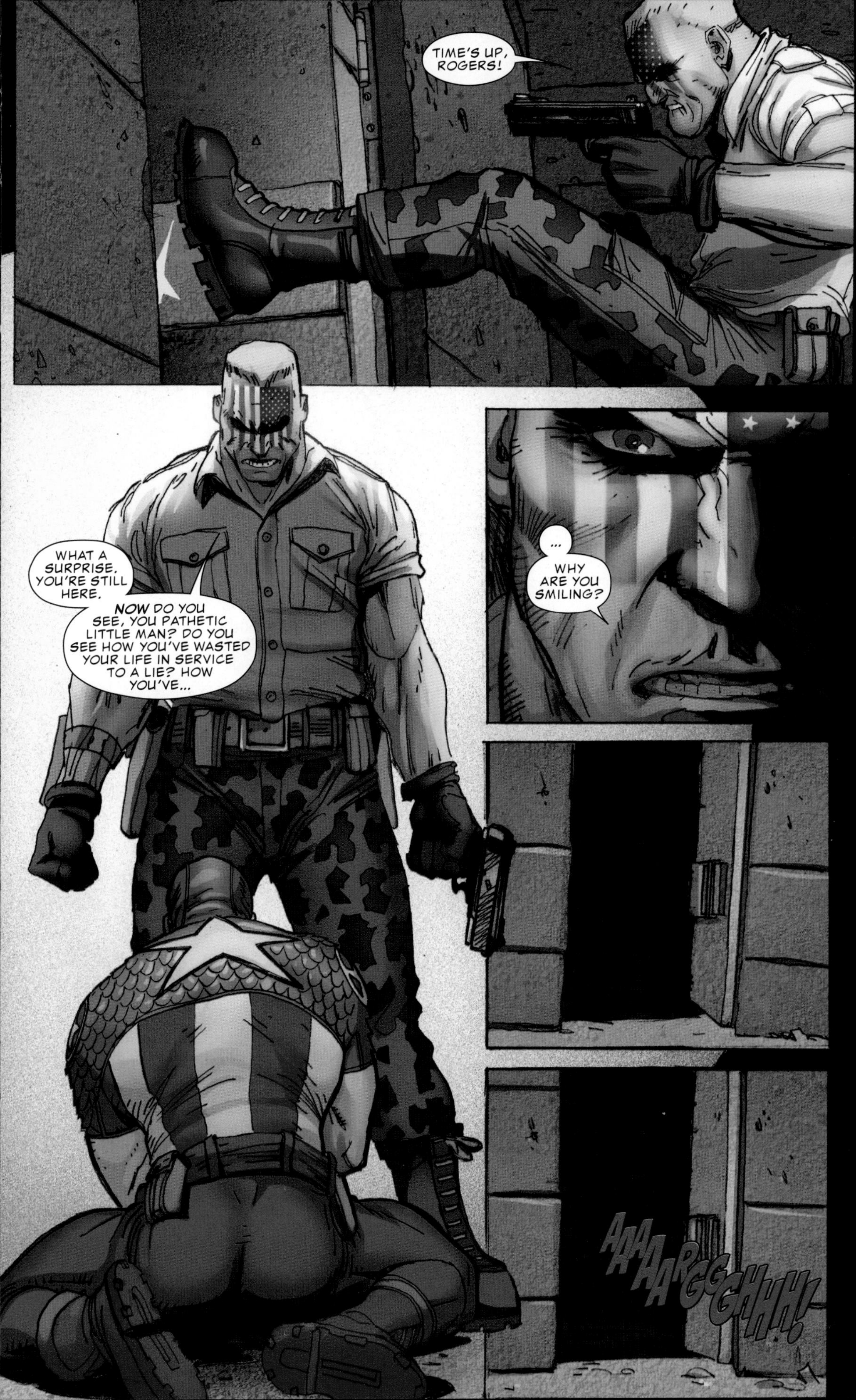
TIME'S UP, ROGERS!
WHAT A SURPRISE. YOU'RE STILL HERE.
NOW DO YOU SEE, YOU PATHETIC LITTLE MAN? DO YOU SEE HOW YOU'VE WASTED YOUR LIFE IN SERVICE TO A LIE? HOW YOU'VE...
...
WHY ARE YOU SMILING?
AAAAARGGGHHH!

4

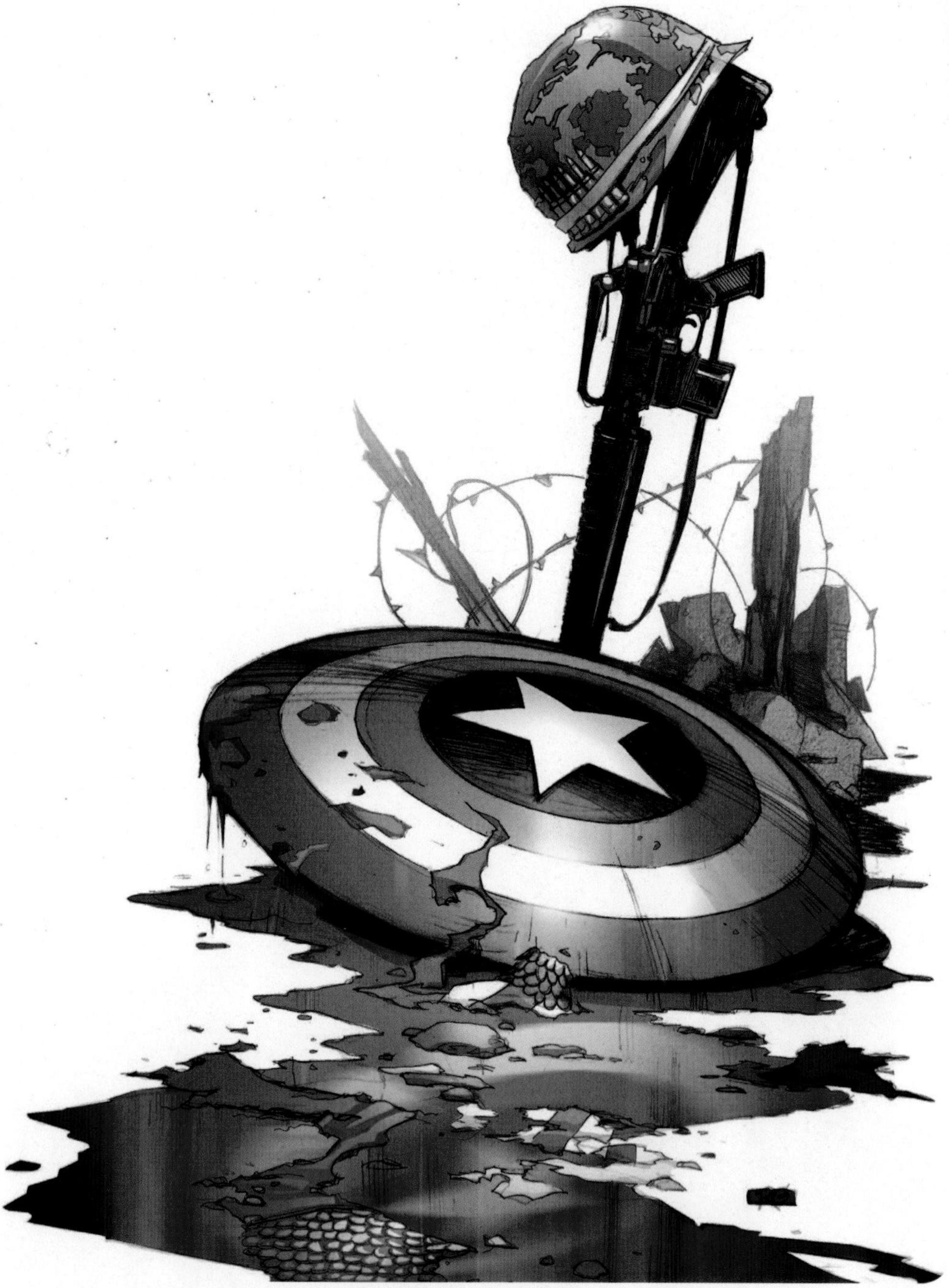

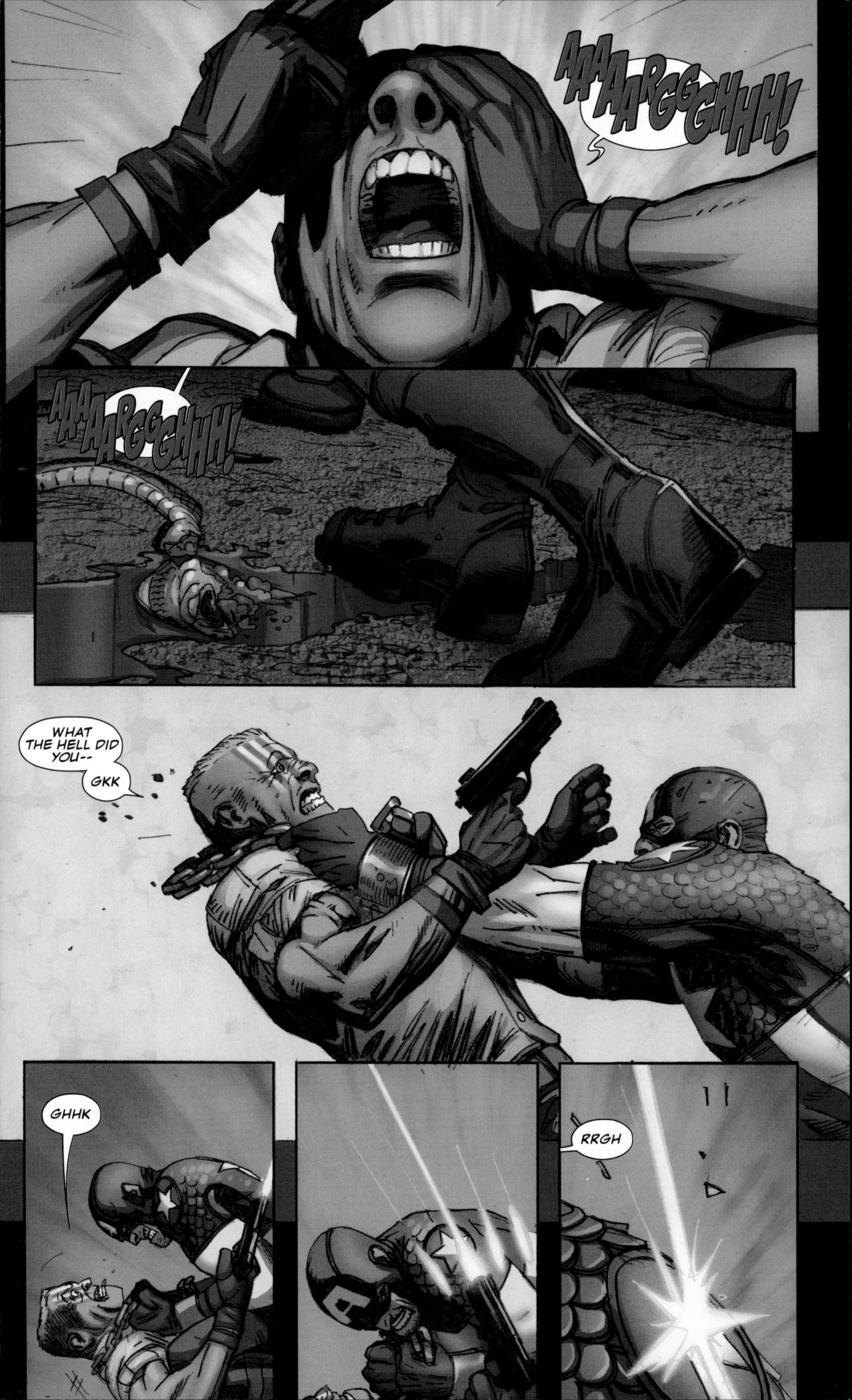
AAAAARGGGHHHH!
AAAAARGGGHHHH!
WHAT THE HELL DID YOU--
GKK
GHHK
RRGH

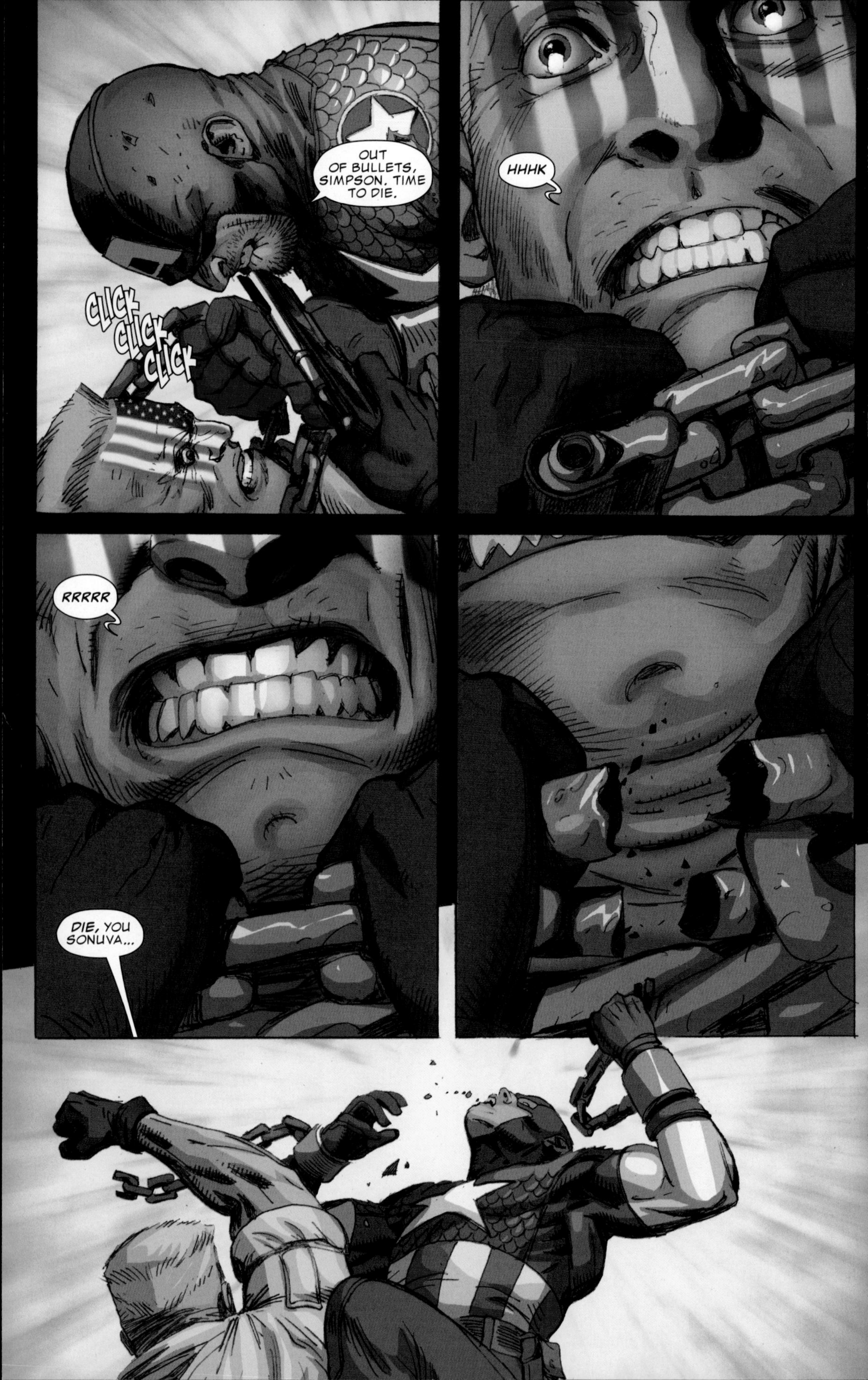
OUT OF BULLETS, SIMPSON. TIME TO DIE.
CLICK CLICK CLICK
HHHK
RRRRR
DIE, YOU SONUVA...

GAAA...YOU PIG-HEADED SON OF A BITCH...

YOU COULD'VE HAD AN *EASY* [DEA]TH, COULD'VE LEFT [SOM]ETHING BEHIND FOR [T]HEM TO BURY IN [A]RLINGTON.

BUT NOW [I']M GONNA FEED [YOU] TO MY *PIGS*, ONE [PAT]HETIC LITTLE SCRAP AT A TIME.

C'MON!

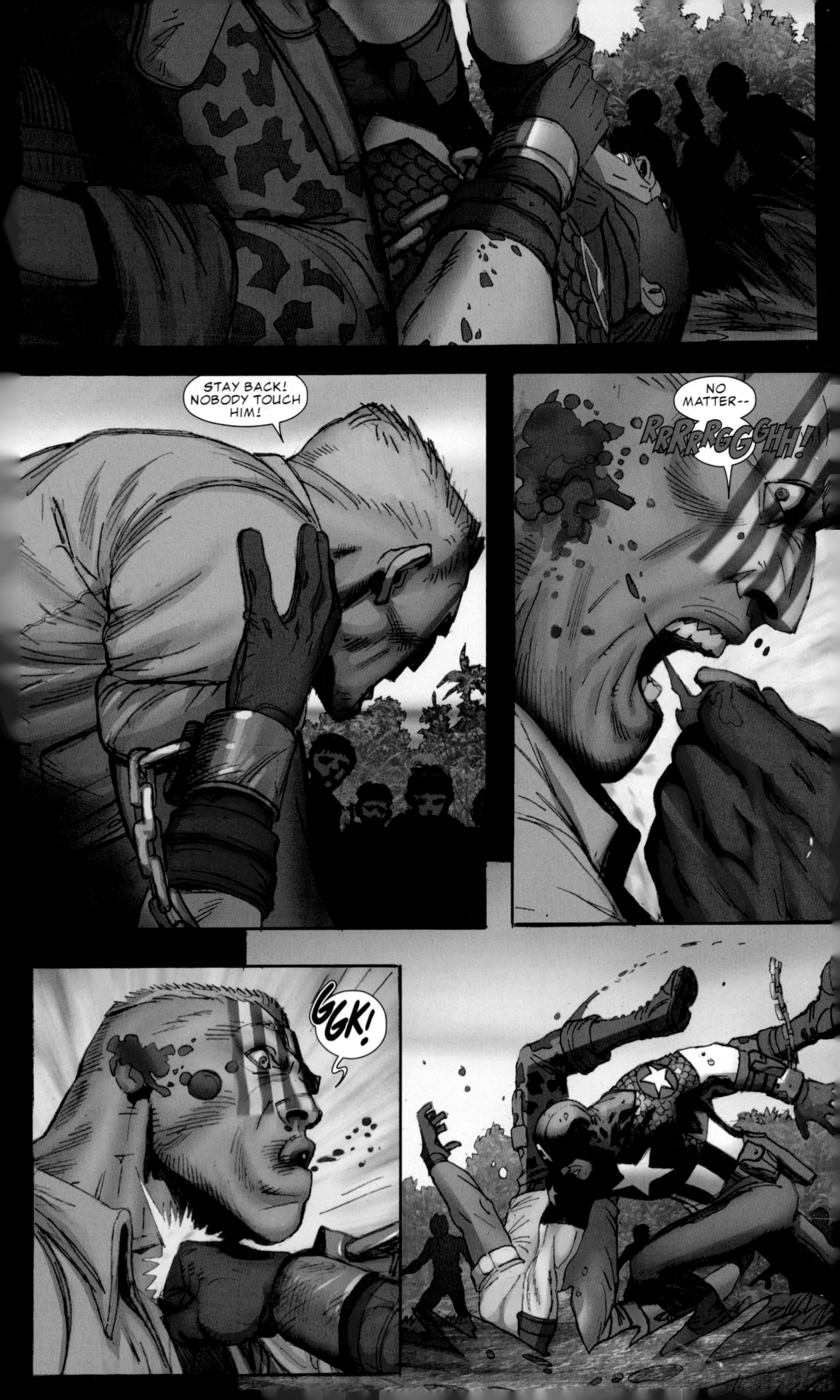
STAY BACK! NOBODY TOUCH HIM!
NO MATTER--
RRRRRGGGHH!
GGK!

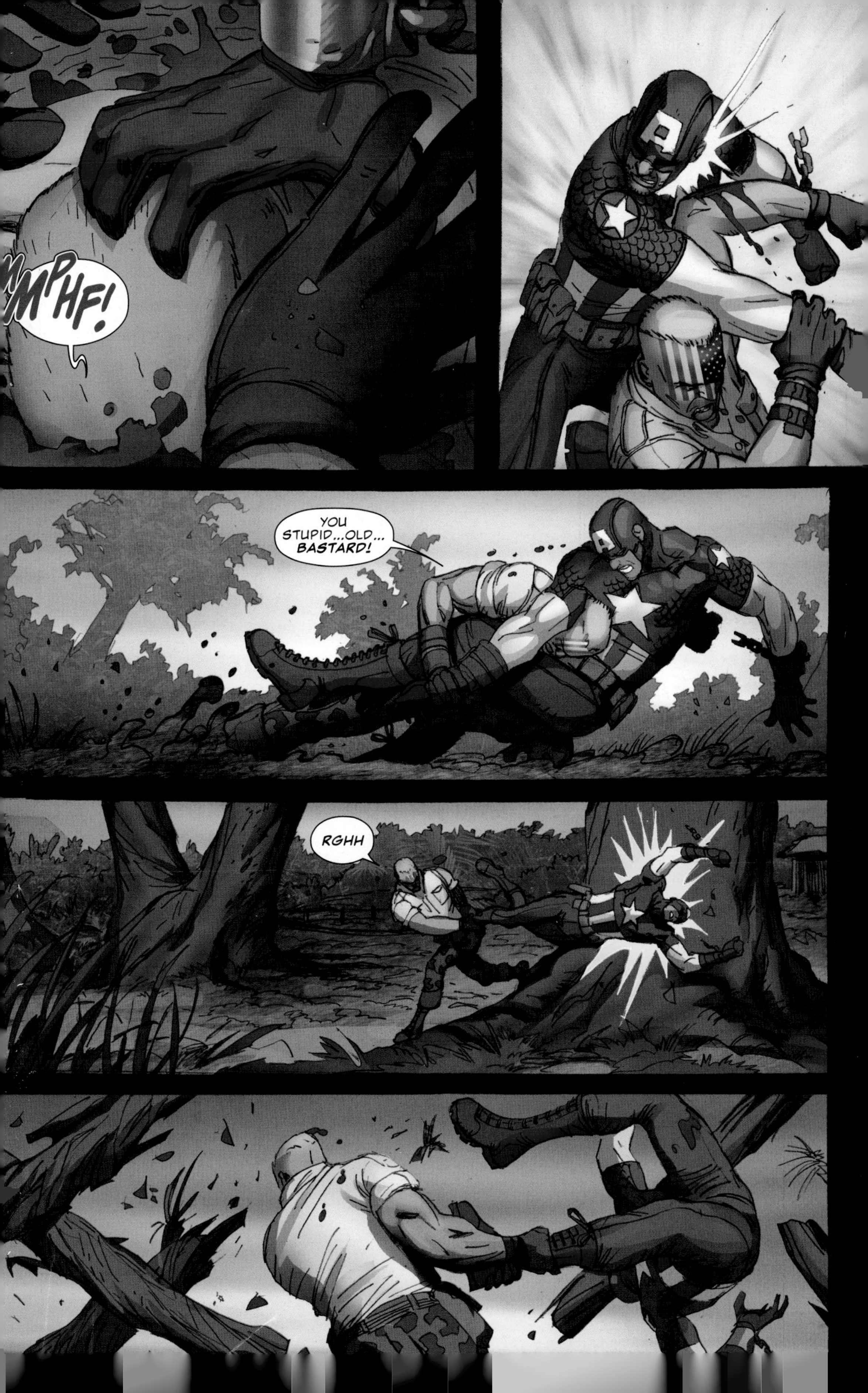

MMPHF!
YOU STUPID...OLD... BASTARD!
RGHH

AFTER I BASH YOUR BRAINS IN, ROGERS, I'M GONNA HANG YOU UP AND BLEED YOU OUT LIKE A DEER.

AND THAT *BLOOD* WILL FEED THE CAUSE FOR YEARS TO COME.

YOU'VE GOTTEN ENOUGH BLOOD OUTTA ME ALREADY, SIMPSON.

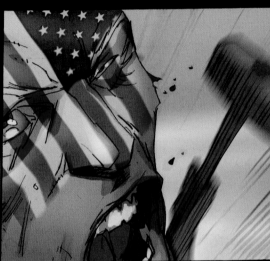

BUT I'LL TAKE A BIT MORE OF *YOURS.*

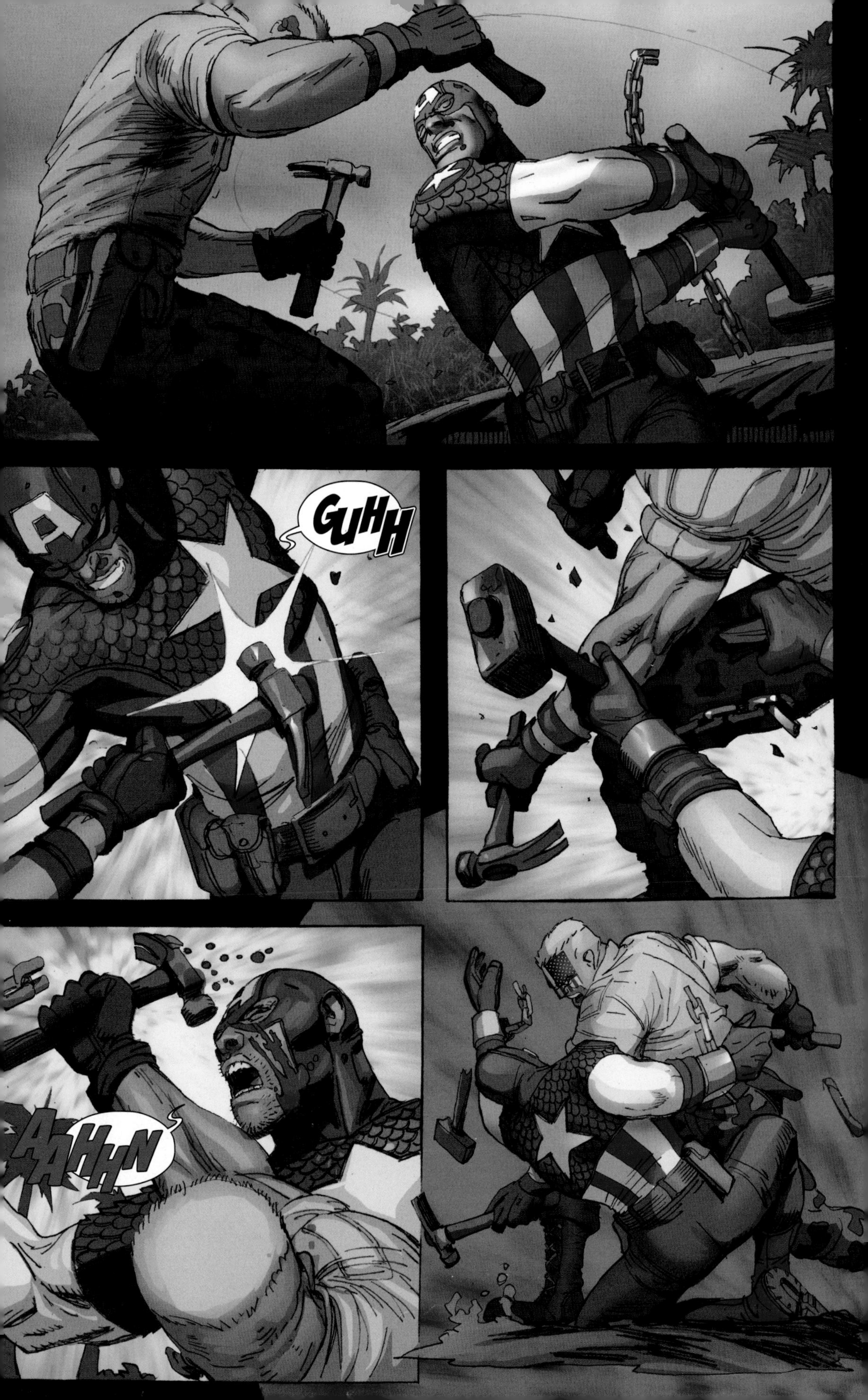
GUHH
AAHHN

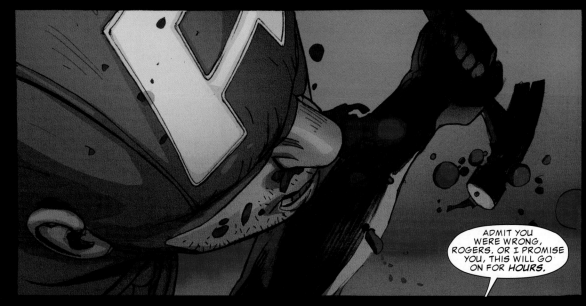

ADMIT YOU WERE WRONG, ROGERS. OR I PROMISE YOU, THIS WILL GO ON FOR *HOURS*.

ADMIT YOU'RE THE TOOL OF AN IMPERIALIST REGIME. THAT ALL YOU KNOW ARE *LIES* AND PROPAGANDA.

THAT AMERICA IS DEAD. AND *YOU* HELPED KILL IT.

ADMIT YOU WERE WRONG, ROGERS! WHILE YOU STILL HAVE TIME! ADMIT IT!

OKAY...

OKAY, I ADMIT IT. I WAS WRONG. ABOUT ONE THING AT LEAST.

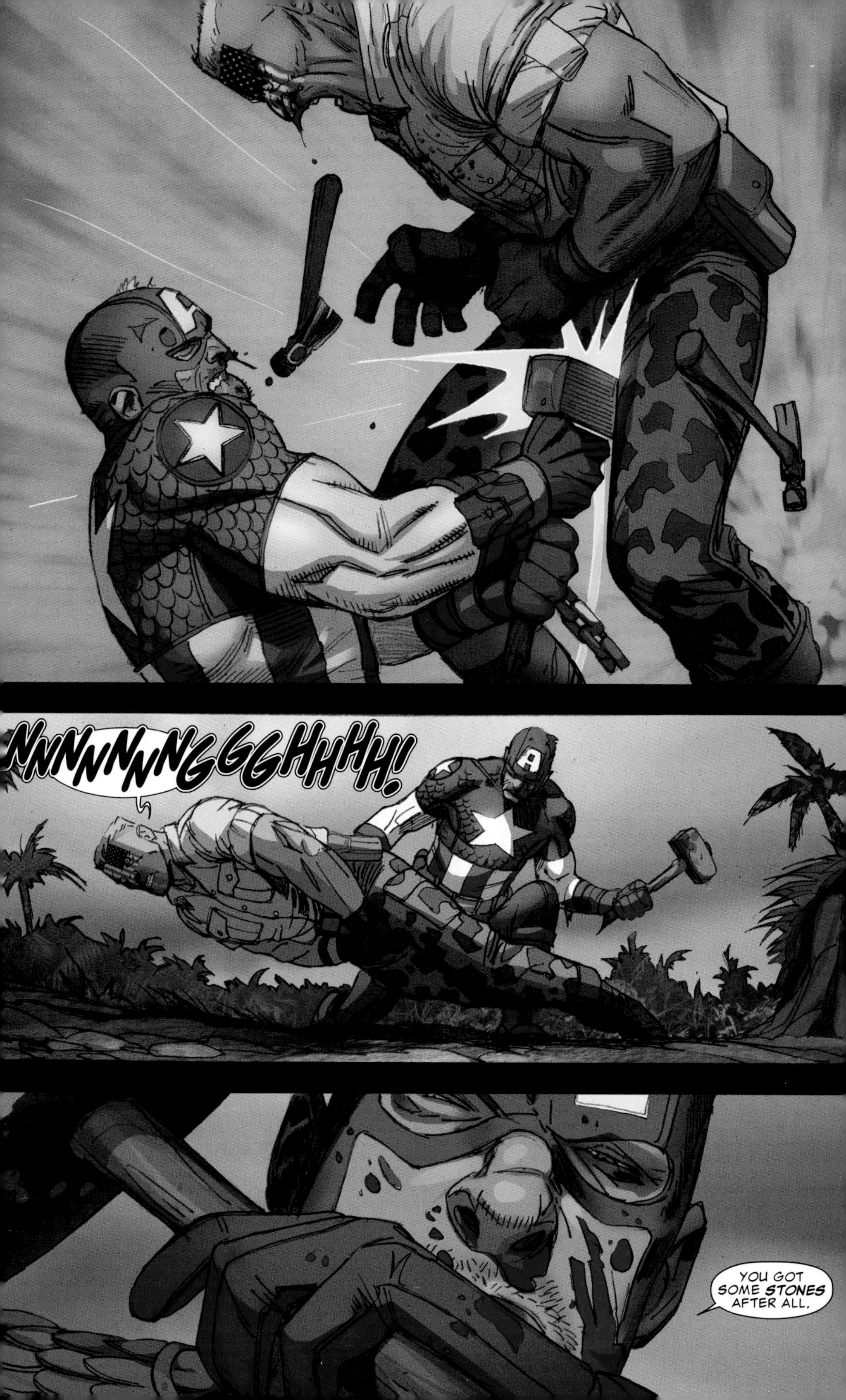
NNNNNNNGGGHHHHH!
YOU GOT SOME STONES AFTER ALL.

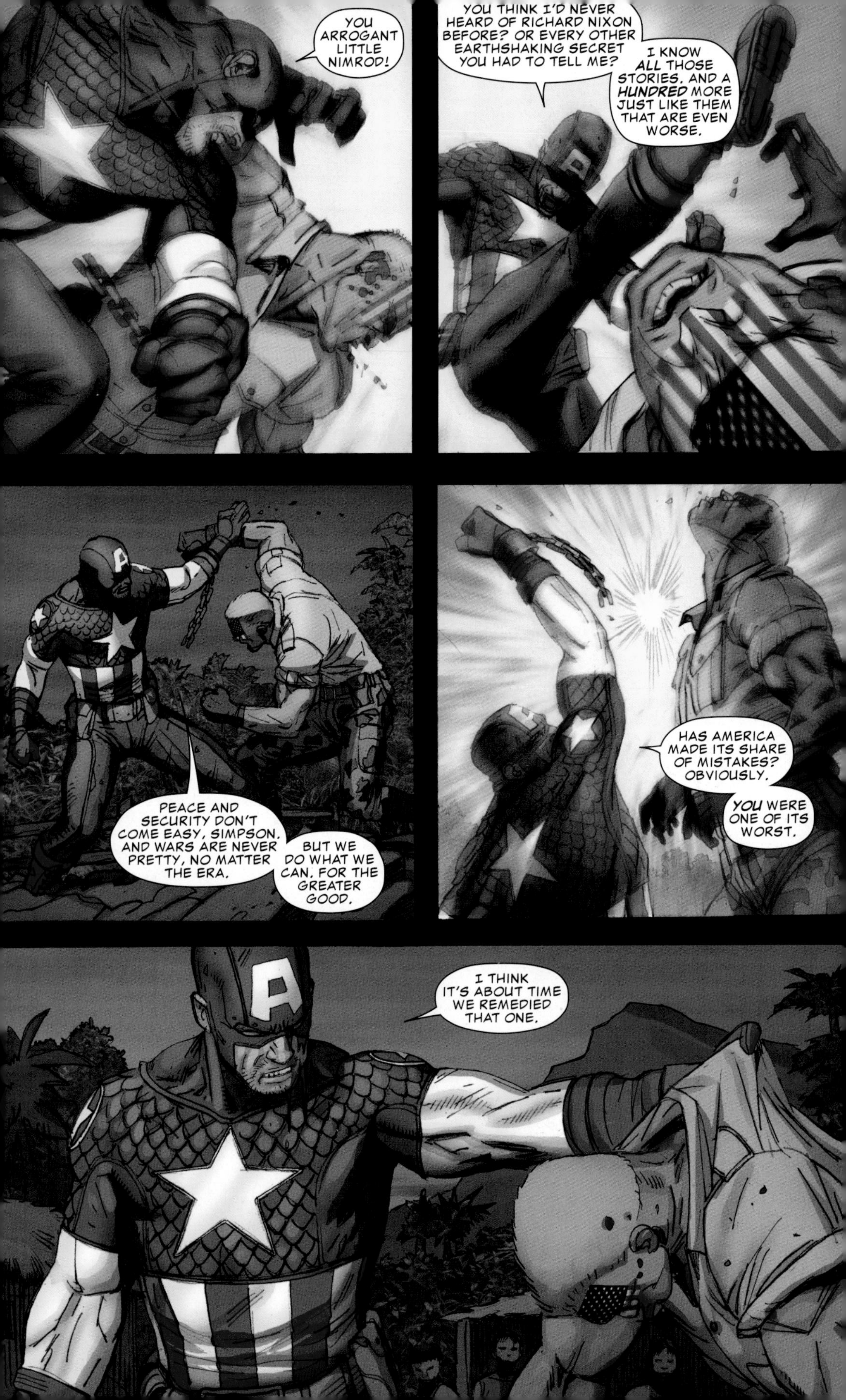

YOU ARROGANT LITTLE NIMROD!
YOU THINK I'D NEVER HEARD OF RICHARD NIXON BEFORE? OR EVERY OTHER EARTHSHAKING SECRET YOU HAD TO TELL ME?
I KNOW ALL THOSE STORIES. AND A HUNDRED MORE JUST LIKE THEM THAT ARE EVEN WORSE.
PEACE AND SECURITY DON'T COME EASY, SIMPSON. AND WARS ARE NEVER PRETTY, NO MATTER THE ERA.
BUT WE DO WHAT WE CAN. FOR THE GREATER GOOD.
HAS AMERICA MADE ITS SHARE OF MISTAKES? OBVIOUSLY.
YOU WERE ONE OF ITS WORST.
I THINK IT'S ABOUT TIME WE REMEDIED THAT ONE.

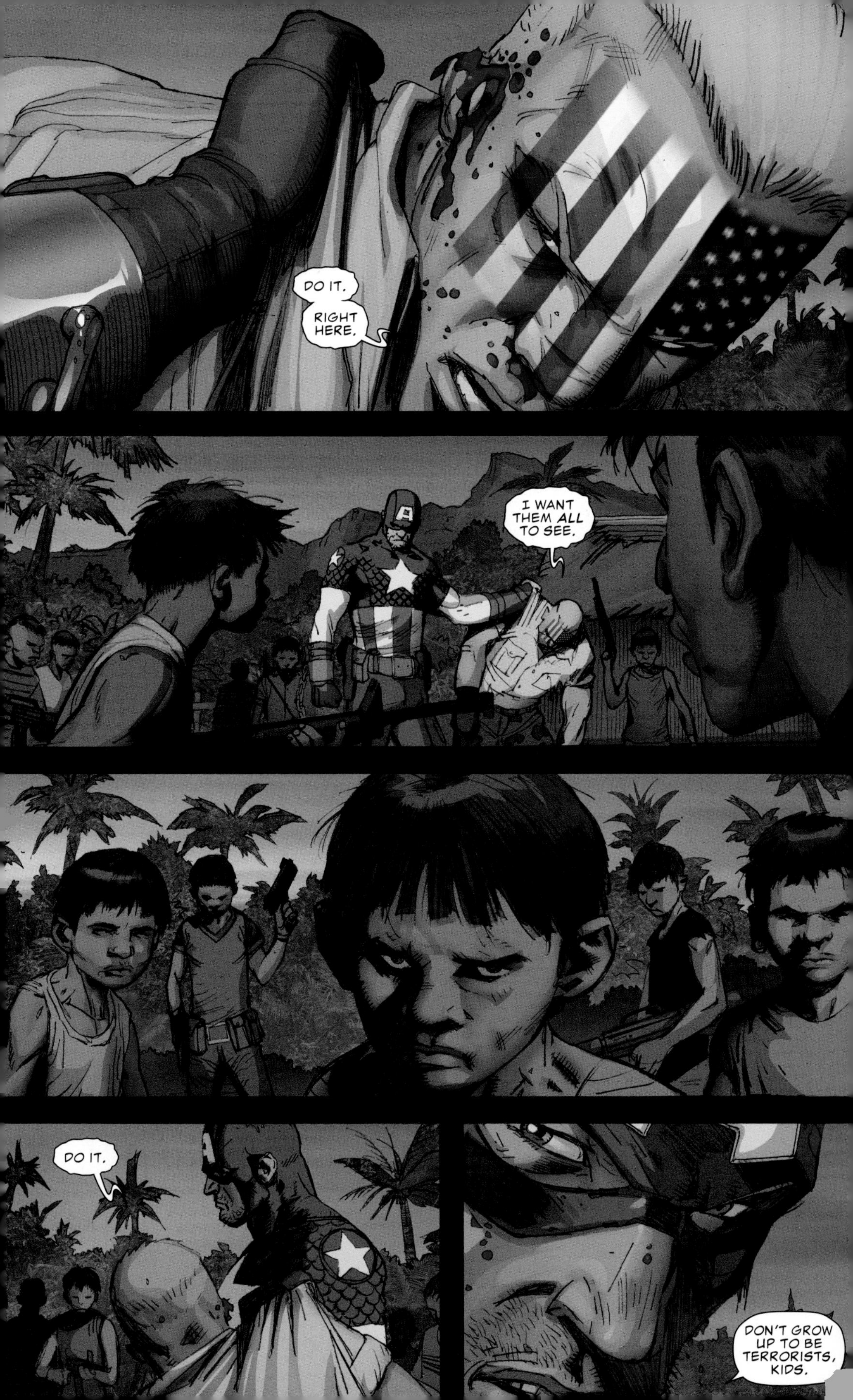
DO IT.
RIGHT HERE.
I WANT THEM ALL TO SEE.
DO IT.
DON'T GROW UP TO BE TERRORISTS, KIDS.

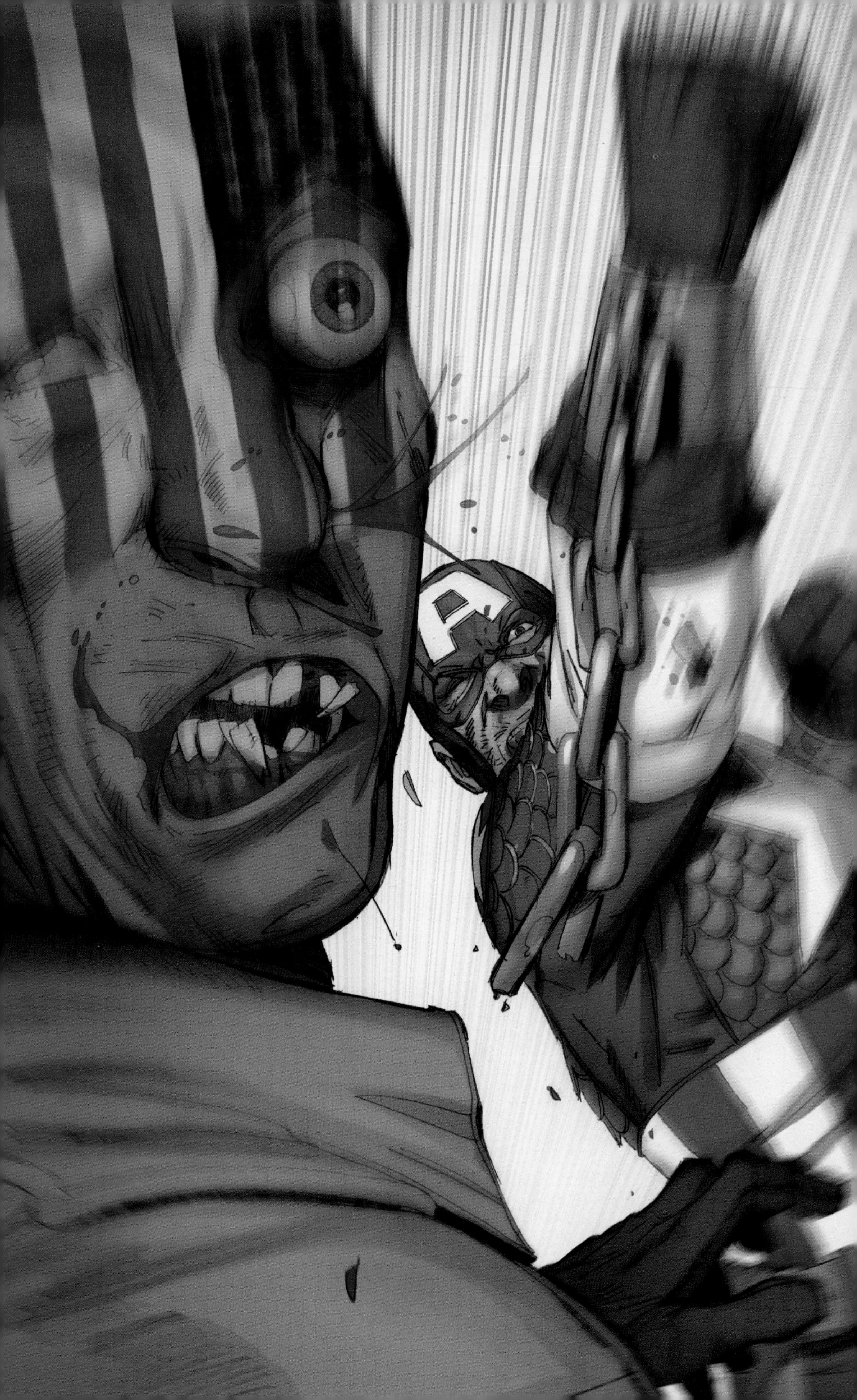

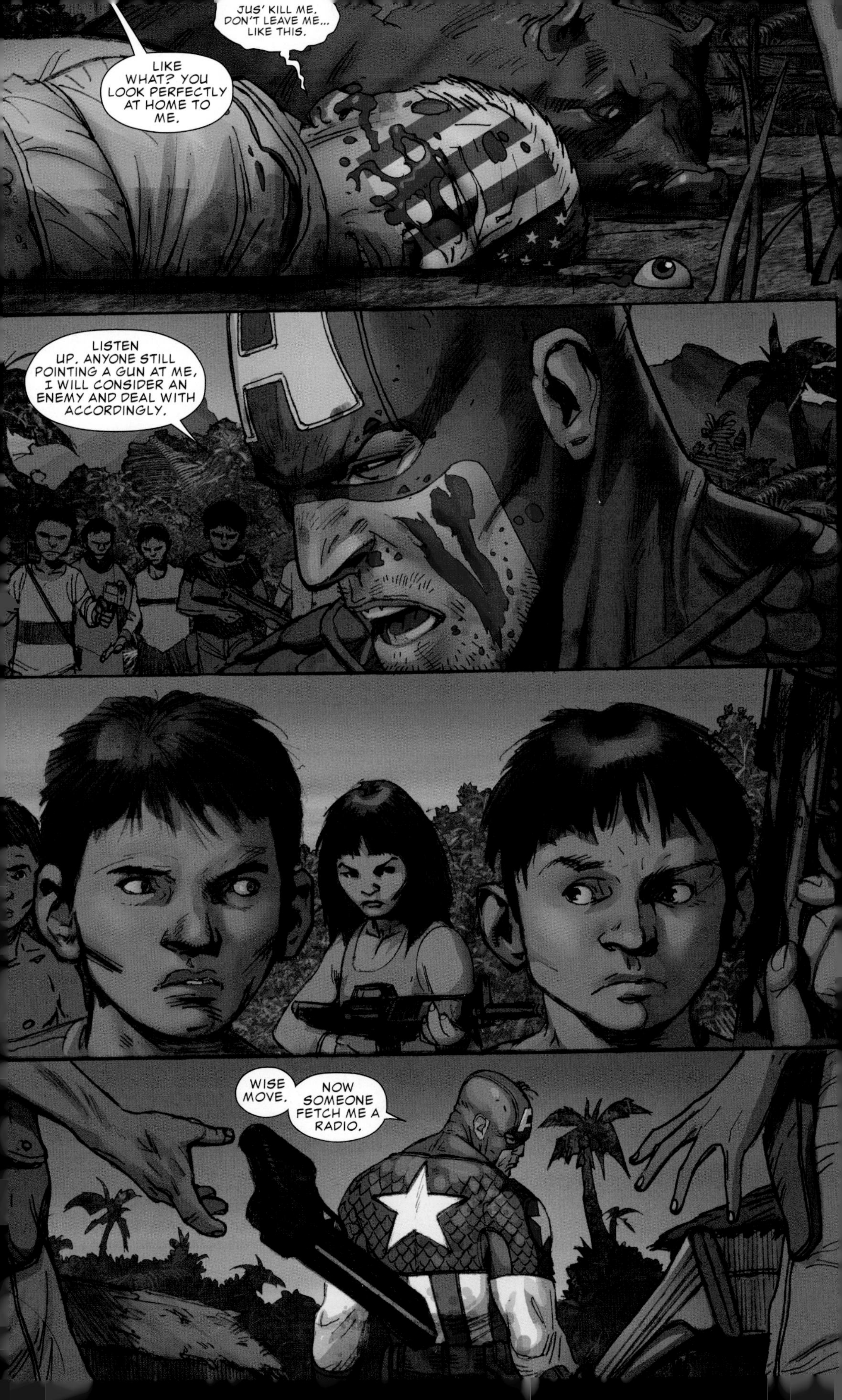

JUS' KILL ME. DON'T LEAVE ME... LIKE THIS.
LIKE WHAT? YOU LOOK PERFECTLY AT HOME TO ME.
LISTEN UP. ANYONE STILL POINTING A GUN AT ME, I WILL CONSIDER AN ENEMY AND DEAL WITH ACCORDINGLY.
WISE MOVE.
NOW SOMEONE FETCH ME A RADIO.

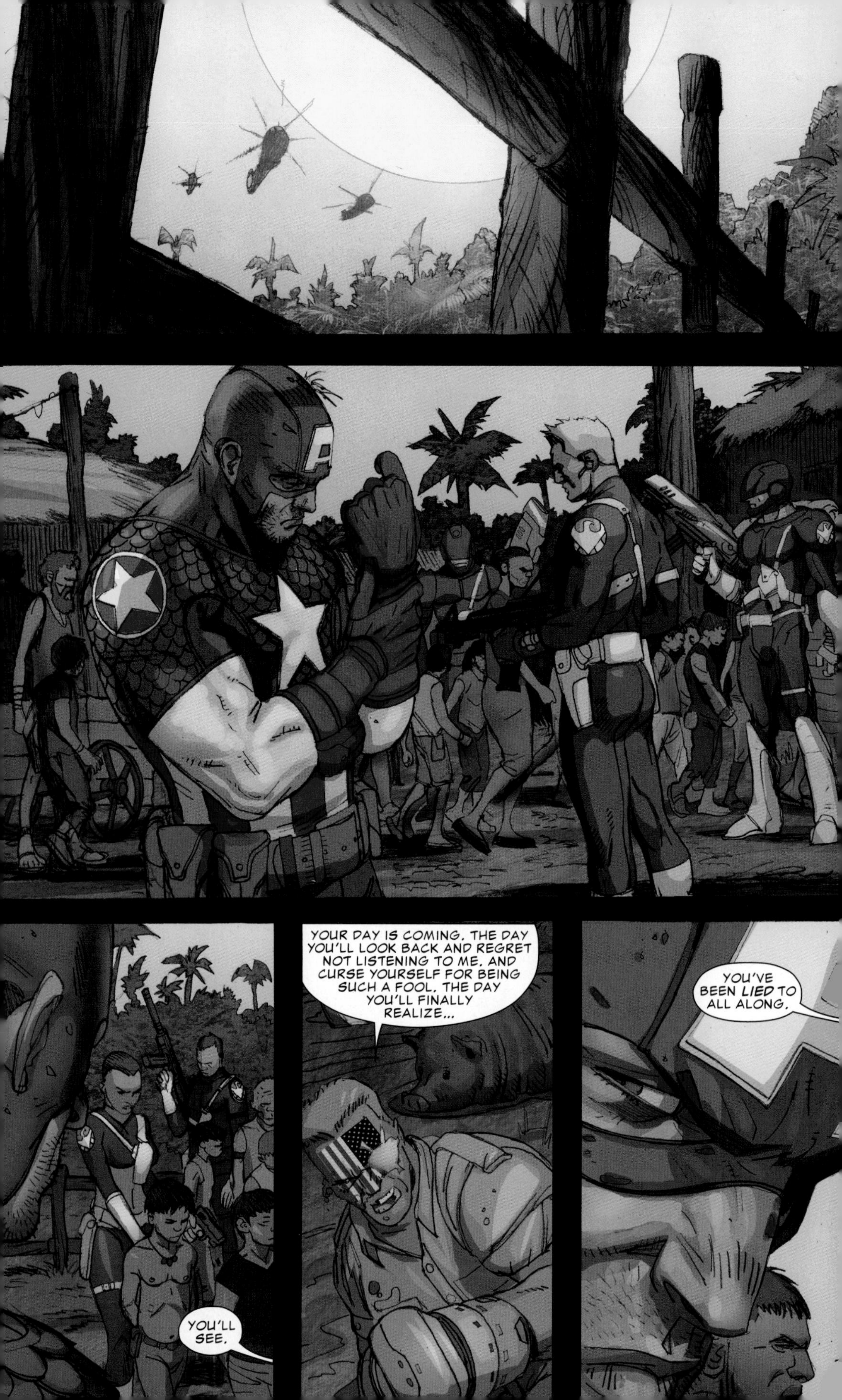
YOU'LL SEE.
YOUR DAY IS COMING. THE DAY YOU'LL LOOK BACK AND REGRET NOT LISTENING TO ME. AND CURSE YOURSELF FOR BEING SUCH A FOOL. THE DAY YOU'LL FINALLY REALIZE...
YOU'VE BEEN LIED TO ALL ALONG.

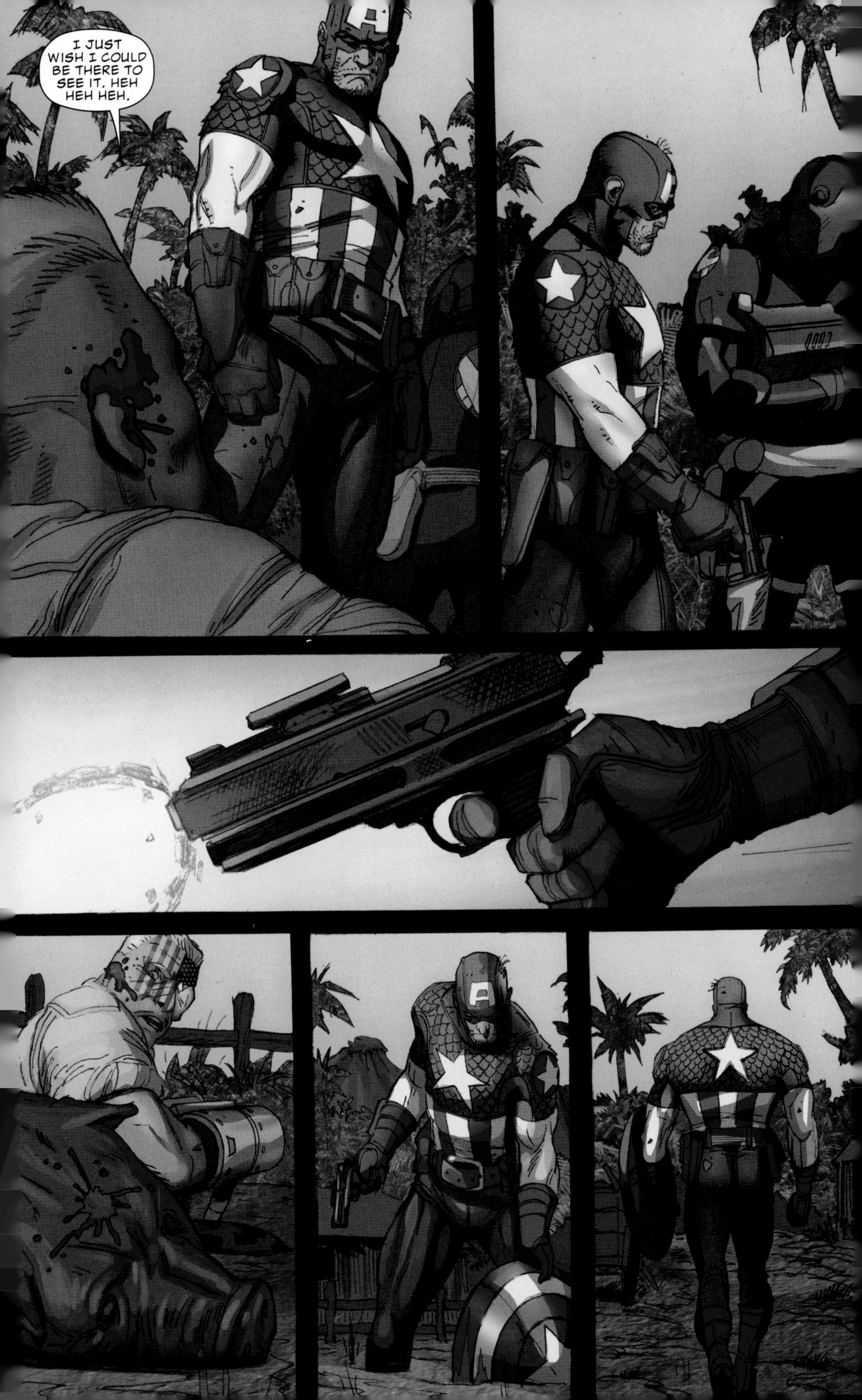
I JUST WISH I COULD BE THERE TO SEE IT. HEH HEH HEH.

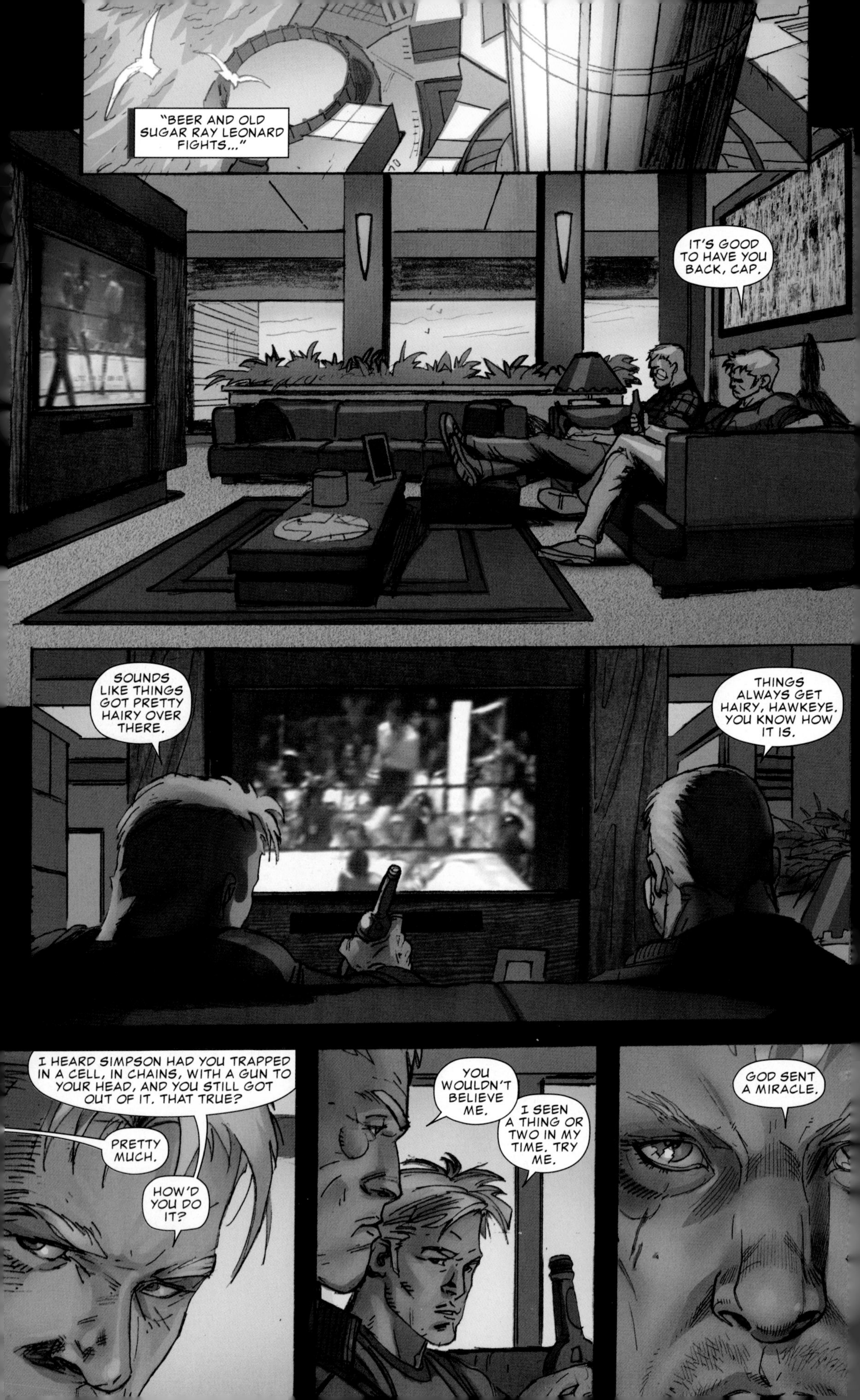
"BEER AND OLD SUGAR RAY LEONARD FIGHTS..."
IT'S GOOD TO HAVE YOU BACK, CAP.
SOUNDS LIKE THINGS GOT PRETTY HAIRY OVER THERE.
THINGS ALWAYS GET HAIRY, HAWKEYE. YOU KNOW HOW IT IS.
I HEARD SIMPSON HAD YOU TRAPPED IN A CELL, IN CHAINS, WITH A GUN TO YOUR HEAD, AND YOU STILL GOT OUT OF IT. THAT TRUE?
PRETTY MUCH.
HOW'D YOU DO IT?
YOU WOULDN'T BELIEVE ME.
I SEEN A THING OR TWO IN MY TIME. TRY ME.
GOD SENT A MIRACLE.

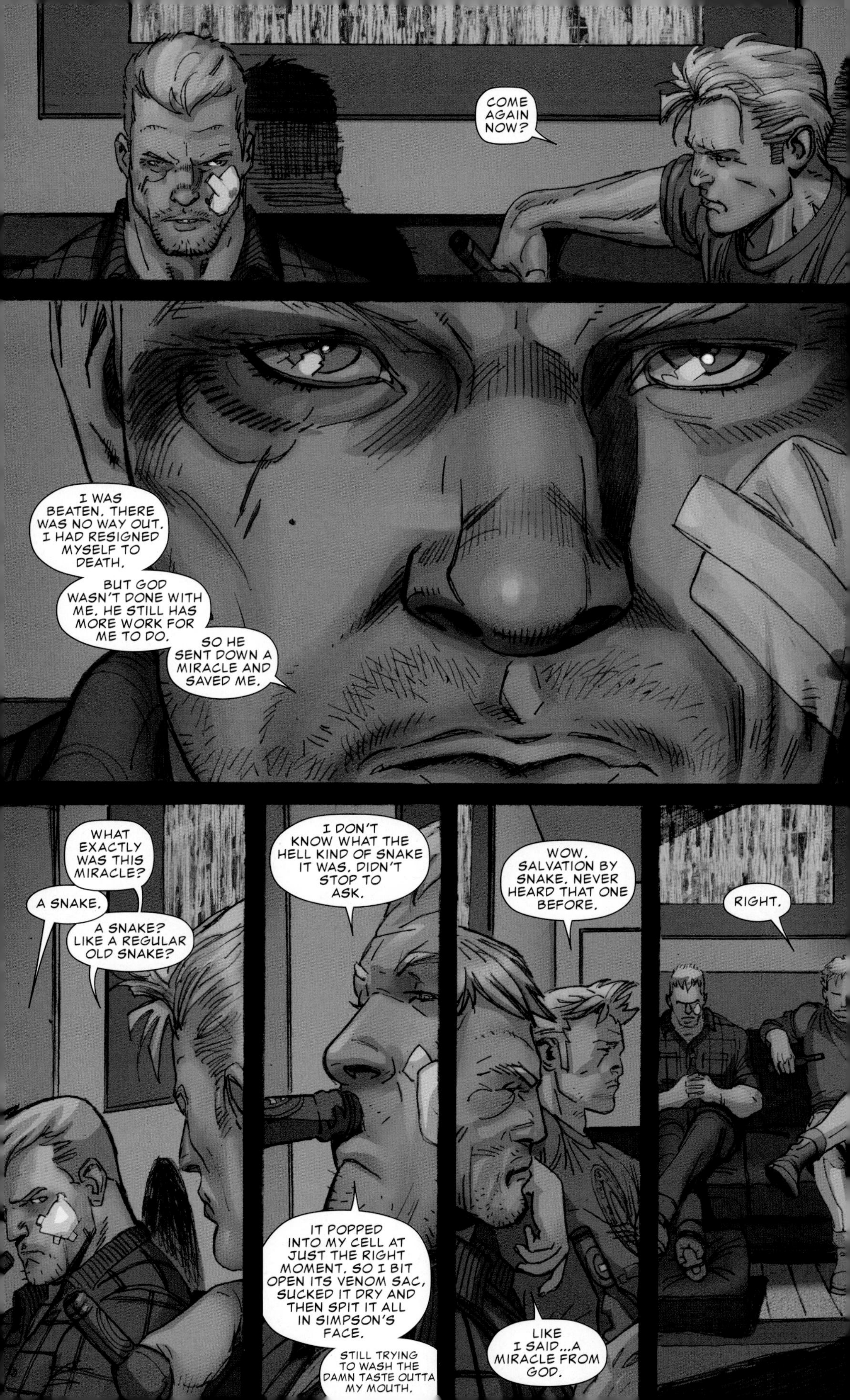
COME AGAIN NOW?
I WAS BEATEN. THERE WAS NO WAY OUT. I HAD RESIGNED MYSELF TO DEATH.
BUT GOD WASN'T DONE WITH ME. HE STILL HAS MORE WORK FOR ME TO DO.
SO HE SENT DOWN A MIRACLE AND SAVED ME.
WHAT EXACTLY WAS THIS MIRACLE?
A SNAKE.
A SNAKE? LIKE A REGULAR OLD SNAKE?
I DON'T KNOW WHAT THE HELL KIND OF SNAKE IT WAS. DIDN'T STOP TO ASK.
IT POPPED INTO MY CELL AT JUST THE RIGHT MOMENT. SO I BIT OPEN ITS VENOM SAC, SUCKED IT DRY AND THEN SPIT IT ALL IN SIMPSON'S FACE.
STILL TRYING TO WASH THE DAMN TASTE OUTTA MY MOUTH.
WOW. SALVATION BY SNAKE. NEVER HEARD THAT ONE BEFORE.
LIKE I SAID...A MIRACLE FROM GOD.
RIGHT.

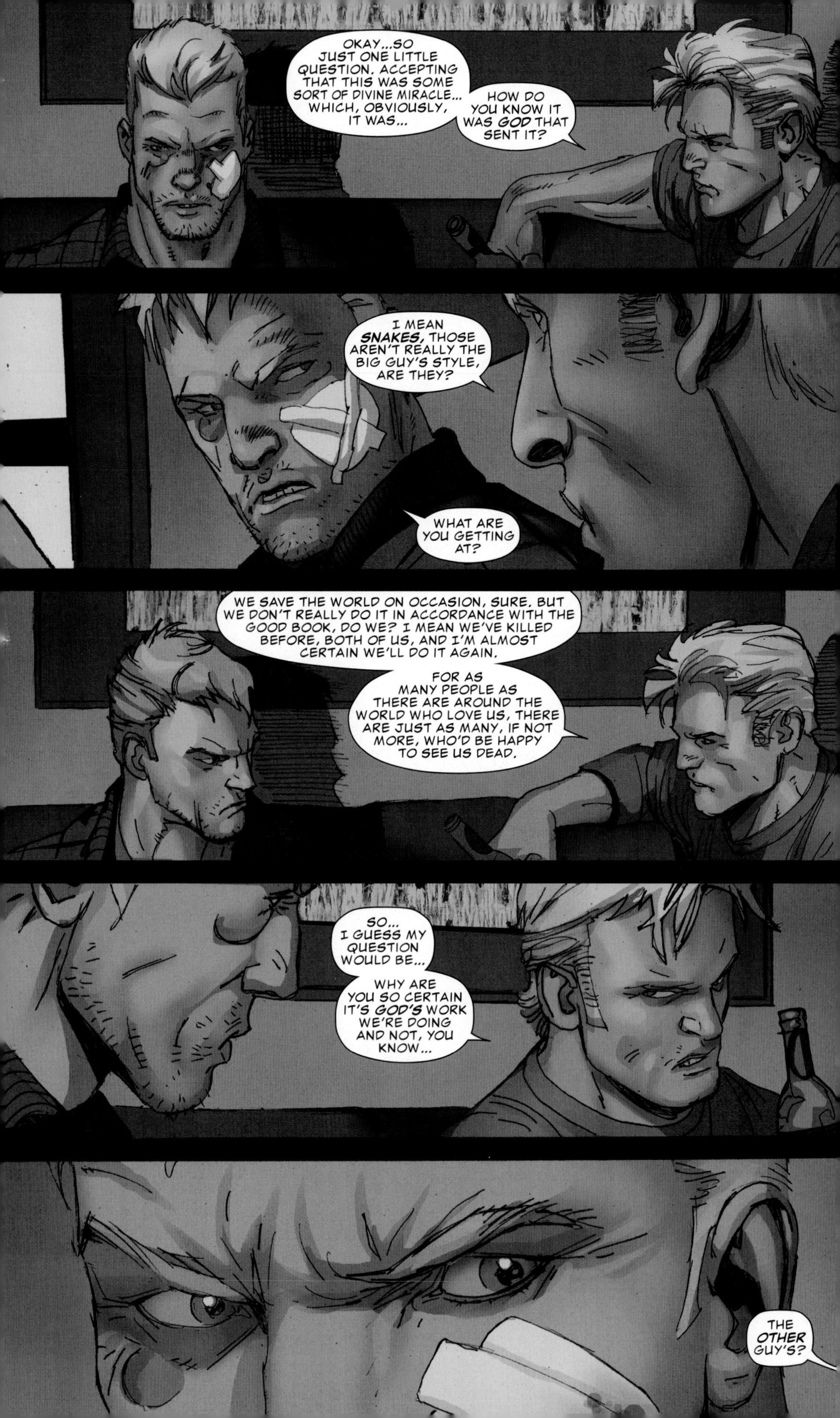
OKAY...SO JUST ONE LITTLE QUESTION. ACCEPTING THAT THIS WAS SOME SORT OF DIVINE MIRACLE... WHICH, OBVIOUSLY, IT WAS...
HOW DO YOU KNOW IT WAS GOD THAT SENT IT?
I MEAN SNAKES, THOSE AREN'T REALLY THE BIG GUY'S STYLE, ARE THEY?
WHAT ARE YOU GETTING AT?
WE SAVE THE WORLD ON OCCASION, SURE. BUT WE DON'T REALLY DO IT IN ACCORDANCE WITH THE GOOD BOOK, DO WE? I MEAN WE'VE KILLED BEFORE, BOTH OF US, AND I'M ALMOST CERTAIN WE'LL DO IT AGAIN.
FOR AS MANY PEOPLE AS THERE ARE AROUND THE WORLD WHO LOVE US, THERE ARE JUST AS MANY, IF NOT MORE, WHO'D BE HAPPY TO SEE US DEAD.
SO... I GUESS MY QUESTION WOULD BE...
WHY ARE YOU SO CERTAIN IT'S GOD'S WORK WE'RE DOING AND NOT, YOU KNOW...
THE OTHER GUY'S?

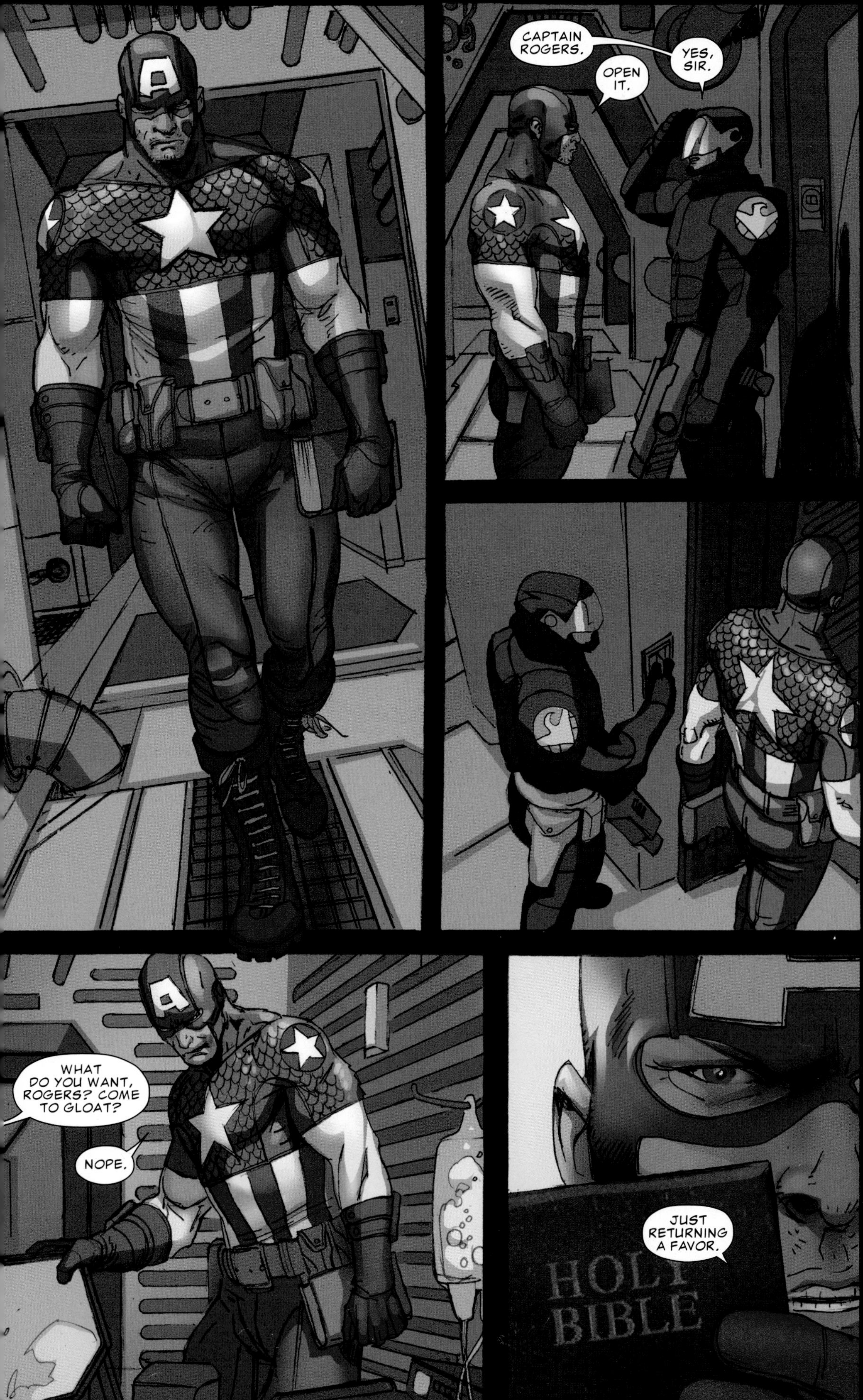
CAPTAIN ROGERS.
YES, SIR.
OPEN IT.
WHAT DO YOU WANT, ROGERS? COME TO GLOAT?
NOPE.
JUST RETURNING A FAVOR.
HOLY BIBLE

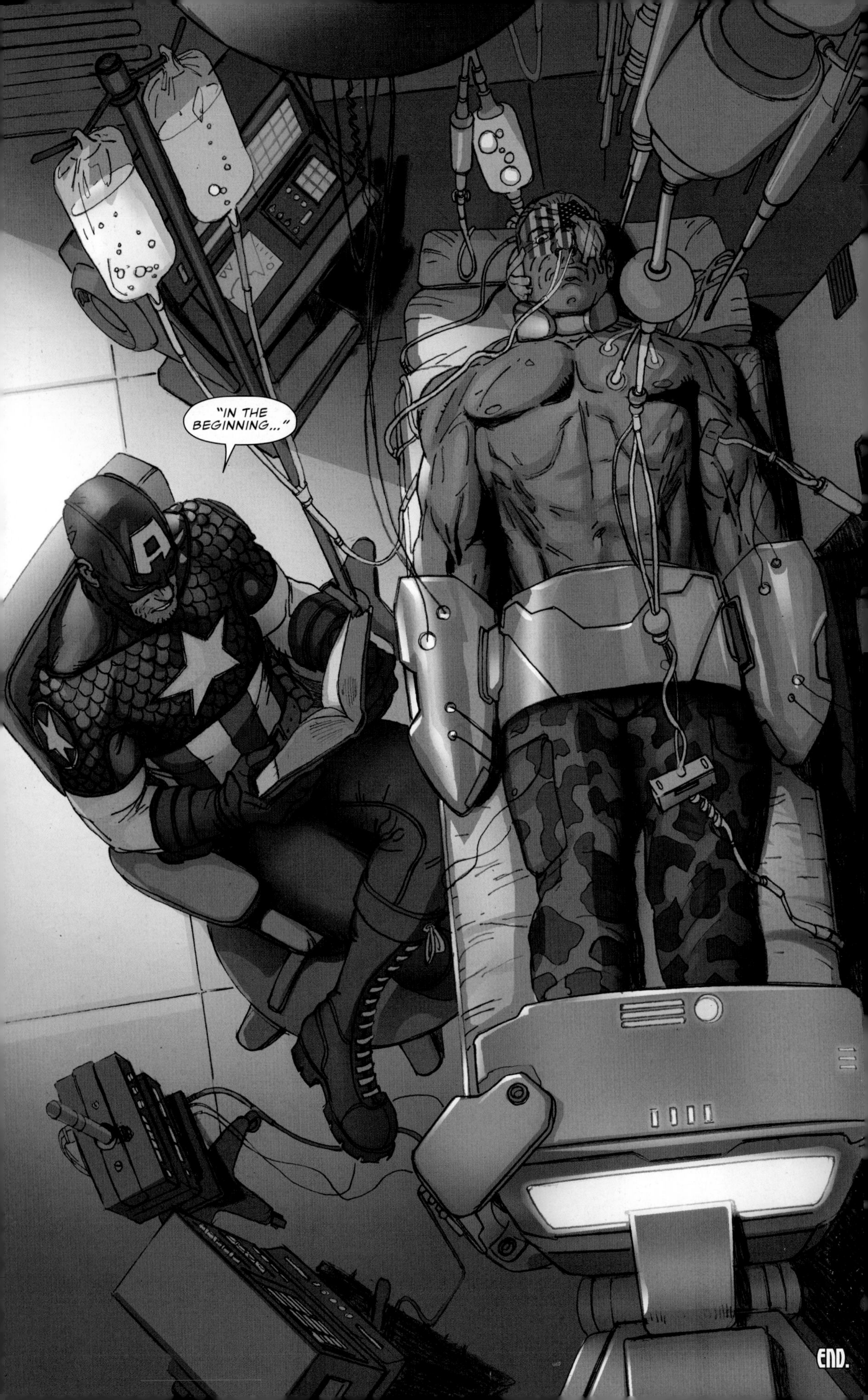
"IN THE BEGINNING..."
END.

1 VARIANT
BY ED McGUINNESS, DEXTER VINES & BOO COOK

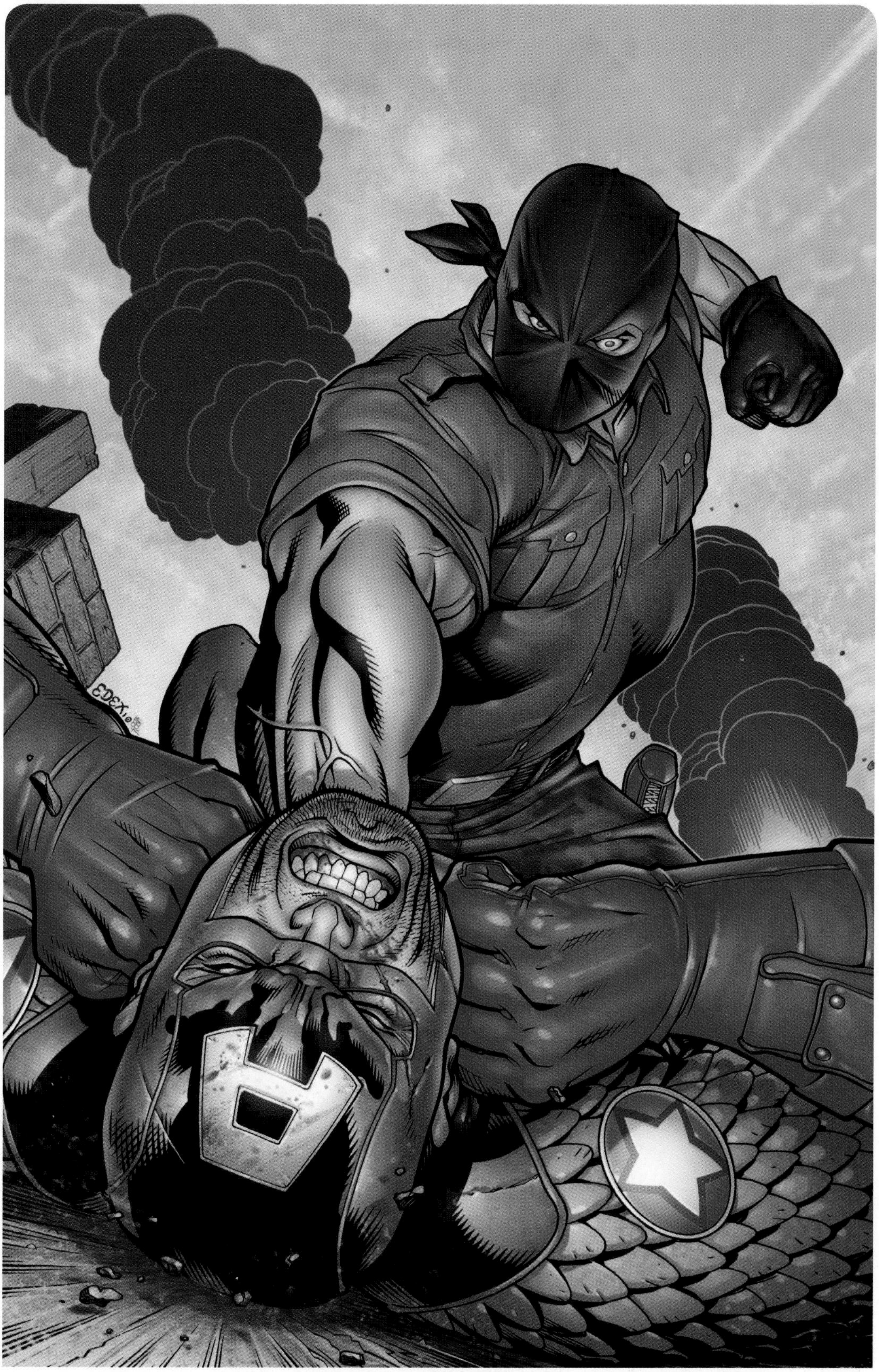

GOING TO WAR WITH ULTIMATE CAPTAIN AMERICA!

WRITER **JASON AARON** TAKES UP ARMS WITH A DECIDEDLY DIFFERENT STEVE ROGERS

BY JESS HARROLD

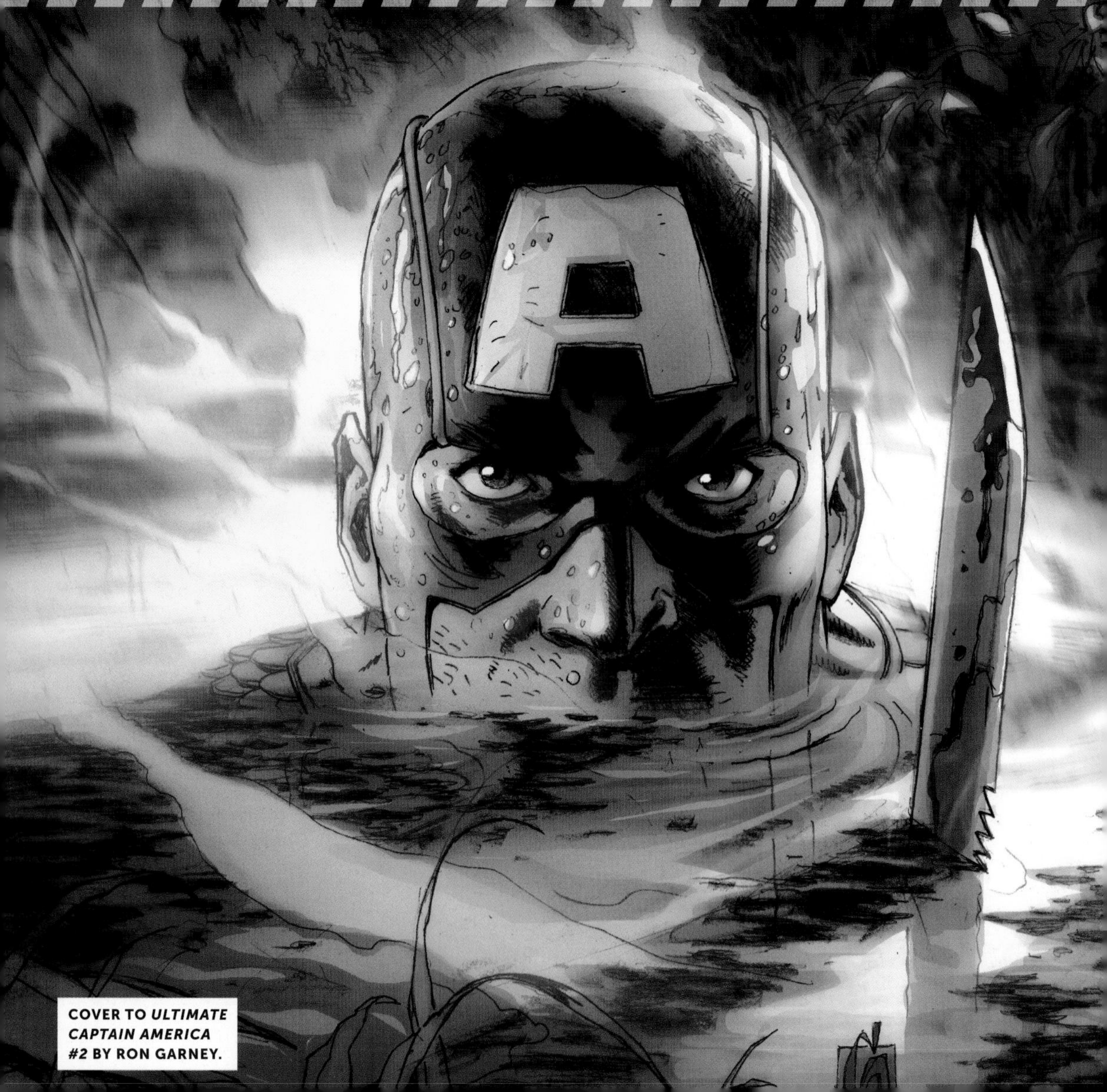

COVER TO *ULTIMATE CAPTAIN AMERICA* #2 BY RON GARNEY.

Like your Captain America with a little more edge? A Sentinel of Liberty who'll do anything — and everything — to get the job done? Jack Bauer with an "A" on his head? Then Ultimate Cap is the man for you. The Super-Soldier star of *The Ultimates* and *Ultimate Avengers* finally has his own limited series in *Ultimate Comics Captain America,* and who better to write it than Marvel Architect Jason Aaron — no stranger to tough-guy super heroics after his stints chronicling the all-action adventures of Wolverine, Ghost Rider and the Punisher. Reunited with *Wolverine: Weapon X* collaborator Ron Garney for the high-octane, four-issue series, Jason pits Ultimate Cap against his Vietnam War-era counterpart in a battle to keep the Super-Soldier serum out of enemy hands. *Spotlight* caught up with Jason partway through the series to rap about Ultimate Cap!

SPOTLIGHT: *Ultimate Comics Captain America* marks your debut in the Ultimate Universe. Are you a fan of what has come before, particularly how Mark Millar has developed the character in *The Ultimates* and *Ultimate Avengers*?

JASON: Yeah, I'm a big fan of the Ultimate Universe, going all the way back to the beginning. And Mark's *Ultimates* run is obviously one of the defining super-hero runs of the last several years.

SPOTLIGHT: When we spoke to Mark about Ultimate Cap, he said he "looks like Brad Pitt, but sort of smells like your granddad." What's your take on the character?

JASON: Part Boy Scout. Part grumpy old man. All hero. But with an edge. And with very definite ideas of how the world should work, ideas he doesn't accept will ever be outdated. I also see him as a guy who's still a "man out of time." He missed out on a lot over the years, a lot of important chunks of American history, and he's still catching up on that — or at times stubbornly refusing to catch up. Marvel Universe Cap has pretty much moved past the "man out of time" phase by this point, but Ultimate Cap still grapples with it. Because of that, I think Ultimate Cap can seem a bit more cantankerous and pigheaded. But at the end of the day, they're both still the greatest heroes their world has ever seen.

SPOTLIGHT: You highlight the markedly different role Cap plays in the Ultimate Universe in his scene with Carol Danvers in the second issue, which must have been fun to write.

JASON: Yeah, it was nice to poke a little fun at the idea of "Cap going rogue" being something he seems to do every other Tuesday.

SPOTLIGHT: There's also a nice touch in that story where you play on Ultimate Cap's famous disdain for the French.

JASON: I, personally, have nothing but goodwill for the French. Cap? Not so much.

WRITER JASON AARON.

SPOTLIGHT: Your series pits Steve against Frank Simpson, America's Super-Soldier of the Vietnam era, the Ultimate version of the flag-faced Frank Miller character longtime readers know as Nuke. For those who have yet to check out the book, what's his story in the Ultimate Universe, and in what ways does the stark contrast between Steve and Frank allow you to explore Ultimate Cap's character?

JASON: Frank Simpson started out much like Steve Rogers. He was just a patriotic kid who wanted to do his part for his country. He volunteered to follow in Steve's

★ ★ ★ HIT LIST ★ ★ ★

JASON AARON

Like the cut of Jason Aaron's jib? Want to learn more? Check out the following collected editions and series, and tell your comic shop *Spotlight* sent you!

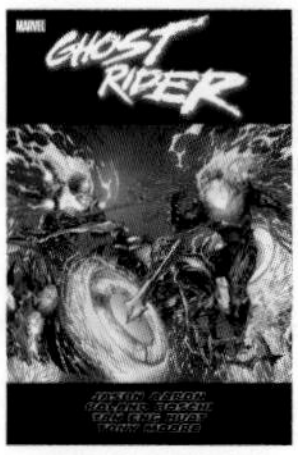
GHOST RIDER

GHOST RIDER

It's a case of "Ghost Riders in the sky" as blazing-skulled brothers Johnny Blaze and Danny Ketch race to the gates of heaven to stave off an assault by a rogue angel and a veritable antichrist. Gun-toting nuns, a villain with an eyeball for a head and Daimon Hellstrom — an Aaron favorite — round out a high-octane grindhouse epic spanning sixteen issues of *Ghost Rider* and the climactic *Heaven's on Fire* limited series.

Collected editions: Get it *all* in the *Ghost Rider by Jason Aaron Omnibus HC!*

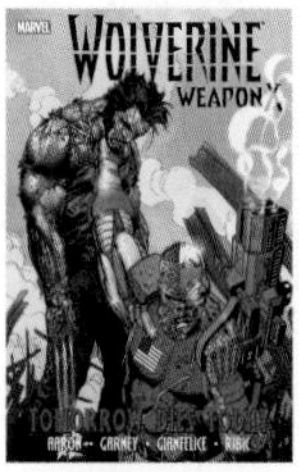
WOLVERINE
WEAPON X

WOLVERINE: WEAPON X

After clicking on the entertaining chase tale "Get Mystique" in the pages of *Wolverine*, Jason and Ron Garney launched this title. Adamantium soldiers! Logan in an insane asylum! A new girlfriend! Two Captain Americas! And a boatload of Deathloks! All capped off with a touching final-issue tribute to the dearly departed Nightcrawler.

Collected editions: See the *Wolverine Weapon X Vol. 1: Adamantium Men, Vol. 2: Insane in the Brain* and *Vol. 3: Tomorrow Dies Today Premiere HCs/TPBs!*

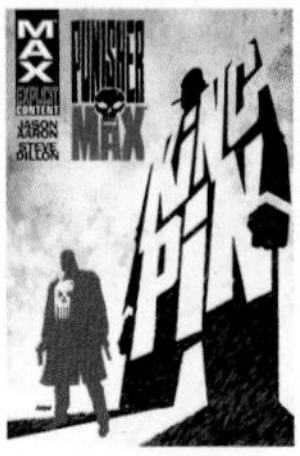
MAX
PUNISHER
MAX
JASON AARON
STEVE DILLON

PUNISHERMAX

United with renowned *Punisher* artist Steve Dillon, Jason gets twisted in this brutal, adults-only series. Witness the rise of Wilson Fisk, a Kingpin of Crime more ruthless than ever before, and a maniacal take on Bullseye not to be missed! Jason and Steve ratchet up the violence as the blood flows, the bodies pile up and readers beg for more!

Collected editions: See the *PunisherMAX: Bullseye and PunisherMAX: Kingpin Premiere HCs/TPBs!*

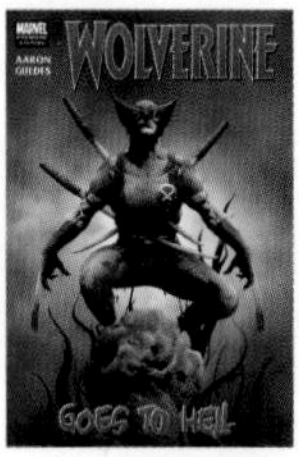
WOLVERINE
AARON
GUEDES
GOES TO HELL

WOLVERINE

For years, writers have been putting Logan through hell — but only Jason has done it literally. Relaunching *Wolverine* with artist Renato Guedes, Jason sent the Avenging X-Man to the fiery underworld and forced him to claw his way back out. Meanwhile, a demon wearing his flesh targets his loved ones. As Daimon Hellstrom — told you! — pops up to help out up top, it's Puck to the rescue down below!

Collected editions: Start out with the wonderfully violent *Wolverine: Get Mystique TPB* and move on to the aptly named *Wolverine: Wolverine Goes to Hell Premiere HC/TPB!*

footsteps, to become a new sort of Captain America in the years after Steve disappeared. But instead of World War II, Frank Simpson got the moral quagmire of the Vietnam War. And at one point in the midst of that war, he just walked off into the jungle, feeling like he'd been lied to and betrayed by his country. He hasn't been seen since, until he pops up in the modern day — apparently helping to spread the Super-Soldier serum among America's enemies, wanting to arm the rest of the world against what he sees as America's imperialism. When Cap and Nuke finally come face-to-face, Nuke feels like he needs to educate Cap on some of the lessons that he missed while he was trapped in ice — the lessons of Vietnam, of Watergate, etc. Cap, as you can imagine, isn't much interested in listening, but instead has some lessons of his own to lay down.

SPOTLIGHT: This isn't the first comic you've written with ties to the Vietnam War. It's clearly a period that interests you and provides fertile ground for storytelling.

JASON: My cousin, Gustav Hasford, was a Vietnam vet and an author. His book, *The Short-Timers*, was the basis for Stanley Kubrick's *Full Metal Jacket*. And my first-ever comic series was a Vietnam War miniseries for Vertigo called *The Other Side*. So yeah, it's a subject that I feel a real connection to, and one I'll likely continue to explore from time to time over the course of my career.

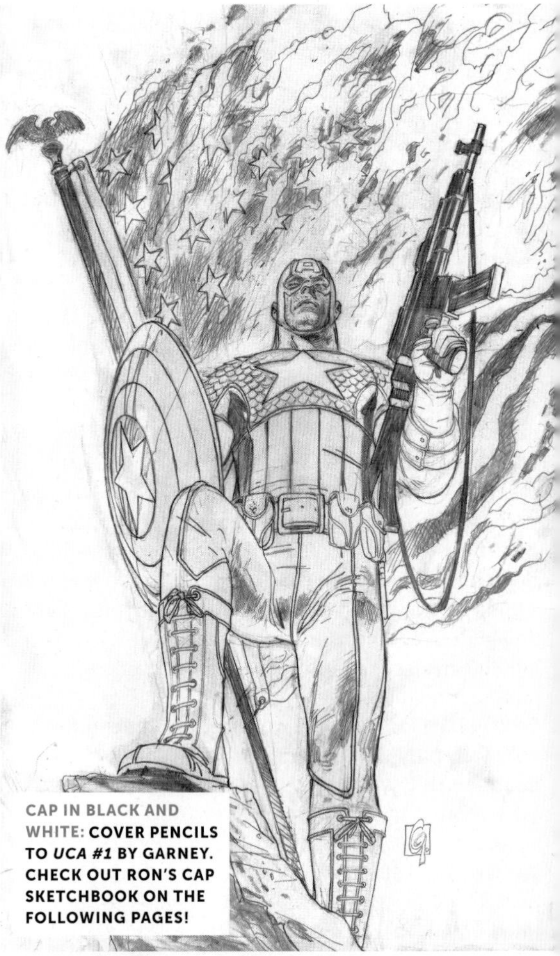

CAP IN BLACK AND WHITE: COVER PENCILS TO *UCA #1* BY GARNEY. CHECK OUT RON'S CAP SKETCHBOOK ON THE FOLLOWING PAGES!

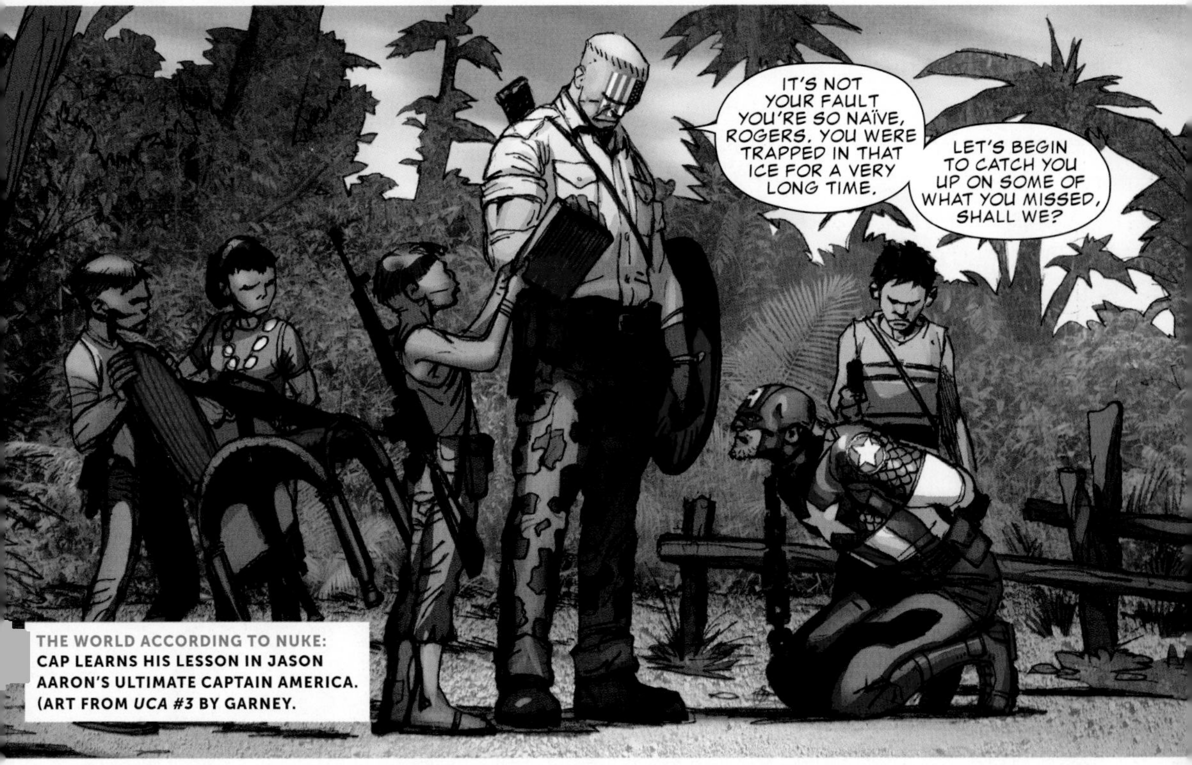
IT'S NOT YOUR FAULT YOU'RE SO NAÏVE, ROGERS. YOU WERE TRAPPED IN THAT ICE FOR A VERY LONG TIME.
LET'S BEGIN TO CATCH YOU UP ON SOME OF WHAT YOU MISSED, SHALL WE?

THE WORLD ACCORDING TO NUKE: CAP LEARNS HIS LESSON IN JASON AARON'S ULTIMATE CAPTAIN AMERICA. (ART FROM *UCA #3* BY GARNEY.

"(Ultimate Cap has) definite ideas of how the world should work, ideas he doesn't accept will ever be outdated."

SPOTLIGHT: You mention the plot also involves Frank's version of the serum falling into the hands of enemies of the United States as a kind of Super-Soldier arms race develops. As a writer, do you particularly enjoy rooting super heroics in real-world events and politics?

JASON: I think that's a part of what has always made the Ultimates interesting: looking at them as living and breathing WMDs, and figuring how that would play out on an international scale. This story is very much a story about the legacy of the Vietnam War, but it's also a story about today's global climate.

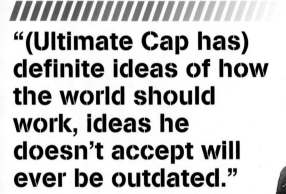

SPOTLIGHT: You obviously get on well with Ron Garney and like to see him draw the shield after writing Bucky Cap into your *Wolverine: Weapon X* run. What makes him such a great artist for Cap?

JASON: Ron's just a great artist no matter what he's drawing. His penchant for action is unparalleled in my opinion, and I still feel like he's doing some of the best work of his career right now. I'm just happy that I've been a part of that and get to keep working with him.

SPOTLIGHT: Finally, imagine Marvel calls offering you *Captain America* or an *Ultimate Cap* ongoing: Which do you choose?

JASON: Either one would be a thrill, quite honestly. But trust me, I've already got enough on my plate as is.

Check out some of the tasty morsels on Jason's overflowing plate each month in the pages of PunisherMAX *and* Wolverine*! And speaking of* Ultimate Cap *artist Ron Garney? Just turn the page, Friends of Old Marvel!* ■

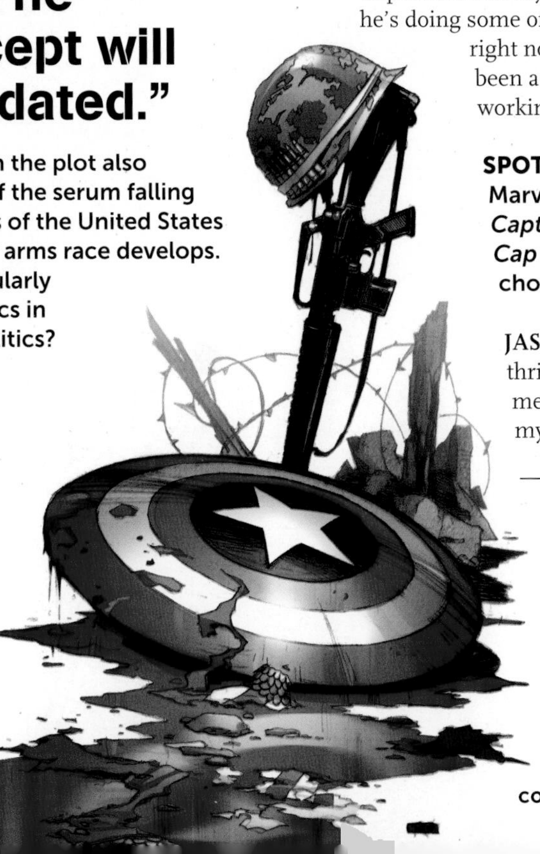

COVER TO *UCA #4* BY GARNEY.

During a Marvel career spanning two decades, Ron Garney has soared the spaceways with the Silver Surfer, gone on a rollicking rampage with the Incredible Hulk, sliced and diced with Wolverine, and put Spider-Man back in black. But to many fans, Ron's kinetic style will forever be associated with one man: the star-spangled Avenger, Captain America. While it took the controversial "Heroes Reborn" experiment and the resulting "Heroes Return," to bring books like *Avengers*, *Iron Man* and *Thor* back to greatness, the ideal combination of Ron and writer Mark Waid had already restored the shine to Cap's shield in 1995. Their well-received run cut short by "Heroes Reborn," Waid and Garney came back to *Captain America* with "Heroes Return" — but the reunion only lasted five issues, as well as six more of the spinoff series *Sentinel of Liberty*. Fans have wondered ever since what might have been had Waid and Garney's run continued uninterrupted. Now, after years in which his natural affinity for drawing Cap has been glimpsed only in guest appearances, Ron has returned to the character — this time with an Ultimate twist. Here, the artist throws open his archives to reveal sketches and pencils that prove no matter which Cap you're talking about, Ron's the man to draw him.

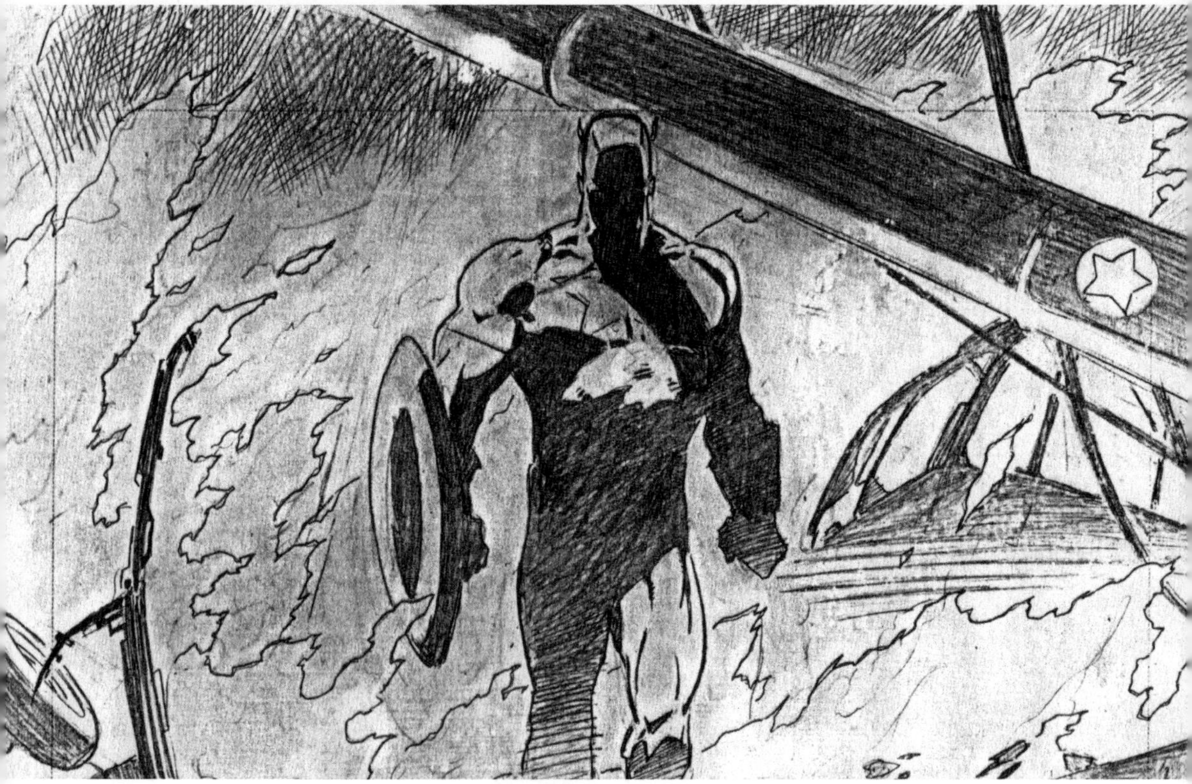

ON CAP: "I enjoy doing action storytelling — and all the way back to the Kirby era, that's what you get when you read a Cap book: a lot of kinetic action. I think that's a strength of my work. I'm also drawn to the character based on what he represents. I like doing iconic characters. I think it appeals to the mythology in me. We gravitate toward characters we can look up to and follow. Captain America is a character like that, as opposed to a character like Deadpool. Deadpool is a cool character, but he's not iconic."

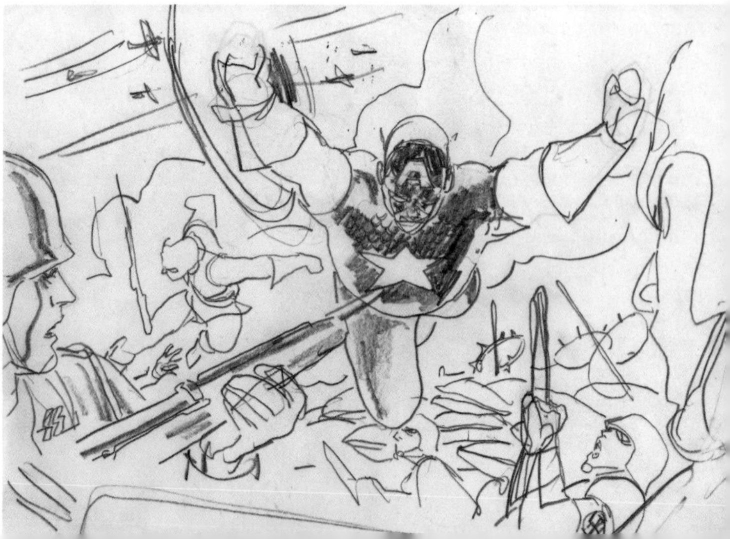

A Captain America Classicist Shares A Presentation Of His Best

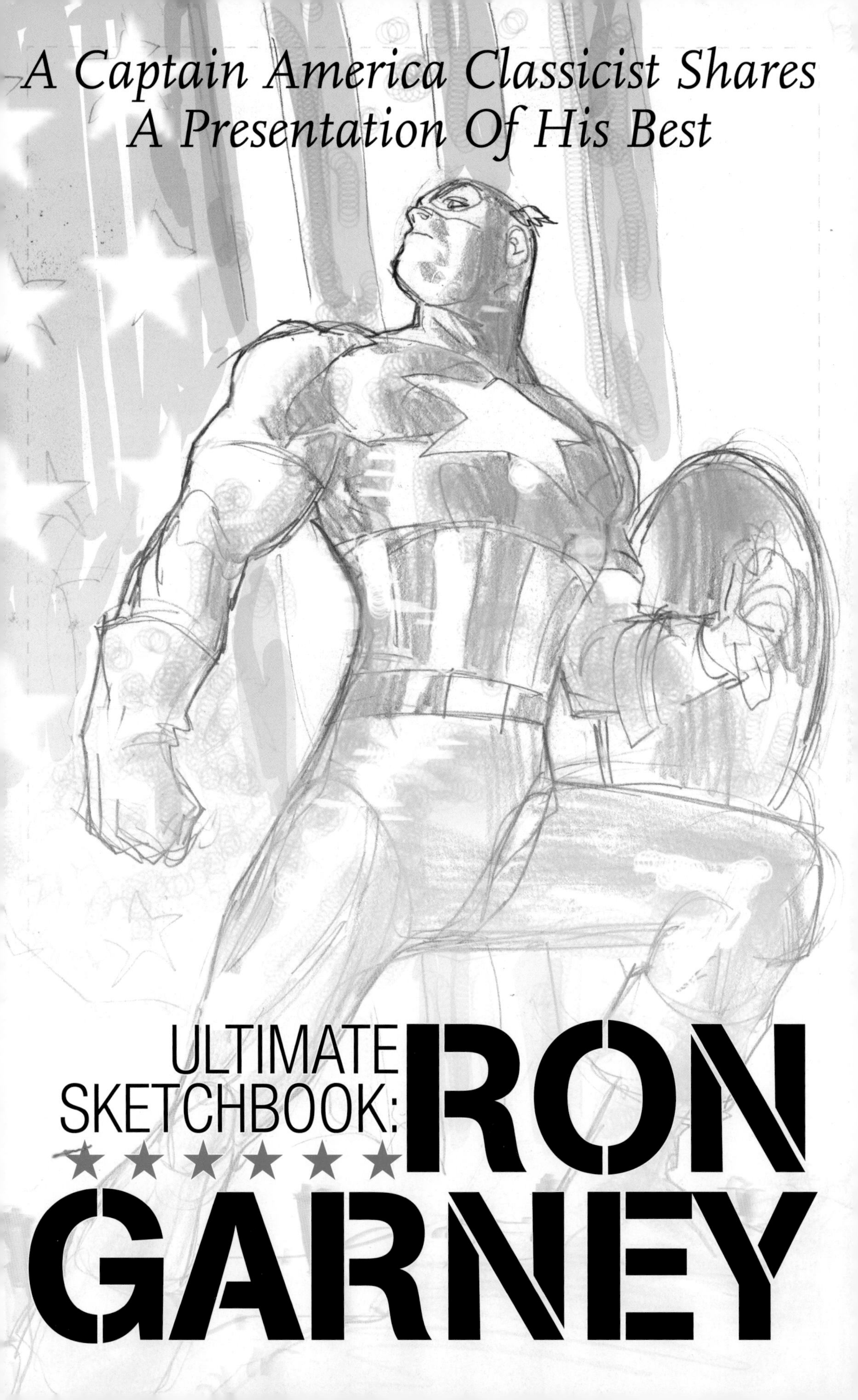

ULTIMATE SKETCHBOOK: RON GARNEY

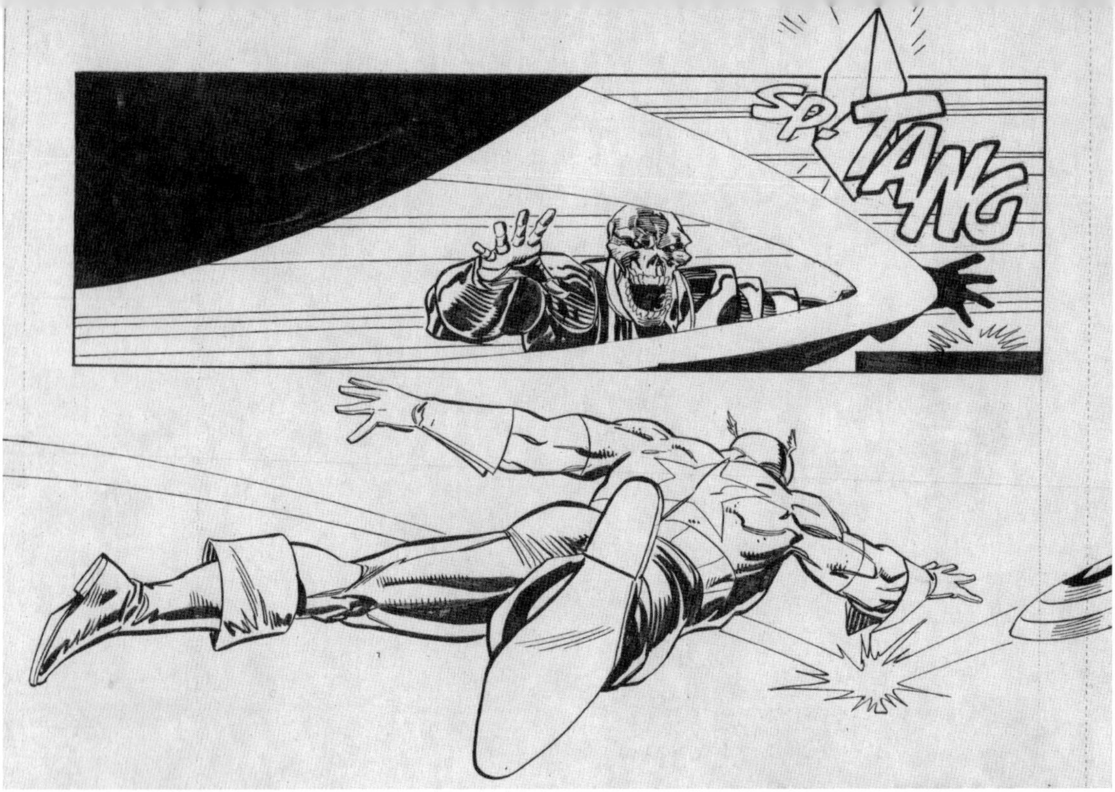
SP-TANG

ON CHOREOGRAPHING CAP: "My style is somewhere between old-school and contemporary. I have a particular way that I see the action moving and the dynamics of the shield. There's a lot of left-to-right movement in my work, and the way you have to pace the action in Cap — when he throws the shield and how he throws it — is very tricky to pull off. You have to time it correctly."

ON BUCKY CAP: "Even though I drew Bucky in *Wolverine: Weapon X*, he's not really Cap to me. He's an homage to Cap. It's not Superman without Clark Kent, it's not Spider-Man without Peter Parker, and it's not Captain America without Steve Rogers. Bucky can move well, but he could be in any other costume. You don't have the same iconography in the artwork. The iconic images I feel more with Steve Rogers."

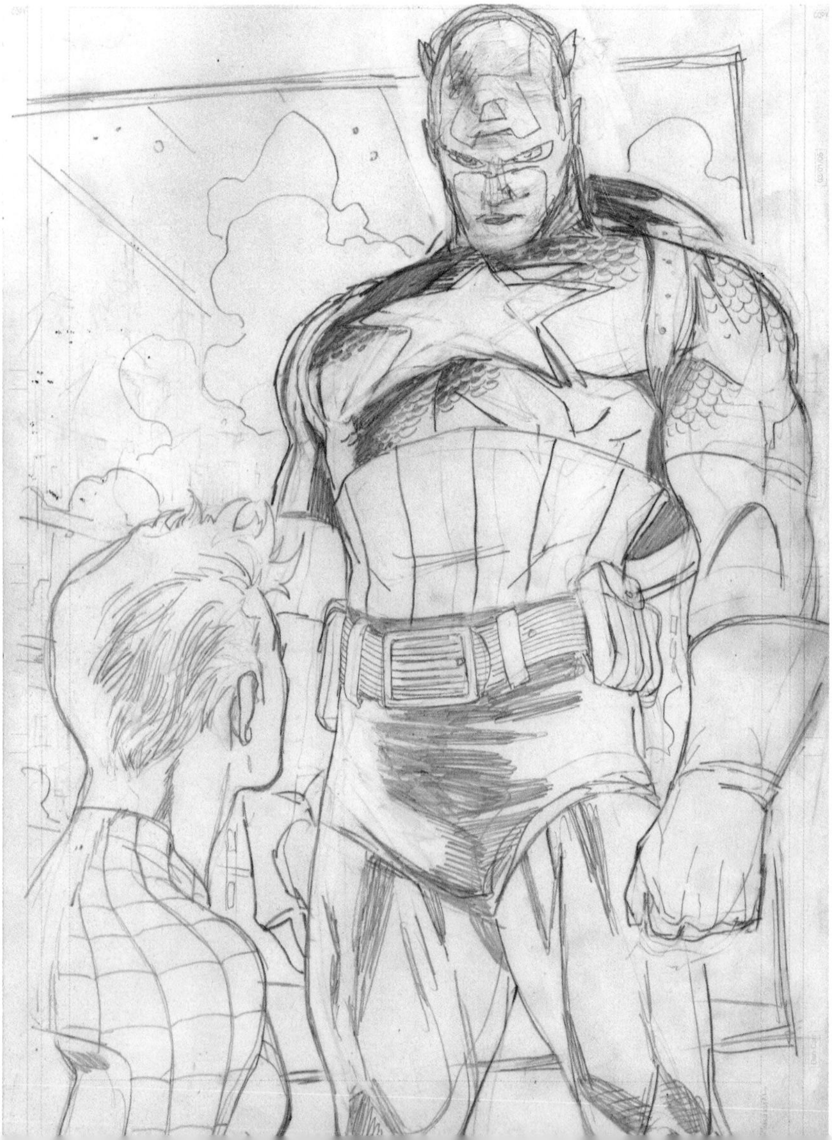

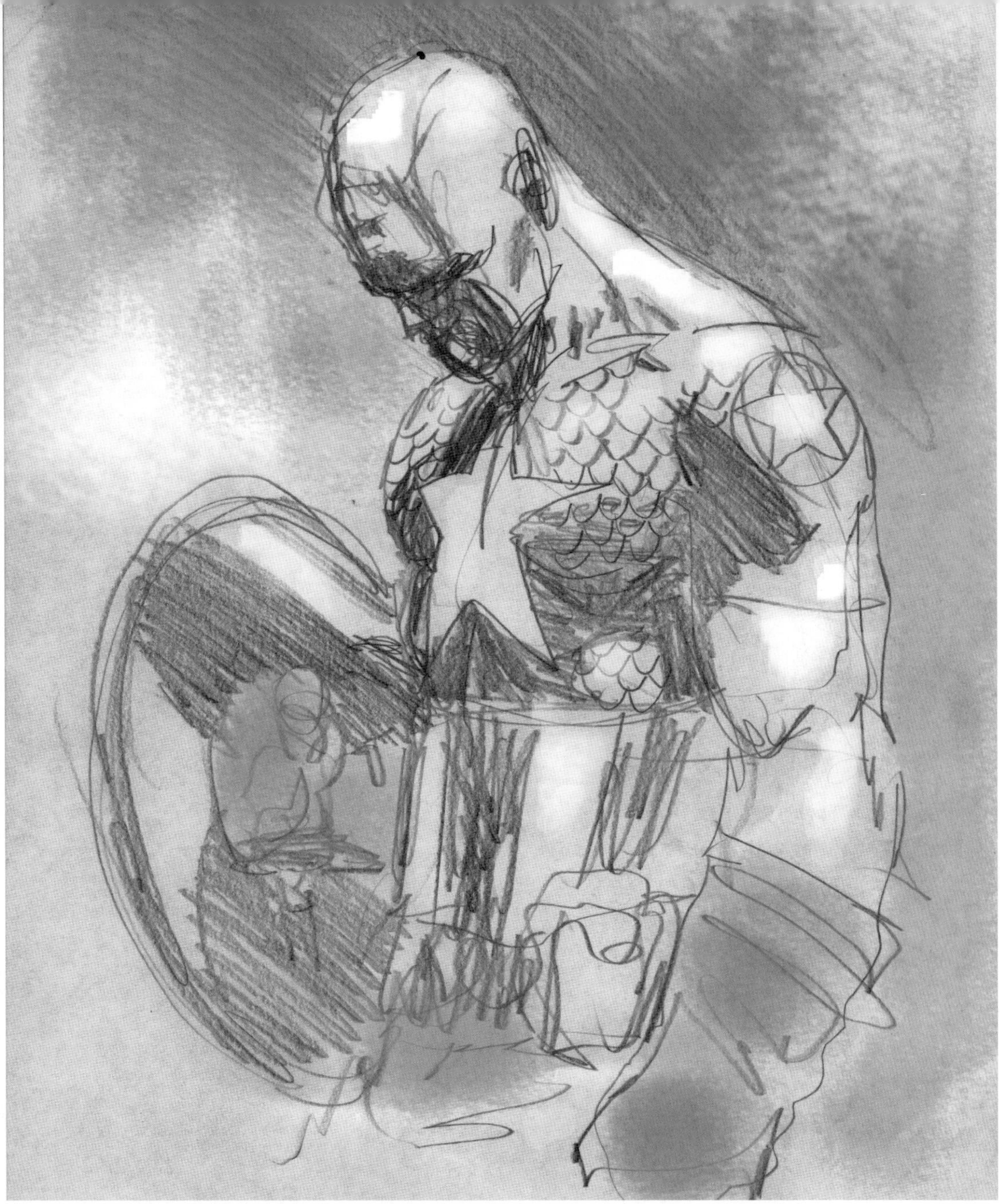

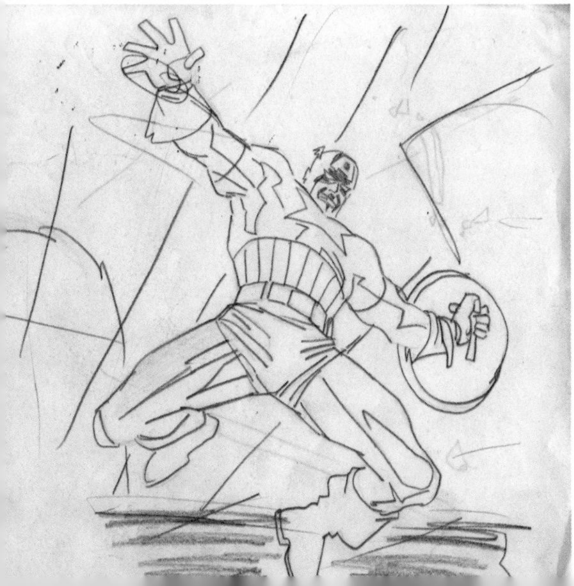

ON CAP'S COSTUME: "Spider-Man's probably my favorite, but Cap's costume is up there in my top five. I think it's a very handsome design, especially the red and white around the waist, which I think is unique. Scales or no scales, that is the question! The chainmail has been rendered in more detail over the years. Especially with the *Ultimate Cap* stuff, we have to see all the scales. With the older Cap, we used to see just a rendering of it. Back in the '70s, you couldn't afford to sit there and render each scale like you can now."

MARVEL

Book Issue Story

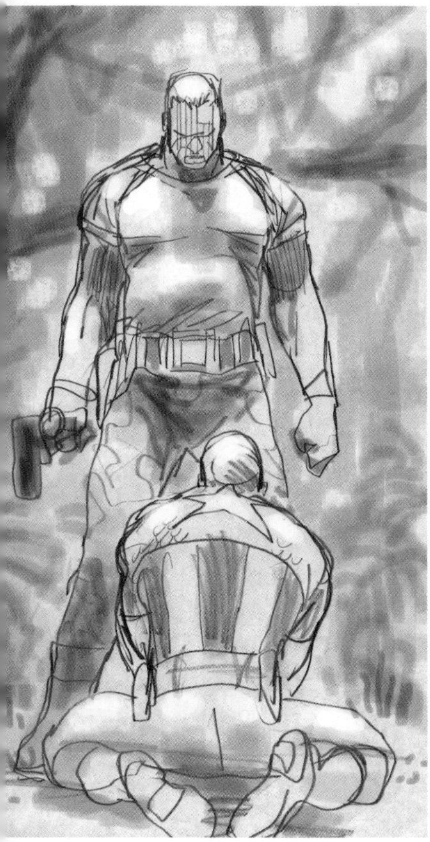

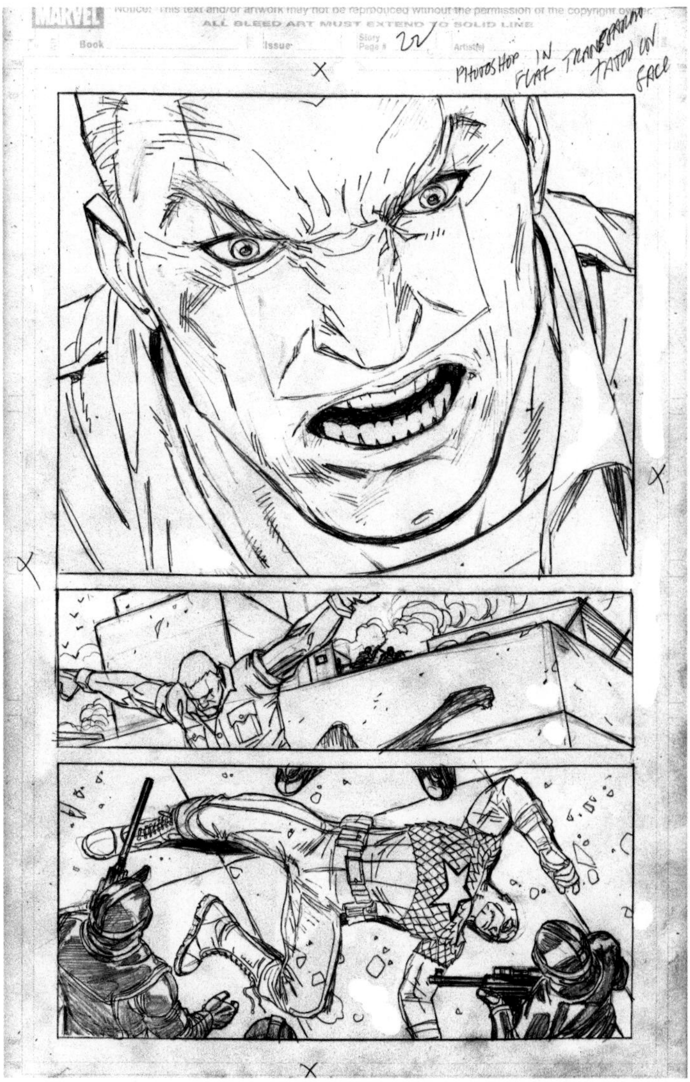
MARVEL
ALL BLEED ART MUST EXTEND TO SOLID LINE
Book
Issue
Story Page # 22
Artist(s)
PHOTOSHOP IN FLAT TRANSPARENT TATOO ON FACE

ON ULTIMATE CAP: "When I first started working on *Ultimate Cap*, it was very odd because of the attitude difference. In the first issue, I think my style of drawing Cap felt weird with Jason's writing. But as the issues went along, I think that fleshed itself out. I felt like I was getting more into the idea of this guy's facial expressions. He talks and fights in a more raw way than the Marvel Universe Cap. In the last issue, you'll see a big difference. There are a couple of things that happen in that fight scene that would be pretty uncharacteristic for the Marvel Universe Steve Rogers."

ON NUKE: "I thought it was a great choice to use him. It's fun creating some lore for a character from such a legendary run as Frank Miller's 'Born Again.' Visually, all he's got is that tattoo on his face and military fatigues, and that's what makes it work. He doesn't need any more than that. I started out by drawing the tattoo in, and it took a few emails back and forth with the colorist, Jason Keith, to get it to look right. At first, it looked like a plastic sticker on his face. But once we got it to look right, I would basically put the outline of the rectangle on there and leave it up to Jason to color."

ON ULTIMATE CAP'S COSTUME: "Drawing the Ultimate Cap costume made it more fun than rehashing the same old stuff I'd done fifteen years ago. The extra detail in the costume and its more military flavor felt a little more real to me. Having drawn Ultimate Cap and the 616 Cap, I enjoy drawing him without the wings. When you put the wings on him, he becomes the 616 Cap. It's not that you can't take him seriously with the wings, but he becomes less of a bastard than the Ultimate Cap when he has them. They make him a bit lighter. It's easier to take Ultimate Cap seriously. You're more likely to see a guy like Cap one day than Thor, so I think this costume lends itself to that believability. This guy could really exist."

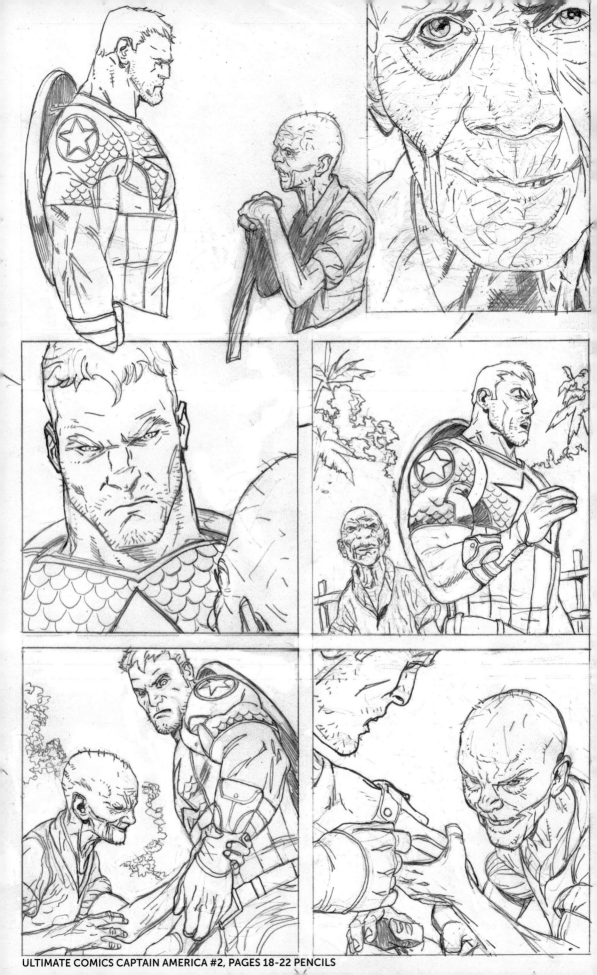

ULTIMATE COMICS CAPTAIN AMERICA #2, PAGES 18-22 PENCILS

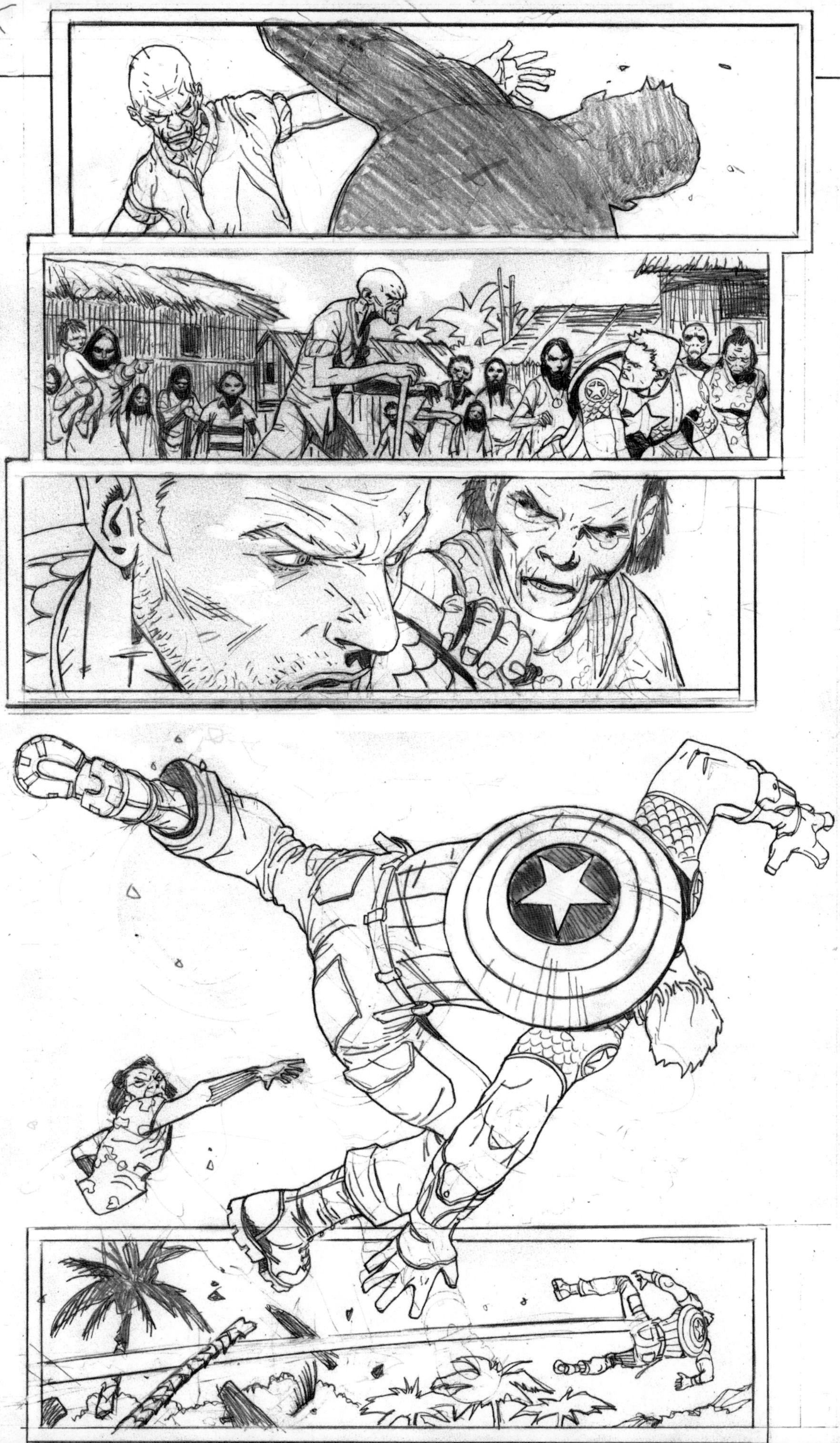

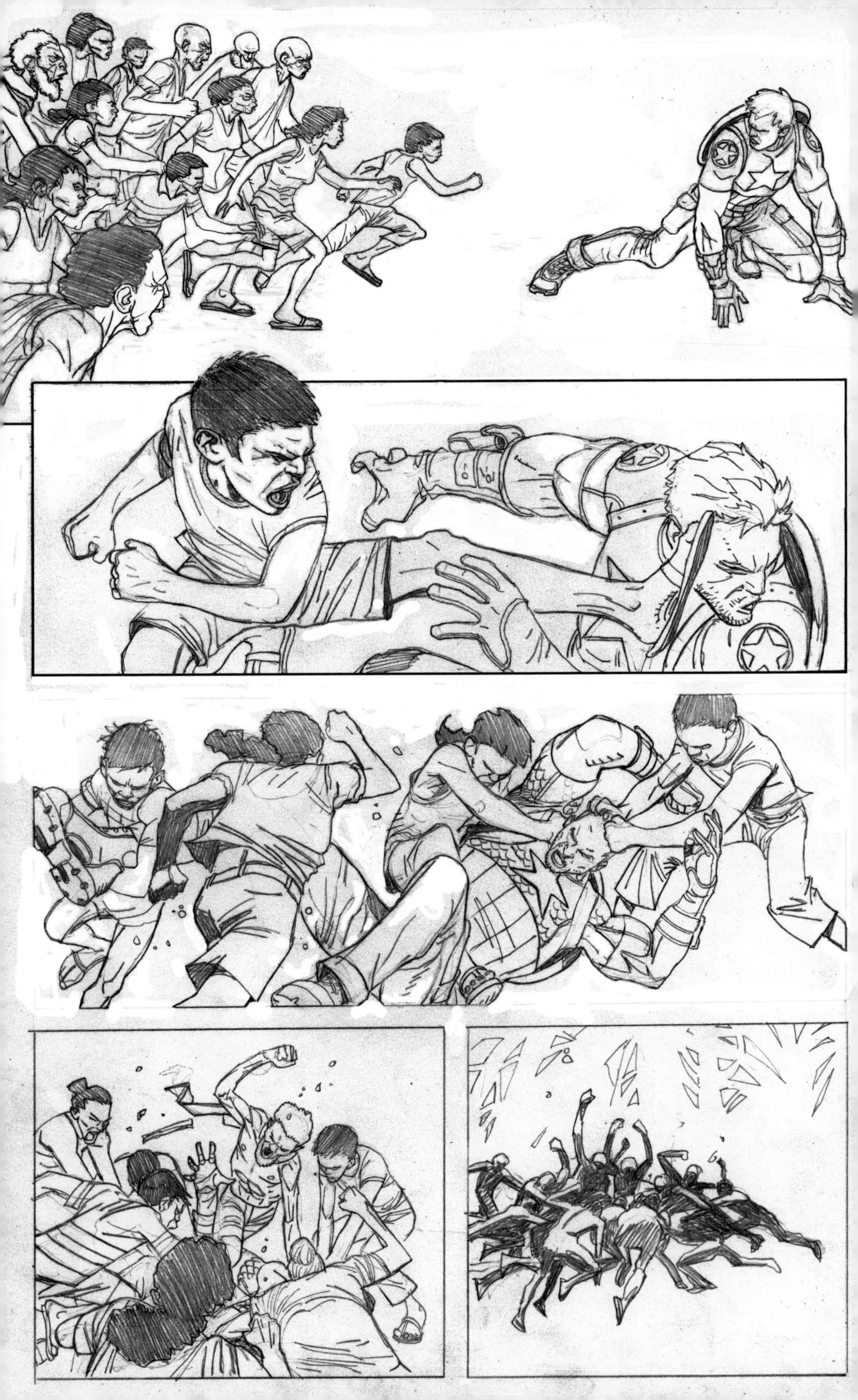

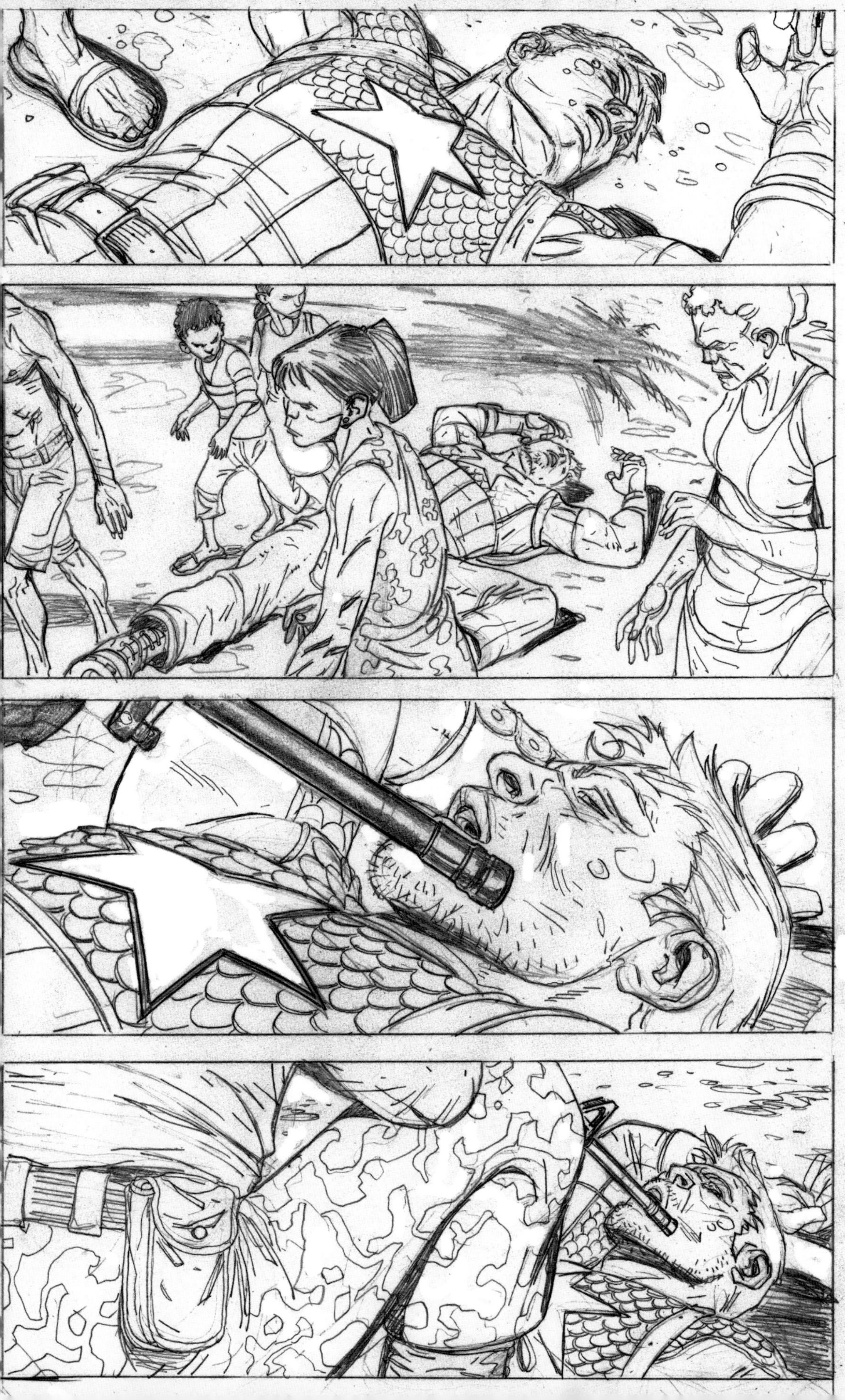

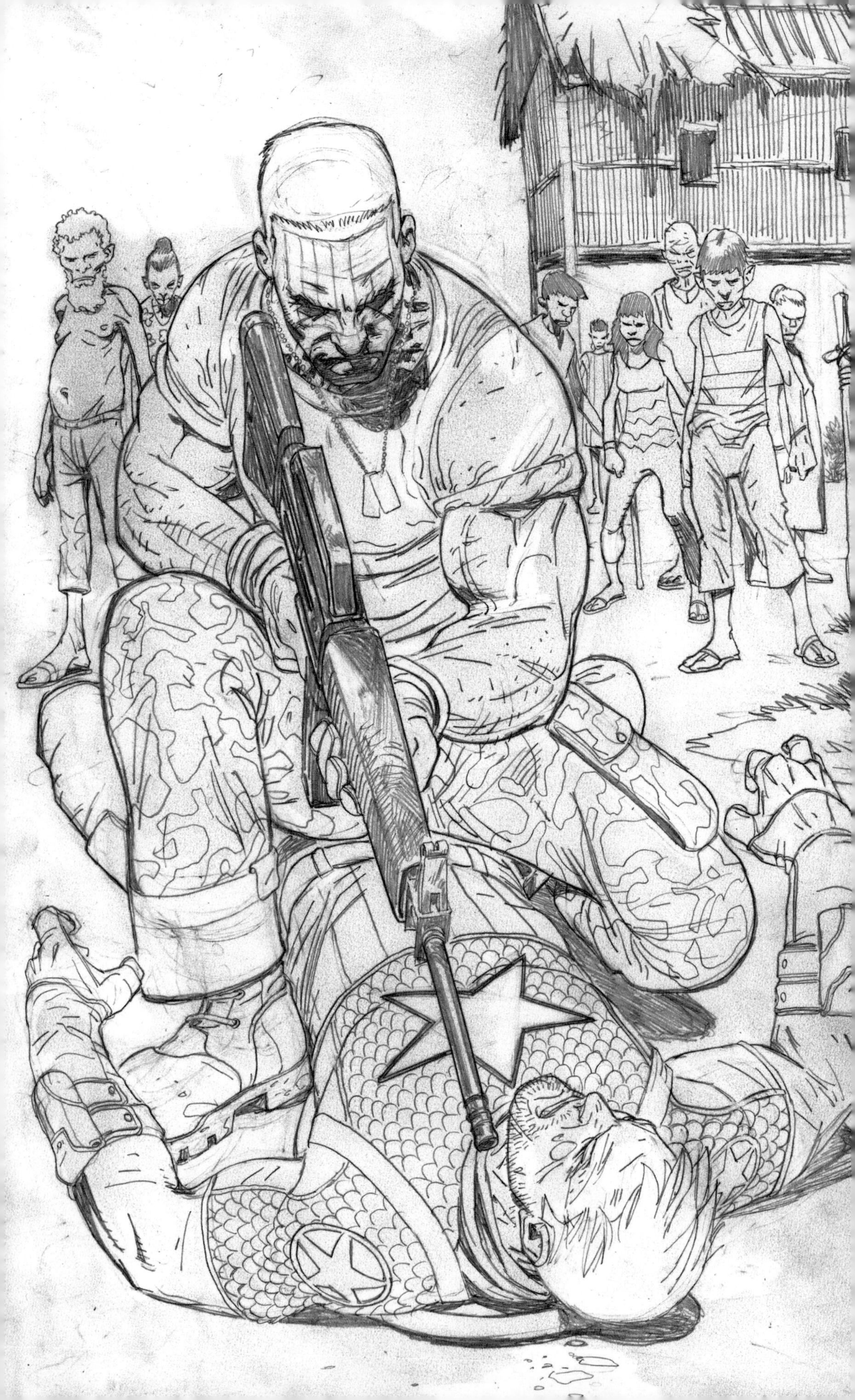